T0330982

Economic Development, Agriculture and Climate Change

World Scientific Lecture Notes in Economics and Policy

ISSN: 2630-4872

Series Editors: Ariel Dinar *(University of California, Riverside, USA)*
Dirk Bergemann *(Yale University, USA)*
Devashish Mitra *(Syracuse University, USA)*
James S. Shortle *(Pennsylvania State University, USA)*
Kar-Yiu Wong *(University of Washington, USA)*
David Grabowski *(Harvard Medical School, USA)*

The World Scientific Lecture Notes in Economics and Policy series is aimed to produce lecture note texts for a wide range of economics disciplines, both theoretical and applied at the undergraduate and graduate levels. Contributors to the series are highly ranked and experienced professors of economics who see in publication of their lectures a mission to disseminate the teaching of economics in an affordable manner to students and other readers interested in enriching their knowledge of economic topics. The series was formerly titled World Scientific Lecture Notes in Economics.

Published:

Vol. 15: *Economic Development, Agriculture and Climate Change*
by Antonio Yúnez-Naude and Jorge Mora-Rivera

Vol. 14: *Lectures in the Microeconomics of Choice: Foundations, Consumers, and Producers*
by William David Anthony Bryant

Vol. 13: *Advanced Mathematical Methods in Environmental and Resource Economics*
by Anastasios Xepapadeas

Vol. 12: *Lecture Notes in Global-Local Policy Interactions*
by Ariel Dinar

Vol. 11: *Lecture Notes in Water Policy*
by David Feldman

Vol. 10: *Lecture Notes in International Trade Theory: Classical Trade and Applications*
by Larry S. Karp

For the complete list of volumes in this series, please visit
www.worldscientific.com/series/wslnep

World Scientific Lecture Notes in Economics and Policy – Vol. 15

Economic Development, Agriculture and Climate Change

Antonio Yúnez-Naude
El Colegio de México, Mexico

Jorge Mora-Rivera
Tecnologico de Monterrey, Mexico

World Scientific

NEW JERSEY • LONDON • SINGAPORE • BEIJING • SHANGHAI • HONG KONG • TAIPEI • CHENNAI • TOKYO

Published by

World Scientific Publishing Co. Pte. Ltd.
5 Toh Tuck Link, Singapore 596224
USA office: 27 Warren Street, Suite 401-402, Hackensack, NJ 07601
UK office: 57 Shelton Street, Covent Garden, London WC2H 9HE

Library of Congress Cataloging-in-Publication Data
Names: Yúnez-Naude, Antonio, author. | Mora-Rivera, Jorge, author.
Title: Economic development, agriculture and climate change / Antonio Yúnez-Naude, El Colegio de Mexico, Jorge Mora-Rivera, Tecnologico de Monterrey, Mexico.
Description: New Jersey : World Scientific, [2023] | Series: World scientific lecture notes in economics and policy, 2630-4872 ; Vol. 15 | Includes bibliographical references and index.
Identifiers: LCCN 2022053788 | ISBN 9789811269516 (hardcover) | ISBN 9789811269523 (ebook) | ISBN 9789811269530 (ebook other)
Subjects: LCSH: Economic development. | Economic development--Developing countries. | Sustainable development. | Agriculture--Environmental aspects. | Climatic changes--Economic aspects.
Classification: LCC HD82 .Y86 2023 | DDC 338.9--dc23/eng/20221205
LC record available at https://lccn.loc.gov/2022053788

British Library Cataloguing-in-Publication Data
A catalogue record for this book is available from the British Library.

Copyright © 2023 by World Scientific Publishing Co. Pte. Ltd.

All rights reserved. This book, or parts thereof, may not be reproduced in any form or by any means, electronic or mechanical, including photocopying, recording or any information storage and retrieval system now known or to be invented, without written permission from the publisher.

For photocopying of material in this volume, please pay a copying fee through the Copyright Clearance Center, Inc., 222 Rosewood Drive, Danvers, MA 01923, USA. In this case permission to photocopy is not required from the publisher.

For any available supplementary material, please visit
https://www.worldscientific.com/worldscibooks/10.1142/13238#t=suppl

Desk Editors: Sanjay Varadharajan/Geysilla Jean

Typeset by Stallion Press
Email: enquiries@stallionpress.com

Printed in Singapore

Dedication

We dedicate this book to Guillermo Ortega Rangel and to Olga Torres Arroyo for their patience, love, and support that allowed us to commit the time required to prepare this volume and update our lectures following recent research results on global warming, as well as last year climate change events and international discussions on policy design to promote sustainable global development.

Preface

This lecture notes book is based on our lectures on economic development and policies, climate change, and agricultural sustainable growth to senior B.A. and junior graduate students in economics. The target audience includes students in social sciences and professionals interested in the above areas of knowledge.

Our main purpose is to present the state-of-the-art of the knowledge with regard to the relationships between development and climate change (CC from now on), with special reference to agriculture and to policies aimed to promote its sustainable development, i.e., to attain inclusive human welfare while maintaining the ability of natural systems to provide the natural resources and ecosystem services on which the economy and society depend. We also give special attention to the situation in low and medium-income countries and, in particular, to rural households and subsistence small farmers prevailing in these countries. The reason is because there are billions of these agents whose livelihoods depend on their use of natural resources and whose particular economic behavior is frequently ignored in the design and application of agricultural and rural sustainable development policies.

The study of agriculture, CC, and sustainability require a consideration of natural resources and their uses (land, fresh water, forests, etc.), as well as the rural sector, since land for agricultural production often expands at the expense of forests. In addition, the use of water for agricultural production affects the availability of this resource for other uses in the urban, industrial, and services sectors.

The above means that the knowledge of sustainable agricultural development under global CC requires an interdisciplinary or at least a multidisciplinary approach. In this book we do our best to deal with this challenge by focusing on issues and topics related to agriculture and its use of natural resources in the context of CC, but without ignoring the interrelations of these phenomena with other issues of sustainability beyond agriculture.

The book has eight chapters. In Chapter 1 we present the meaning of CC, its major drivers, recent changes, and consequences; we also include the definition of natural resources or "natural capital" and the problems in evaluating such concepts.

We dedicate Chapter 2 to presenting the main issues addressed in the book, including the definition of sustainable development: evidence that a major driver of CC since the industrial revolution is strongly related to anthropogenic activities. We also discuss the risks caused by global warming and CC with special reference to food production and food security. In Chapter 2, we include also a summary of the scientific contributions of the Intergovernmental Panel on CC (IPCC), part of the United Nations Conferences on CC (UNFCC) with respect to tendencies and pathway to achieve sustainability and evidence about the growing gap between the targets to reduce greenhouse gas (GHG) emissions and urgent actions that governments, the private sector, and civil society must undertake in order to comply with international commitments to reduce global warming.

In Chapter 3, we begin to focus our attention on agriculture through a review of the role of agriculture in economic development, based on literature published since the mid-20th century. In this chapter we give special attention to development policies, and the role of markets as well as to the incorporation of the rural sector, rural households, and sustainability aspects in the literature.

In Chapter 4, we adopt the IPCC approach to consider Agriculture, Forestry, and Other Land Uses (AFOLU), aware that land use for agricultural production is deeply connected with other land uses such as forestry. We begin the chapter by presenting what we know about the role of the AFOLU sector in GHG emissions and as a sink of carbon dioxide (CO_2). Based on the importance of fresh water for agricultural production, in addition to the IPCC analyses of the AFOLU sector we discuss issues related to freshwater availability and use.

We then dedicate Chapter 4 to discussing necessary actions in agriculture and in the AFOLU sectors to mitigate global warming as well as adaptation strategies to deal with CC, including the vulnerability the rural population faces due to this phenomenon. Since few studies explicitly consider the specific characteristics of rural households in medium- and low-income countries, in this chapter we discuss the specific behavior of these economic agents and its implications for sustainability and development policies.

In Chapter 5, we present economic development models relevant to the agricultural and rural sectors, covering human migration models, partial equilibrium models, multisectoral modes, and eco-physical models. The chapter has a technical character, but should be easy to understand for the target audience of the book.

Chapter 6 is dedicated to presenting evaluations of international commitments to reduce global warming under the UNFCC, starting with the Kyoto Protocol adopted in late 1997. In this chapter we include negotiations between the United Nations participants at the 26th Conference of the Parties held in Glasgow, United Kingdom in 2021, known as COP26. We contrast commitments and trends in global warming, with special attention to agriculture and the rural sectors, adding our reflection on the importance of taking into consideration the specificities of the functioning and behavior of rural households in policies and actions aimed to attain sustainability in agricultural and food production.

Based on the gap between commitments and trends in global warming as discussed in Chapter 6, our purpose in Chapter 7 is to explore the reasons underlying this gap. We do so by presenting major challenges humans face in attaining sustainable development, again putting special emphasis on agriculture and rural areas. These challenges range from the valuation of priceless natural resources to the appropriate institutions, governance, and democracy.

The book ends in Chapter 8, with a summary of the book contents, a discussion of policies required to halt global warming, and with reflections on the necessary steps we must take to avoid global disasters that can occur if global warming is not halted. Chapter 8 ends with a series of questions as homework assignments with the purpose to motivate students and readers' knowledge and reflections.

With regard to the use of this publication as a textbook, we have designed it to follow an academic term. We also offer the flexibility of distributing its components by lecture. This because, notwithstanding that the book content is self-contained, students may require additional background readings and/or may be interested in learning more about themes treated in the book. So, we refer to a considerable number of publications. In many cases we present a summary of the contents of papers we use instead of quoting exactly the original text, and so, we just include the reference of the source.

We hope that this lecture book will contribute to understanding the challenges that agriculture and food production face and with this to the discussion of the commitments and actions that we must implement to attend the urgent need to reduce global warming.

In the preparation of the book, we received the valuable assistance of Ligia Figuerola Brunet, Miguel Calderón Giorguli, Gina González García, Fátima Rangel Mendoza, Genaro Cruz Salas, Lidia Ceballos Valencia, and María Antonieta Pérez Landgrave.

Antonio Yúnez-Naude
Jorge Mora-Rivera

About the Authors

Antonio Yúnez-Naude is Professor at the Center for Economic Studies, El Colegio de Mexico (COLMEX) since 1976. He has obtained his Ph.D. in Economics from the London School of Economics and Political Science, University of London and M.A. in Economics from the University of Essex and El Colegio de México. He is Emeritus National Researcher, Mexico and member of the Governing Committee, COLMEX as well as Director of the Center for Economic Studies, COLMEX (2009–2012). Yúnez-Naude's teaching and theses supervision include economic development, natural resources and CC, rural out-migration, trade, agriculture, rural poverty and income distribution; applied partial and general equilibrium models. Several of Prof. Yúnez-Naude's M.A. students have obtained the Ph.D. from prestigious US programs in agriculture and natural resource economics, such as those at Texas A&M and the University of California-Davis. They are now working in Mexican research institutions or hold high government posts, among others, in the Central Bank of Mexico and the National Institute of Statistics, Geography and Informatics. Research areas include sustainable development, with special attention to the rural sector of low and medium-income countries, migration, CC, and natural resources. The following are some of his selected recent research works: (1) Trends of labor migration from Mexico and from Northern Central American countries to the USA and migration policy options; (2) Mexico's corn imports from the United States and the impact on migration trends under NAFTA; (3) Incorporating natural resources in social accounting matrixes for economic-wide analyses of the impacts of CC and policies; (4) Economy-wide effects of policies to mitigate the COVID-19 pandemic; and (5) Economy-wide effects of COVID-19 on Mexico's employment, poverty, and income distribution. Yúnez-Naude has been the Director of the Program for the Study of Economic Change of Mexico's Agriculture (PRECESAM, Spanish acronym) during 1998–2009; Codirector of Rural Economies of The Americas (REAP), University of California-Davis, from 1997 to 2015; Member of the Advisory Board, *Agricultural Economics* between 2004 and 2009; Member of editorial committee of books in economics and public administration, *Fondo de Cultura Economica* from 2003; Member of the editorial committee *Lecturas de Economía*, University of Antioquia, Colombia, from 2009.

Yúnez-Naude's selected recent publications include: (1) With Dyer, G. and Lopez-Feldman, A. (2018). Maize (Zea mays L.) management in Yaxcaba, Yucatan, during the twenty first century's first decade is consistent with and overall loss of landrace diversity in Southeast Mexico. *Genetic Resources and Crop Evolution (GRES), 65*, p. 29–54, https://doi.org/10.1007/s10722-017-0507-3. (2) With Mora-Rivera, J. and Govea-Vargas, Y. (2021). What is the relationship between US–Mexico migration and trade in agriculture? In R. Hinojosa-Ojeda and E. Telles (eds.), *The Trump Paradox Migration, Trade, and Racial Politics in US–Mexico Integration* (Chapter 10, pp. 148–158). University of California Press. https://doi.org/10.1525/9780520972513-014. (3) With López, A. (2021). La política agrícola en México: Evaluación a partir de una tipología de productores. *Estudios Sociológicos*, https://www.scielo.org.mx/pdf/es/v39n116/2448-6442-es-39-116-495.pdf, and in *Estudios Sociológicos, 39*(116), 495–532. (4) With Hernández-Solano, A., López-López, A., and Govea-Vargas, Y. (2022). Socioeconomic effects of COVID-19 in Mexico: A multisectoral approach and policy options. *Latin American Economic Journal, 31*, 1–20.

Jorge Mora-Rivera has a Ph.D. in Economics from El Colegio de México. He works as Professor and Researcher at the School of Social Science and Government in the Economics Department at Instituto Tecnologico y de Estudios Superiores de Monterrey (ITESM). Mora-Rivera's work has appeared in various international journals, including *World Development*, *Telecommunication Policy*, *Journal of Travel Research*, *New Media and Society*, *Journal of International Migration and Integration*, *Technology in Society*, and other prestigious publications. He is a member of Mexico's National System of Researchers (SNI) and has served as a consultant for the Mexican government and international organizations, including the World Bank, Inter-American Development Bank, ECLAC, UNDP, and FAO. His areas of interest are economic development, natural resources, international migration, CC, poverty, inequality and food security in the rural sector, and applied econometrics. Some of his recent publications are: (1) Mora-Rivera, J. and García-Mora, F. (2021). International remittances as a driver of domestic tourism expenditure: Evidence from Mexico. *Journal of Travel Research, 60*(8), 1752–1779. https://doi.org/10.1177/0047287520962222. (2) Mora-Rivera, J. and van Gameren, E. (2021). The impact of remittances on food insecurity: Evidence from Mexico. *World Development, 140*. https://doi.org/10.1016/j.worlddev.2020.105349. (3) García-Mora, F. and Mora-Rivera, J. (2021). Exploring the impacts of Internet access on poverty: A regional analysis of rural Mexico. *New Media and Society*. https://doi.org/10.1177/14614448211000650. (4) Mora-Rivera, J. and García-Mora, F. (2021). Internet access and poverty reduction: Evidence from rural and urban Mexico. *Telecommunication Policy, 45*(2). https://doi.org/10.1016/j.telpol.2020.102076. (5) Guerrero-Carrera, J., Jaramillo, J. L., Mora-Rivera, J., Bustamante, A., and Chulin, N. (2020). Impact of CC on coffee production. *Tropical and Subtropical Agroecosystems, 23*(3). (6) Martínez-Domínguez, M. and Mora-Rivera, J. (2020). Internet adoption and usage patterns in rural Mexico. *Technology in Society, 60.* https://doi.org/10.1016/j.techsoc.2019.101226.

Contents

List of Figures

List of Tables

List of Boxes

Acronyms and Abbreviations

AFOLU	Agriculture, Forestry, and Other Land Uses
AR6	Sixth Assessment Report
AR5	Fifth Assessment Report
B20	Business 20
BECCS	Bioenergy Carbon Capture and Storage
°C	Celsius
CC	Climate Change
CCUS	Carbon Capture Utilization and Storage
CAIT	Climate Data Explores
CES	Constant Elasticity of Substitution
CIS	Commonwealth Independent Countries
CDM	Clean Development Mechanism
CEOs	Chief Executive Officers
CET	Constant Elasticity of Transformation
CGEM	Computable General Equilibrium Models
CH_4	Methane
CO_2	Carbon Dioxide
COPs	Conference of the Parties
DREM	Disaggregated Rural Economywide Models
ES	Earth Summit
EIT	Economies in Transition
F-gases	Hydrofluorocarbons HFCs, perfluorocarbons PFCs, and sulphur hexafluoride, SF_6
FABLE	Food, Agriculture, Biodiversity, Land, and Energy

FAO	Food and Agriculture Organization of the United Nations
FOLU	Forestry and Other Land Uses
FFRC	Forest Finance Risk Consortium
FVA	Framework of Various Approaches of the UNFCC
GDP	Gross Domestic Product
GHG	Greenhouse Gas
GIZ	German Agency for International Development
GMST	Global Mean Surface Temperature
GTAP	Global Trade Analysis Project
Gt CO_2-eq yr^{-1}	Carbon Dioxide Equivalent per Year
$GTCO_2e$	Gigatons of Equivalent Carbon dioxide emissions
ha	Hectares
ICSU	International Council of Scientific Unions
IFAD	International Fund for Agricultural Development
IFPRI	International Food Policy Research Institute
IMO	International Meteorological Organization
IMOMM	Input–Output Multiplier Model
INDCs	Intended Nationally Determined Contributions
INC	Intergovernmental Negotiating Committee
IPBES	Intergovernmental Science-Policy Platform on Biodiversity and Ecosystem Services
IT	International Transparency
IOT	Input–Output Table
IAD	Institutional Analysis and Development
IPCC	Intergovernmental Panel on Climate Change
ITMOs	Internationally Transferred Mitigation Outcomes
IRP	International Resource Panel
KJWA	Koronivia Joint Work on Agriculture
LDCs	Less-Developed Countries
LUC	Land-Use Change
LULUCF	Land-Use Change and Forestry

MIROC	Interdisciplinary Research on Climate
N_2O	Nitrous Oxide
NELM	New Economics of Labor Migration
NDCs	Nationally Determined Contributions
NGOs	Non-Governmental Organizations
OECD	Organization for Economic Cooperation and Development
PACC	Paris Agreement on Climate Change
PBS USA	Public Broadcasting Service
PPP	Purchasing Power Parity
PT	Productive Territories
PoU	Prevalence of Undernourishment
RCPs	Representative Concentration Pathways
SAM	Social Accounting Matrix
SAMMM	SAM-Based Multiplier Model
SAMs	Social Accounting Matrixes
SBSTA	Subsidiary Body for Scientific and Technological Advice
SDGs	Sustainable Development Goals
SPM	Summary for Policymakers
SSPs	Shared Socioeconomic Pathways
TEEB	The Economics of Ecosystems & Biodiversity
TFP	Total Factor Productivity
UN	United Nations
UNGA	United Nations General Assembly
UNEP	United National Environment Programme
UNCTAD	United Nations Conference on Trade and Development
UNFCCC	United Nations Framework Convention on Climate Change
USA	United States of America
WB	World Bank
WMO	World Meteorological Organization
WTO	World Trade Organization
WWF	World Wildlife Fund for Nature
WSSD	World Summit for Sustainable Development

Chapter 1

Introduction

Climate change is the shift in climate patterns caused primarily by greenhouse gas (GHG) emissions. GHG emissions are trapped by the earth's atmosphere and have been the main driving force of global warming. We can divide the principal forces behind GHG emissions into two: natural systems and human activities. Natural system emissions include those from forest fires, wetlands, oceans, volcano activities and mud, permafrost, and earthquakes. GHG emissions from human activities are related to energy production, industry, forestry and land use, and land use changes. Based on the results of a statistical analysis of global GHG emissions, Yue and Gao (2018) conclude that natural systems can be considered as self-balancing and that emissions from human activities add additional pressure to the earth's system.

Global warming is a fact: The average global temperature is estimated to be 1.1°C (±0.1°C) above the average level reached during 1850–1900. Scientific evidence point to human influence on the climate system and to increases in global warming, with impacts observed across all continents and oceans.

According to the Intergovernmental Panel on Climate Change (IPCC),[1] human activities are estimated to have caused approximately 1.0°C of global warming above pre-industrial levels in 1750 (IPCC, 2018).

As a consequence of global warming, in 2018, the world suffered 315 cases of natural disasters mainly related to the climate. Approximately 68.5 million people were affected, and economic losses amounted to $131.7 billion, of which storms, floods, wildfires, and droughts accounted for approximately 93%. Economic losses attributed to wildfires in 2018 alone are almost equal to the collective losses from wildfires incurred over the past decade, which is quite alarming. Furthermore, food, water, health, ecosystems, human habitat, and infrastructure have been identified as the most vulnerable sectors under attack by the climate (Fawzy *et al.*, 2020).

During recent years, several regions around the world have witnessed extreme climate conditions, such as drought, temperatures reaching 50°C, and fires on the western coast of North America (British Colombia, California, Oregon, and the State of Washington); drought followed by extreme rains in southern Australia; a 4-year drought in southern Madagascar, Mozambique, and Jordan; extreme temperatures and/or floods in Europe and Southeast Asia (see https://knoema.es/atlas/sources/WMO?topic=Climate%20Change and https://public.wmo.int/en/about-us/who-we-are, consulted on December 20, 2021).

Major contributors to CC are anthropogenic GHG emissions (carbon dioxide (CO_2), methane (CH_4), and nitrous oxide (N_2O) that have increased since the pre-industrial period, caused largely by economic and population growth, and are now higher than ever. This has led to unprecedented atmospheric concentrations of GHG emissions.

[1] In association with the World Meteorological Organization (WMO, https://public.wmo.int/en.) and the United Nations Environment Programme (UNEP), the IPCC was created in 1988 with the purpose to provide governments at all levels with scientific knowledge that they can use to develop climate policies and to supply regular assessments of the scientific basis of climate change, its impacts, and future risks (https://www.ipcc.ch).

Their effects, together with those of other anthropogenic drivers, have been detected throughout the climate system and are likely to have been the dominant cause of the observed warming since the mid-20th century. For example, carbon dioxide emissions grew by 2% and reached a record high of 37 billion tons of CO_2 in 2018 (https://www.ipcc.ch/report/, consulted on December 20, 2021).

Remarkable economic growth since the Industrial Revolution has shown that conditions from the middle of the past century to date have not been sustainable since they have been based on the increasing use of fossil fuels and the depletion of natural resources or natural capital (see Box 1.1). In addition, economic growth has not equally benefited all populations, regions, and countries, and poverty prevails throughout the world. In addition, most communities whose inhabitants live in poverty are in rural areas and many of them depend on natural resources.

Global warming causes extreme weather events, such as heatwaves, record-breaking fires, tropical cyclones, floods, and drought. These events are increasing and have a profound impact on socio-economic development and the environment.

Box 1.1. Natural Capital: Definition, Relevance and Valuation

What is natural capital? Natural capital can be defined as the world's stocks of natural assets: geology, soil, air, water, and all living things. It is from this natural capital that humans derive a wide range of services, often called ecosystem services, which make human life possible. The most obvious ecosystem services include the food we eat, the water we drink, and the plant materials we use for fuel, building materials and medicines. There are also many less visible ecosystem services such as the climate regulation and natural flood defenses provided by forests, the billions of tons of carbon stored by peatlands, and the pollination of crops by insects. Even less visible are cultural ecosystem services such as the inspiration we take from wildlife and the natural environment [*].

(*Continued*)

Box 1.1. (*Continued*)

Why is natural capital an issue? In terms of financial capital, overspending causes debt, which if left unchecked can result in bankruptcy. With natural capital, using excess stock from our natural environment can also lead to debt which must be repaid, for example, by replanting forests or allowing aquifers to replenish. If we continue to reduce stocks of natural capital without allowing or encouraging nature to recover, we risk local, regional, or even global ecosystem collapse. Poorly managed natural capital therefore becomes not only an ecological liability but a social and economic liability as well. Working against nature by overexploiting natural capital can be catastrophic not only in terms of biodiversity loss but also catastrophic in human terms, as ecosystem productivity and resilience decline and some regions become more prone to extreme events like floods and droughts. Ultimately, overexploitation makes sustainability more difficult for human communities, particularly in already stressed ecosystems, potentially leading to starvation, conflict over resource scarcity, and displacement of populations.

Is natural capital really valuable in financial terms? Nature is priceless though not valueless, as proven by many studies that have calculated the value of natural capital in financial terms. For example, street trees in California provide $1 billion per year in ecosystem services, through atmospheric regulation and flood prevention, and Mexico's mangrove forests provide an annual $70 billion to the economy through storm protection, fisheries support, and ecotourism. In 2013, the TEEB for Business Coalition published a well-known report that estimated that the world's primary production and processing sectors are responsible for "environmental externality" costs totaling a staggering $7.3 trillion annually. A year later, a study published in the journal of *Global Environmental Change* revealed that the total value of the world's ecosystem services amounted to twice as much as global aggregate GDP — as much as $124.8 trillion per year.

Box 1.1. (*Continued*)

Source: Natural Capital Forum, https://naturalcapitalforum.com/about/ (consulted on July, 22, 2021; see also https://naturalcapitalforum.com/).

[*] The International Resource Panel (IRP) considers that natural resources are formed by metals, minerals, fossil fuels, biomass, water, and land. It adds that these resources can be tracked as flows through the economy: from extraction, through processing and consumption, to point of reuse or discarding at end-of-life (IRP, 2021, p. 3).

References

Fawzy, S., Osman, A. I., Doran, J., and Rooney, D. (2020). Strategies for mitigation of climate change: A review. *Environmental Chemistry Letters, 18*, 2069–2094. https://doi.org/10.1007/s10311-020-01059-w.

International Resource Panel (IRP). (2021). *Building Biodiversity: The Natural Resource Management Approach.* J. Potočnik and I. Teixeira (eds.). A think piece of the International Resource Panel Co-Chairs, 42 p.

Intergovernmental Panel on Climate Change (IPCC). (2018). Summary for Policymakers. In V. Masson-Delmotte, P. Zhai, H.-O. Pörtner, D. Roberts, J. Skea, P. R. Shukla, A. Pirani, W. Moufouma-Okia, C. Péan, R. Pidcock, S. Connors, J. B. R. Matthews, Y. Chen, X. Zhou, M. I. Gomis, E. Lonnoy, T. Maycock, M. Tignor, and T. Waterfield (eds.), *Global Warming of 1.5°C.* An IPCC Special Report on the impacts of global warming of 1.5°C above pre-industrial levels and related global greenhouse gas emission pathways, in the context of strengthening the global response to the threat of climate change, sustainable development, and efforts to eradicate poverty. https://www.ipcc.ch/sr15/chapter/spm/.

Yue, X.-L. and Gao, Q.-X. (2018). Contributions of natural systems and human activity to greenhouse gas emissions. *Advances in Climate Change Research, 9*, 243–252. www.sciencedirect.com/science/article/pii/S1674927818300376.

Chapter 2

The Framework

In this chapter, we present the context of the chapters that follow by discussing the notion of sustainable development and provide a summary of the evidence pointing to anthropogenic roots as a major cause of global warming since the Industrial Revolution, and the risks climate change (hereinafter referred to as CC) pose to humans. We also refer to the commitments undertaken by the United Nations member countries to contain global warming and compare them with actual trends, as well as the actions required to limit average global temperature by 2030 to 1.5°C (2.7°F) with respect to pre-industrial levels.

2.1 Sustainable Development

In 2015, all United Nations member states adopted the 2030 Agenda for Sustainable Development based on 17 Sustainable Development Goals (SDGs). All countries (high, middle, and low income)[1] recognize that ending poverty and other deprivations must go hand-in-hand with strategies that improve health and education, reduce

[1]To distinguish countries by income levels is preferable than using the notions of developed and less-developed countries because income is a less subjective way to measure differences between groups of countries. However, as we will see throughout the book, the traditional distinction of countries by development levels remains.

inequality, and spur economic growth while tackling CC and working to preserve our oceans and forests (https://sdgs.un.org/es/goals, consulted on July 26, 2021).[2]

The goals for 2030 are: (1) End poverty in all its forms everywhere; (2) end hunger, achieve food security,[3] and improve nutrition while promoting sustainable agriculture; (3) ensure healthy living and promote well-being; (4) ensure inclusive and equitable quality education and promote lifelong learning opportunities for all; (5) achieve gender equality and empower all women and girls; (6) ensure availability and sustainable management of freshwater and sanitation for all; (7) ensure access to affordable, reliable, sustainable, and modern energy; (8) promote sustained, inclusive and sustainable economic growth, full and productive job opportunities, and decent work for all; (9) build resilient infrastructure, promote inclusive and sustainable industrialization, and foster innovation; (10) reduce inequality within and among countries; (11) make cities and human settlements inclusive, safe, resilient, and sustainable; (12) ensure sustainable consumption and production patterns; (13) take immediate measures to combat CC and its impacts; (14) conserve and sustainably use the oceans, seas, and marine resources for sustainable development; (15) protect, restore, and promote sustainable use of terrestrial ecosystems, sustainably manage forests, combat desertification, and inhibit and reverse land degradation, and halt biodiversity loss (see Box 2.1); (16) promote peaceful and inclusive societies

[2]The SDGs build on decades of work by countries and the UN, beginning in June 1992 with the Earth Summit in Rio de Janeiro, Brazil, where more than 178 countries adopted the Agenda, a comprehensive plan of actions to build a global partnership for sustainable development to improve human lives and protect the environment, followed by the Paris Agreement on Climate Change signed in December 2015. Now, the annual High-level Political Forum on Sustainable Development serves as the central UN platform for the follow-up and review of the SDGs.

[3]According to the Food and Agriculture Organization of the United Nations (FAO), food security exists when all people, at all times, have physical and economic access to sufficient safe and nutritious food that meets their dietary needs and food preferences for an active and healthy life (https://www.fao.org/3/al936e/al936e00.pdf) (fao.org, consulted on October 31, 2021).

for sustainable development; provide access to justice for all and build effective, accountable, and inclusive institutions at all levels; (17) strengthen the means of implementation and revitalize the Global Partnership for Sustainable Development.

Box 2.1. Biodiversity

Biodiversity is the diversity within species, between species and ecosystems. It offers our world untold richness. It delivers crucial services for human health and societal resilience, while also providing clear intrinsic value … [*]. The advantages of a biodiverse planet are widespread and varied; from reducing the likelihood of zoonotic diseases, to mitigating the impacts of flooding. Biodiversity underpins our food systems by aiding crop pollination and promoting healthy soil formation.

> [Biodiversity] … boosts ecosystem productivity and resilience, ensuring every resource that humanity relies on from the natural world is amplified and protected from system shocks. Two-thirds of our marine life is under threat from plastic pollution and overfishing, and global recorded populations of animals, mammals, birds, fish, amphibians and reptiles have fallen by 68 per cent over the last half century … In less than half a century we have witnessed the disappearance of about half of Earth's forests and one million animal and plant species are threatened with extinction. …

We know that the primary cause of biodiversity loss is the inefficient use in production of natural resources. The International Resource Panel (IRP) Global Resources Outlook 2019 found that the extraction and processing of biomass drives over 80% of land-use-related biodiversity loss. Biomass — crops, crop residues, grazed biomass, timber, and wild catch of fish — is used for food, material, feedstock, and for energy, of which the unsustainable production and consumption of agricultural commodities is a major culprit … (IRP, 2019). Three-quarters of the Earth's surface has been altered by humans, leading to an unprecedented decline of forest and natural spaces …

(*Continued*)

Box 2.1. (*Continued*)

This approach is self-destructive: the food system relies heavily on the ecosystem services provided by biodiversity, such as pollination, healthy soils, and clean water. These provisioning ecosystem services all depend on healthy, biodiverse, and natural environments. Their true value remains unknown [see Chapter VI], but the costs of ecosystem degradation are beginning to stack up. The Food and Agriculture Organization of the United Nations (FAO) estimates that [by the end of 2010's], globally, $240–560 billion worth of crops rely on honey bee pollination ..., yet in the USA over the past 60 years honey bee hives have declined by 60%. Mangrove forests help avoid an estimated $80 billion each year globally in coastal flooding damage, yet they continue to be cleared for better sea views, coastal aquaculture, and maritime access.

We have failed to manage natural capital in a manner that maintains resilience and prosperity. Increased extraction of natural capital will now therefore come at the expense of future provision of the services nature provides.

Nature is a resource keeping each of us alive; but it is degrading rapidly and being shared unfairly. High-income countries, representing one-third of the global population, have material consumption footprints that are 60% higher than middle-income countries, and 13 times the level of low-income countries (IRP, 2019).

While the poor rely on biodiversity and natural resources for their basic survival, it is the wealthier nations whose consumption of these resources lead to the greatest negative environmental impact.

[*] "Intrinsic value defined as the true value of an asset not determined by market prices. In the case of nature, recognizing that it has value in its own right, independent of human use."

Source: International Resource Panel (IRP) (2021, pp. 6–8).

(*Continued*)

Box 2.1. (*Continued*)

Authors note: Trends of biodiversity loss contrast with the commitments under the United Nations Convention on Biological Diversity whose three main objectives are the following: conservation of biological diversity, sustainable use of its components, and equitable and fair sharing of the benefits arising from genetic resources. The Convention was adopted in Nairobi back in May 1992 and was signed by 168 countries at Rio de Janeiro in mid-1992 June 1993.

In regard to biodiversity loss the IRP proposes that: "To the world's efforts to restore and regenerate nature, ... the single-biggest missing piece [is]: natural resource management. The picture that emerges is one of opportunity: for biodiversity-rich nations to be recognized for the value of their natural wealth and be rewarded for maintaining ecosystem services, and for countries with high resource footprints to invest in global natural resource management as an efficient strategy to reduce their indirect pressure on biodiversity to ensure an environmentally secure future" (IRP, 2021, Foreword).

In order to measure progress in achieving these goals, the United Nations (UN) designed a framework of global indicators for SDGs and targets. The UN member states are committed to providing the necessary data for the UN to estimate progress (see Section 2.3).

2.2 The Anthropogenic Roots of Climate Change: Facts and Risks[4]

During the past two centuries and a half economic and population growth have led to atmospheric concentrations of greenhouse gas (GHG) emissions, largely consisting of carbon dioxide (CO_2),

[4]This section is mainly based on IPCC 2014 and 2018.

methane (CH_4), and nitrous oxide (N_2O). These emissions are unprecedented in at least the last 800,000 years. Their effects, together with those of other anthropogenic drivers, have been detected throughout the climate system and are, according to the Intergovernmental Panel on Climate Change (IPCC) *extremely likely* to have been the dominant cause of the observed warming since the mid-20th century.[5]

Between 1750 and 2011 about 40% of anthropogenic CO_2 emissions to the atmosphere have remained in the atmosphere; the rest was stored on land (in plants and soils) and in the oceans causing ocean acidification. Emissions of CO_2 from fossil fuel combustion and industrial processes contributed about 78% of the total GHG emissions increase from 1970 to 2010. Between 2000 and 2010 the contribution on CO_2 emissions of population growth remained similar to the previous three decades, while the contribution of economic growth has risen sharply. These tendencies have been present despite a growing number of CC mitigation policies.

GHG emissions impact the climate system leading to CC. In recent decades, changes in climate have affected natural and human systems on all continents and across the oceans. CC is strongest and most comprehensive for natural systems: e.g., freshwater quantity and quality and many animal species have migrated, whereas the effects of CC on humans differ among populations (e.g., many studies covering wide ranges of regions and crops show that negative impacts of CC on crop yields have been more common than positive impacts (results for the case of corn in Mexico show in Box 2.2).[6]

[5]The IPCC was created in 1988 by the World Meteorological Organization (WMO) and the United Nations Environment Programme (UNEP) to provide policymakers assessments of the scientific basis of climate change, its impacts, and future risks, and options for adaptation and mitigation. In Section 4.2, we present these two actions agents may take regarding CC.

[6]See Section 5.3.3 of Chapter 5 for a description of the model used in the study summarized in Box 5.1.

Box 2.2. Climate Change and Corn in Mexico

In rural areas the effects of climate change (CC) are and will differ between regions and between rural household types. In our study we estimate the direct and indirect likely impacts of CC on Mexico's five rural regions and rural households. For this we apply a microeconomy-wide model using survey data representing Mexican rural households (Taylor and Filipski, 2014).

Based on the information resulting from the survey, rural households are distinguished according to their involvement in agricultural production, agricultural plot size, access to water, and the destination of the corn they cultivate: for family-owned consumption and/or to feed their livestock and for the market. In the model we incorporate transaction costs in corn markets. We also model market failures in Mexico's land and labor markets and consider rural households' production of crops other than corn, livestock, non-agricultural activities, and other income sources (i.e., we consider rural households' diversification of activities and income sources).

The model comprises five types of households: (1) not involved in agricultural production; (2) landless leasing land for crop production; (3) subsistence household farmers owning less than two hectares of land and using their produced corn for family-animal consumption (they are units of production and consumption; (4) commercial medium-sized farmers with plots between 2 and 5 hectares; and (5) commercial big farmers with plots of 4 hectares or more.

Based on these features of the micro-general equilibrium model, we construct social accounting matrixes (SAMs) for the five rural regions of Mexico, calibrate the model, and perform a simulation to measure the likely multisectoral effects of CC on rural households' corn production and income [details of the model in Chapter 4]. The simulated shock is based on regional estimations of the impacts

(*Continued*)

Box 2.2. (*Continued*)

of CC on corn yields using predictions of CC for the period 2040–2069 resulting from the Model for Interdisciplinary Research on Climate (MIROC) developed by the Center for Climate System Research of the University of Tokyo (Table A).

Table A. Projected Impacts of Climate Change in Corn Yields

Region	Corn under irrigation (%)	Rainfed corn (%)
South-southeast	−15.50	−33.00
Central	71.40	11.90
Central-west	−21.80	−27.50
North-west	−27.50	−28.40
North-east	0.00	6.10

Among others, our findings indicate that, in addition to the expected regional heterogeneity of the simulated corn yield changes, we find that CC effects on rural households' production and incomes widely differ between the types of households. Table B illustrates this result as regards the income; e.g., the most negatively impacted by CC are subsistence households in the south–southeast, medium-sized households in the central–west rural region and big farmers in the north–west (with respect to the base, calibrated SAM, the income of these households decreased by more than 14%).

Table B. Effects of Climate Change in Rural Households' Income

	Landless households		Land-holders' farmers			
			Subsistence	Medium	Big	
Region	Leasing in Ag. land (%)	Non-farmers (%)	[0,2) has (%)	[2,5) has (%)	[+5) has (%)	Regional (%)
South-southeast	−0.70	0.10	−14.20	−12.10	−4.40	−8.00
Central	1.00	0.70	9.40	4.60	9.80	5.80
Central-west	−1.10	−0.80	11.80	−14.30	−10.60	−5.50
North-west	0.10	−1.50	−3.40	−8.70	−14.90	−3.90
North-east	0.50	0.20	2.40	2.70	2.00	1.30

(*Continued*)

Box 2.2. (*Continued*)

Notwithstanding that some households could be benefited by corn yield changes, the net impact of these modifications would be a reduction in the income of rural Mexico households by around $600 million, as well as a decline in corn production, the major staple food in Mexico.

In Table C, we present our results for household activities located in the south-southeast region, because it could be the most affected region by corn yields reductions resulting from CC. This region is the most affected by the incidence of poverty and is also where most of Mexico's jungles are located. We also intend to illustrate the details captured by our disaggregated-microeconomy-wide applied model.

Table C. Effects of Climate Change in South-southeast Rural Households' Economic Activities*

	Landless households		Land-holders' farmers		
			Subsistence	Medium	Big
Activity	Leasing in Ag. land (%)	Non-farmers (%)	[0,2) has (%)	[2,5) has (%)	[+5) has (%)
Rainfed corn	−39.70	—	−31.90	−36.90	−42.20
Irrigated corn	—	—	−10.70	−23.50	−19.80
Rainfed beans	—	—	1.20	1.30	1.10
Irrigated beans	—	—	2.00	3.00	—
Other rainfed field crops	0.00	—	1.10	1.00	1.00
Other irrigated field crops	—	—	2.20	—	0.00
Coffee	—	—	1.00	1.10	1.00
Sugar cane	—	—	—	—	—
Other perennial crops	—	—	1.20	1.00	1.10
Livestock	0.20	—	−1.00	0.00	0.00
Poultry	10.70	—	−7.14	0.00	0.00
Construction	—	—	—	—	—

(*Continued*)

Table C. (*Continued*)

Activity	**Landless households**		**Land-holders' farmers**		
			Subsistence	**Medium**	**Big**
	Leasing in Ag. land (%)	**Non-farmers (%)**	**[0,2) has (%)**	**[2,5) has (%)**	**[+5) has (%)**
Services (incl. small shops)	0.00	6.60	0.00	0.00	0.00
Natural resources	1.30	2.00	1.10	1.00	1.10
Other activities	3.10	5.40	0.00	0.00	0.00
Domestic migration			0.01		
Migration to the USA			0.01		

*Cells with "—" mean that the household group were not involved in the corresponding activity during the year previous to the survey.

Table C shows that, regardless of farm-household type, the activity most affected in the south-southeast would be that of corn cultivated under rainfed conditions, followed by irrigated corn. Changes in corn production would have an indirect effect, namely, to change land use to cultivate other crops, as well as a more intensive use of natural resources, for land in particular.

Finally, results show that, notwithstanding that CC would bring about losers and winners, the overall effect of the phenomenon would result in the reduction in the income of Mexican rural households, as well as the rise of food insecurity and deforestation.

Source: Hernández Solano and Yúnez Naude (2016). In the writing of the Box the authors summarized and translated these article passages.

During the last decades significant changes in extreme weather and climate events have been observed. Some of them are linked to human influences and include a decrease in cold and/or warm temperature extremes (i.e., a rise in the frequency and intensity of daily temperature extremes); increase in extreme high sea levels and in the number of heavy precipitation events and droughts in several regions of the world. Extreme recent climate-related extremes, such as heat waves, droughts, floods, cyclones and wildfires, reveal significant vulnerability and exposure of some ecosystems and human communities. Extreme climate-related events during 2020 and 2021 are outcome indicators of the effects of global warming (IPCC, 2021a).

There is scientific evidence of human influence on the climate system and that global warming is growing, with impacts observed across all continents and oceans. Anthropogenic GHG emissions have increased since the pre-industrial era, driven largely by economic and population growth, and are now higher than ever. This has led to atmospheric concentrations of carbon dioxide, methane, and nitrous oxide that are unprecedented in at least the last 800,000 years. Their effects, together with those of other anthropogenic drivers, have been detected throughout the climate system and are *extremely likely* to have been the major cause of the observed warming since the mid-20th century.

According to IPCC estimations (2018), human activities are estimated to have caused approximately 1.0°C of global warming above pre-industrial levels, with a *likely* range of 0.8–1.2°C. Global warming is *likely* to reach 1.5°C between 2030 and 2052 if it continues to increase at the current rate (*high confidence*).

If these processes continue, CC caused by humans will lead to higher risks for the present and future generations. Specifically, continued GHG emissions will cause further warming and long-lasting changes in all components of the climate system, increasing the likelihood of severe, pervasive, and irreversible impacts for people and ecosystems. These risks are unevenly distributed and are generally greater for disadvantaged people and communities in countries at all levels of development and are particularly relevant for individual regions.

One major risk is that CC will undermine food security. Global marine species redistribution and marine biodiversity reduction in sensitive regions will challenge the sustained provision of fisheries productivity and other ecosystem services. For major worldwide food staples (wheat, rice, and maize) in tropical and temperate regions, CC without adaptation is projected to negatively impact production for local temperature increases of 2°C or more above the late

20th century levels, although individual locations may benefit (an example is in Box 2.2). Global temperature increases of around 4°C or more above the late 20th century levels, combined with increasing food demand, would pose large risks to food security globally. In addition, CC is projected to reduce renewable surface water and groundwater resources in most dry subtropical regions, intensifying competition for water among sectors. Rural areas are expected to experience major impacts on freshwater availability and supply, food security, infrastructure, and agricultural incomes, including shifts in the production areas of food and non-food crops around the world (IPCC, 2014).

In addition, IPCC projects that CC will also impact human health by exacerbating health problems that already exist, especially in countries with low income and low economic growth. From a poverty perspective, CC will make poverty reduction more difficult, further erode food security, and prolong existing and create new poverty traps. CC will also increase displacement of people.

Since its 2014 Report, the IPCC warned that beyond 2100 CC will be irreversible and experience abrupt changes. Warming will continue beyond 2100 and many aspects of CC and associated impacts will continue for centuries even if anthropogenic emissions of greenhouse gases are stopped. However, the risks of abrupt or irreversible changes will increase as the magnitude of the warming increases (*Ibid.*).

These facts and risks urgently require actions to limit CC, based on substantial and sustained reductions in GHG emissions (mitigation), together with adaptation.

2.3 United Nations Conferences on Climate Change

Global recognition of the consequences of CC began in 1979 during the first world conference held in Geneva where the phenomenon was introduced by the WMO.[7] In 1988 the WMO created the IPCC.

[7]WMO is a specialized agency of the United Nations (UN) with 193 Member States and Territories. WMO originated from the International Meteorological

In collaboration with the UN Environmental Program (UBEP), the IPCC provides governments with information and scientific evidence of CC and its effects, aimed at policy design and actions to reduce global warming. In 1994 UN Parties adopted the United Nations Framework Convention on Climate Change (UNFCCC), whose main purpose is to stabilize greenhouse concentrations in the atmosphere by the designing and application of national policies to limit anthropogenic GHG emissions and to promote GHG sinks. The Convention determines the commitments of all parties involved by establishing major responsibilities on high-income countries, including their financial and technical support to low-income countries. There have been several conferences of the parties (COPs) under the UNFCC. Based on the scope and commitments of the parties, the Kyoto Protocol (Box 2.3), the Paris Agreement, and the recently held Glasgow Conference stand out.

Box 2.3. The Kyoto Protocol

Principal Contents

The Kyoto Protocol was adopted on December 11, 1997. Owing to a complex ratification process, it entered into force only on February 16, 2005. Currently, there are 192 Parties to the Kyoto Protocol.

The Kyoto Protocol operationalizes the UNFCCC by committing industrialized countries and economies in transition to limit and reduce GHG emissions in accordance with agreed individual targets. The Convention itself only requires that those countries adopt policies and measures on mitigation and report periodically. The Kyoto Protocol is based on the principles and provisions of the Convention and follows its annex-based structure. It only binds developed countries, and places a heavier burden on them under

(*Continued*)

Organization (IMO), which was founded in 1873 to facilitate the exchange of weather information across national borders. https://public.wmo.int/en/about-us/who-we-are.

Box 2.3. (*Continued*)

the principle of "common but differentiated responsibility and respective capabilities," because it recognizes that they are largely responsible for the current high levels of GHG emissions in the atmosphere.

In its Annex B, the Kyoto Protocol sets binding emission reduction targets for 37 industrialized countries and economies in transition and the European Union. Overall, these targets add up to an average 5% emission reduction compared to 1990 levels over the 5 year period 2008–2012 (the first commitment).

The Kyoto Protocol does not have an enforcement mechanism, i.e., a legally binding one, in terms of what countries need to do.

Developed countries include both OECD (Organization for Economic Cooperation and Development) and Economies in Transition (EIT) countries. However, a few newly admitted OECD countries are not in Annex I list, including South Korea, Singapore, and Mexico. The group of EIT countries contains several sub-groups: those that are part of the enlarged EU, central Asian Republics, and other members of the Commonwealth Independent Countries (CIS).

Source: United Nations Climate Change (UNCC) (1992), extracts from various pages.

Major Characteristic of the Protocol

- "The Kyoto protocol introduced the emission reduction commitments for developed countries for a five-year commitment period between 2008 and 2012.
- The protocol laid out all related policies, monitoring and reporting systems, as well as introduced three market-based mechanisms to achieve those targets.
- The protocol introduced two project-based mechanisms, clean development mechanism and joint implementation mechanism.

- ◦ The clean development mechanism allows developed country parties to invest and develop emission reduction projects in developing countries, to drive sustainable development in the host country as well as offset carbon emissions of the investing party.
- ◦ Joint implementation projects allow developed country parties to develop similar projects, however, in other developed countries that are protocol parties, offsetting excess emissions of the investing party.

- ... the protocol introduced an emissions trading mechanism as a platform to facilitate the trading of annually assigned emissions that are saved by protocol members to those that exceed their limits ...
- The Kyoto units and general framework introduced and laid the structural foundation of a carbon emissions market and the concept of carbon pricing. Many national and regional governments introduced emissions trading schemes; some are mandatory while others are voluntary. In some cases, such schemes are linked to Kyoto commitments and regulations ...

In 2012, the Doha amendment to the Kyoto protocol was adopted, mainly proposing a second commitment period from 2013 to 2020 as well as updating emissions reduction targets. The amendment proposed a greenhouse gas emissions (GHG) reduction target of at least 18% below 1990 levels. The amendment has not yet entered into force since it has not been ratified by the minimum number of parties required to this date" (Fawzy *et al.*, 2020, pp. 4–5).

The Paris Agreement was negotiated in December 2015 and by July 2021, 191 members of the UNFCCC ratified the agreement.[8] The Agreement recognizes that human-induced CC has already increased the number and strength of some of the climate extreme events and so, global actions are urgently required. The long-term

[8]President Trump withdrew the United States of America (USA) from the Agreement in 2020, but President Biden rejoined in 2021. https://knoema.es/atlas/sources/WMO?topic=Climate%20Change.

temperature goal of the Paris Agreement is to maintain the global average temperature increase below 2°C (3.6°F) above pre-industrial levels and preferably limit the increase to 1.5°C (2.7°F). The Paris Agreement adds that GHS should be reduced and reach net-zero in the second-half of the 21st century and that countries need to increase their ability to adapt to CC impacts and channel financial resources to support CC mitigation and adaptation.

The Paris Agreement is in line with the UN SDGs and recognizes aspects such as: the relationship that CC actions, responses, and impacts have with equitable access to sustainable development and eradication of poverty; the safeguarding of food security and ending of hunger; the protection of human rights, the right to health, the rights of indigenous peoples, migrants, children, persons with disabilities and people in vulnerable situations, gender equality, empowerment of women, and intergenerational equity (more details in Box 2.4 for synergies between the Paris Agreement and the SDGs see UNCC, 2019).

Box 2.4. The Paris Agreement

The Paris Agreement is a United Nations international treaty on climate change, adopted in 2015 where actions for climate change mitigation, adaptation, and finance were accorded. The Agreement was negotiated by 196 Parties at the 2015 United Nations Climate Change Conference that entered into force on November 4, 2016. As of July 2021, 191 members of the United Nations Framework Convention on Climate Change (UNFCCC) are Parties to the Agreement. In the Agreement, the signing countries:

Recognize the need for an effective and progressive response to the urgent threat of climate change on the basis of the best available scientific knowledge.

Recognize the specific needs and special circumstances of developing country Parties, especially those that are particularly vulnerable to the adverse effects of climate change, as provided for in the Convention, and their need of funding and transfer of technology to take actions to reduce anthropogenic GHG missions.

Box 2.4. (*Continued*)

Recognize that Parties may be affected not only by climate change, but also by the impacts of the measures taken in response to it.

Emphasize the intrinsic relationship that climate change actions, responses, and impacts have with equitable access to sustainable development and eradication of poverty.

Recognize the fundamental priority of safeguarding food security and ending hunger, and the particular vulnerabilities of food production systems to the adverse impacts of climate change.

Recognize the need to take into account the imperatives of a just transition of the workforce and the creation of decent work and quality jobs in accordance with nationally defined development priorities,

Acknowledge that climate change is a common concern of humankind, Parties should, when taking actions to address climate change, respect, promote and consider their respective obligations on human rights, the right to health, the rights of indigenous peoples, local communities, migrants, children, persons with disabilities and people in vulnerable situations and the right to development, as well as gender equality, empowerment of women and intergenerational equity.

Recognize the importance:

- of the conservation and enhancement, as appropriate, of sinks and reservoirs of the greenhouse gases referred to in the Convention,
- of ensuring the integrity of all ecosystems, including oceans, and the protection of biodiversity, recognized by some cultures as Mother Earth, and noting the importance for some of the concept of "climate justice," when taking action to address climate change,

(*Continued*)

Box 2.4. (*Continued*)

- of education, training, public awareness, public participation, public access to information and cooperation at all levels on the matters addressed in this Agreement,
- of the engagements of all levels of government and various actors, in accordance with respective national legislations of Parties, in addressing climate change.

Also recognize that sustainable lifestyles and sustainable patterns of consumption and production, with developed country Parties taking the lead, play an important role in addressing climate change.

The Paris Agreement added further objectives, commitments, enhanced compliance and reporting regulations, as well as support mechanisms to the existing climate change combat framework in place under the UNFCC.

- The main objective of the Agreement is to limit the global temperature increase to 2°C by 2100 and pursue efforts to limit the increase to 1.5°C.
- The agreement aims to reach global peaking of greenhouse gases as soon as possible as to strike a balance between human-induced emission sources and greenhouse gas sinks and reservoirs between 2050 and 2100.
- The agreement also introduced new binding commitments, asking all parties to deliver nationally determined contributions and to enforce national measures to achieve, and attempt to exceed such commitments.
- Enhanced transparency, compliance, and clear reporting and communication are advocated under the agreement.

Box 2.4. (*Continued*)

- The Agreement encourages voluntary cooperation between parties beyond mandated initiatives. Moreover, financial support and technological support, as well as capacity building initiatives for developing countries, are mandated by the Agreement. Such obligations are to be undertaken by developed country parties to promote sustainable development and establish adequate mitigation and adaptation support measures within vulnerable countries.
- One of the most important goals established under the Agreement is that of adaptation and adaptive capacity building concerning the temperature goal set.
- Under Article 6 of the Agreement, two international market mechanisms were introduced, cooperative approaches and the sustainable development mechanism. These mechanisms are to be utilized by all parties to meet their nationally determined contributions.
    - Cooperative approaches are a framework that allows parties to utilize internationally transferred mitigation outcomes (ITMOs) to meet nationally determined contribution goals as well as stimulate sustainable development.
    - The sustainable development mechanism is a new approach that promotes mitigation and sustainable development and is perceived as the successor of the clean development mechanism.

Source: Fawzy *et al.* (2020, p. 5).

A fundamental commitment of the Paris Agreement is that the signing states provide information needs relevant to implementing the broader global development agenda, such as synergies between adaptation and mitigation in the context of sustainable development, associated costs, co-benefits and risks, and climate action solution in the context of pursuing the Unite Nations SDGs. Specifically, Article 13, Section 7 states that "(a) Each Party shall regularly provide the following information: (a) A national inventory report of anthropogenic emissions by sources and removals by sinks of greenhouse gases,[9] prepared using good practice methodologies accepted by the IPCC and agreed upon by the Conference of the Parties (COP) serving as the meeting of the Parties to the Paris Agreement. (b) Information necessary to track progress made in implementing and achieving its nationally determined contribution ..." (https://sdgs.un.org/).

To fulfill the UN SDGs and the objectives of the Paris Agreement for reducing global warming, political will is necessary at all levels: worldwide, country, local, and community-wise, etc. It also entails studies on tendencies, causes and effects of global warming, and projections to inform policymakers and civil society. The latter require science, information, and data.

In 2021 the United Nations Environment Programme (UNEP, 2021) published the "Measuring Progress" report with two purposes: (1) to explore the potential and limitations of using a statistical correlation analysis between indicator pairs ("state of the environment" and "drivers of change" indicators; "state of the environment" and "state of society" indicators) to improve the understanding of the interlinkages between SDG indicators (Box 2.5); and (2) to inform on progress being made for those SDG indicators UNEP identified as environment-related since December 2018, based on data from the SDG Global Indicators Database (p. 4).

[9]All green plants take up carbon dioxide from the atmosphere and release oxygen during photosynthesis. When these components of natural capital deteriorate or disappear (e.g., when forests are cut down), much of that stored carbon is released into the atmosphere again as CO_2. This is how deforestation and forest degradation contribute to global warming.

Box 2.5. Selected Goals, Targets and Indicators from the 2030 Agenda for Sustainable Development

Selected goals and targets	Indicators
Goal 6. Ensure availability and sustainable management of water and sanitation for all	
6.4 By 2030, substantially increase water-use efficiency across all sectors and ensure sustainable withdrawals and supply of freshwater to address water scarcity and substantially reduce the number of people suffering from water scarcity	6.4.1 Change in water-use efficiency over time 6.4.2 Level of water stress: Freshwater withdrawal as a proportion of available freshwater resources
6.5 By 2030, implement integrated water resources management at all levels, including through transboundary cooperation, as appropriate	6.5.1 Degree of integrated water resources management 6.5.2 Proportion of transboundary basin area with an operational arrangement for water cooperation
6.6 By 2020, protect and restore water-related ecosystems, including mountains, forests, wetlands, rivers, aquifers and lakes	6.6.1 Change in the extent of water-related ecosystems over time

(*Continued*)

Box 2.5. (*Continued*)

Selected goals and targets	Indicators
Goal 12. Ensure sustainable consumption and production patterns	
12.2 By 2030, achieve the sustainable management and efficient use of natural resources	12.2.1 Material footprint, material footprint per capita, and material footprint per GDP 12.2.2 Domestic material consumption, domestic material consumption per capita, and domestic material consumption per GDP
12.8 By 2030, ensure that people everywhere have the relevant information and awareness for sustainable development and lifestyles in harmony with nature	12.8.1 Extent to which (i) global citizenship education and (ii) education for sustainable development are mainstreamed in (a) national education policies; (b) curricula; (c) teacher education; and (d) student assessment
12.a Support developing countries to strengthen their scientific and technological capacity to move towards more sustainable patterns of consumption and production	12.a.1 Installed renewable energy-generating capacity in developing countries (in watts per capita)

Box 2.5. (*Continued*)

Selected goals and targets	Indicators
12.b Develop and implement tools to monitor sustainable development impacts for sustainable tourism that creates jobs and promotes local culture and products	12.b.1 Implementation of standard accounting tools to monitor the economic and environmental aspects of tourism sustainability
Goal 13. Take urgent action to combat climate change and its impacts	
13.1 Strengthen resilience and adaptive capacity to climate-related hazards and natural disasters in all countries	13.1.1 Number of deaths, missing persons, and directly affected persons attributed to disasters per 100,000 population
	13.1.2 Number of countries that adopt and implement national disaster risk reduction strategies in line with the Sendai Framework for Disaster Risk Reduction 2015–2030
	13.1.3 Proportion of local governments that adopt and implement local disaster risk reduction strategies in line with national disaster risk reduction strategies

(*Continued*)

Box 2.5. (*Continued*)

Selected goals and targets	Indicators
13.2 Integrate climate change measures into national policies, strategies and planning	13.2.1 Number of countries with nationally determined contributions, long-term strategies, national adaptation plans and adaptation communications, as reported to the secretariat of the United Nations Framework Convention on Climate Change
	13.2.2 Total greenhouse gas emissions per year
13.3 Improve education, awareness-raising and human and institutional capacity on climate change mitigation, adaptation, impact reduction and early warning	13.3.1 Extent to which (i) global citizenship education and (ii) education for sustainable development are mainstreamed in (a) national education policies; (b) curricula; (c) teacher education; and (d) student assessment

Box 2.5. (*Continued*)

Selected goals and targets	Indicators
13.a Implement the commitment undertaken by developed-country parties to the United Nations Framework Convention on Climate Change to a goal of mobilizing jointly $100 billion annually by 2020 from all sources to address the needs of developing countries in the context of meaningful mitigation actions and transparency on implementation and fully operationalize the Green Climate Fund through its capitalization as soon as possible	13.a.1 Amounts provided and mobilized in United States dollars per year in relation to the continued existing collective mobilization goal of the $100 billion commitment through to 2025

(*Continued*)

Box 2.5. (*Continued*)

Selected goals and targets	Indicators
13.b Promote mechanisms for raising capacity for effective climate change-related planning and management in least developed countries and small island developing states, including focusing on women, youth and local and marginalized communities	13.b.1 Number of least developed countries and small island developing states with nationally determined contributions, long-term strategies, national adaptation plans and adaptation communications, as reported to the secretariat of the United Nations Framework Convention on Climate Change
Goal 15. Protect, restore and promote sustainable use of terrestrial ecosystems, sustainably manage forests, combat desertification, and halt and reverse land degradation and halt biodiversity loss	
15.1 By 2020, ensure the conservation, restoration and sustainable use of terrestrial and inland freshwater ecosystems and their services, in particular forests, wetlands, mountains, and drylands, in line with obligations under international agreements	15.1.1 Forest area as a proportion of total land area 15.1.2 Proportion of important sites for terrestrial and freshwater biodiversity that are covered by protected areas, by ecosystem type

Box 2.5. (*Continued*)

Selected goals and targets	Indicators
15.2 By 2020, promote the implementation of sustainable management of all types of forests, halt deforestation, restore degraded forests, and substantially increase afforestation and reforestation globally	15.2.1 Progress toward sustainable forest management
15.3 By 2030, combat desertification, restore degraded land and soil, including land affected by desertification, drought and floods, and strive to achieve a land degradation-neutral world	15.3.1 Proportion of land that is degraded over total land area
15.4 By 2030, ensure the conservation of mountain ecosystems, including their biodiversity, in order to enhance their capacity to provide benefits that are essential for sustainable development	15.4.1 Coverage by protected areas of important sites for mountain biodiversity 15.4.2 Mountain Green Cover Index
15.5 Take urgent and significant action to reduce the degradation of natural habitats, halt the loss of biodiversity and, by 2020, protect and prevent the extinction of threatened species	15.5.1 Red List Index

(*Continued*)

Box 2.5. (*Continued*)

Selected goals and targets	Indicators
15.6 Promote fair and equitable sharing of the benefits arising from the utilization of genetic resources and promote appropriate access to such resources, as internationally agreed	15.6.1 Number of countries that have adopted legislative, administrative and policy frameworks to ensure fair and equitable sharing of benefits
15.7 Take urgent action to end poaching and trafficking of protected species of flora and fauna and address both demand and supply of illegal wildlife products	15.7.1 Proportion of traded wildlife that was poached or illicitly trafficked
15.8 By 2020, introduce measures to prevent the introduction and significantly reduce the impact of invasive alien species on land and water ecosystems and control or eradicate the priority species	15.8.1 Proportion of countries adopting relevant national legislation and adequately resourcing the prevention or control of invasive alien species

Box 2.5. (*Continued*)

Selected goals and targets	Indicators
15.9 By 2020, integrate ecosystem and biodiversity values into national and local planning, development processes, poverty reduction strategies and accounts	15.9.1 (a) Number of countries that have established national targets in accordance with or similar to Aichi Biodiversity Target 2 of the Strategic Plan for Biodiversity 2011–2020 in their national biodiversity strategy and action plans and the progress reported towards these targets; and (b) integration of biodiversity into national accounting and reporting systems, defined as implementation of the System of Environmental-Economic Accounting

(*Continued*)

Box 2.5. (*Continued*)

Selected goals and targets	Indicators
15.a Mobilize and significantly increase financial resources from all sources to conserve and sustainably use biodiversity and ecosystems	15.a.1 (a) Official development assistance on conservation and sustainable use of biodiversity; and (b) revenue generated and finance mobilized from biodiversity-relevant economic instruments
15.b Mobilize significant resources from all sources and at all levels to finance sustainable forest management and provide adequate incentives to developing countries to advance such management, including for conservation and reforestation	15.b.1 (a) Official development assistance on conservation and sustainable use of biodiversity; and (b) revenue generated and finance mobilized from biodiversity-relevant economic instruments
15.c Enhance global support for efforts to combat poaching and trafficking of protected species, including by increasing the capacity of local communities to pursue sustainable livelihood opportunities	15.c.1 Proportion of traded wildlife that was poached or illicitly trafficked

Source: UNEP (2021), Annex A, pp. 133–141. https://wedocs.unep.org/bitstream/handle/20.500.11822/36607/SDGMP_EN.pdf (consulted on August 2, 2021).

Two major conclusions follow from the UNEP Report. The first one is that "Many countries are now expending substantial efforts to measure their progress across the environmental dimension of the SDGs and progress in some environmental areas is being made." The second conclusion is that "Overall, progress since 2000 has been insufficient to realize the 2030 Agenda and key environmental areas have continued to deteriorate. This is most obvious regarding the two global issues of biodiversity loss and CC, although these issues are not really holistically captured in the SDGs and thus understanding biodiversity/ecosystem service provisioning or climate change vulnerability requires additional indicators" (UNEP, 2021, pp. 119, 121).[10]

In regard to the purposes of reducing global warming the IPCC published a report for policymakers on the impacts of global warming of 1.5°C above pre-industrial levels and related global GHG emissions pathways contained in the Decision of the 21st Conference of Parties of the UNFCCC to adopt the Paris Agreement (IPCC, 2018).

2.4 Pathway to Achieve Sustainability

Based on scientific evidence, the IPCC concludes that anthropogenic GHG emissions are mainly driven by economic activity, population size, lifestyle, energy use, land use patterns, technology, and climate policy. Using a multi-model mean projection for 2081–2100 relative to 1986–2005, the IPCC uses these drivers to construct Representative Concentration Pathways (RCPs), used for making projections, describing four different 21st century pathways of GHG emissions and atmospheric concentrations, air pollutant emissions, and land use: (1) Stringent mitigation scenario, a scenario that aims to keep global warming below 2°C above pre-industrial temperatures; (2) two intermediate scenarios; (3) one scenario with very high GHG emissions; and (4) scenarios without additional efforts to constrain emissions ("baseline scenarios") that lead to pathways ranging between scenarios 2 and 3 (IPCC, 2014 and 2018).

[10]In Chapter 4, we present the progress made to accomplish the SDGs related to agriculture and food security.

The IPCC results on changes in the climate system indicate that surface temperature will rise over the 21st century under all assessed emission scenarios; heat waves will occur more often and last longer; extreme precipitation events will become more intense and frequent in many regions; the ocean will continue to warm and acidify, and global mean sea level will rise with the strongest warming projected for the surface in tropical and Northern Hemisphere subtropical regions.

However, changes in precipitation will not be uniform. Under the very high GHG emissions scenario: the high latitudes and the equatorial Pacific are *likely* to experience an increase in annual mean precipitation; in many mid-latitude and subtropical dry regions, mean precipitation will *likely* decrease; in many mid-latitude wet regions, mean precipitation will *likely* increase; and extreme precipitation events over most of the mid-latitude land masses and over wet tropical regions will *very likely* become more intense and more frequent (IPCC, 2014).

Up to mid-March 2022 the IPCC *Sixth Assessment Report* (AR6) was still in preparation. However, in the draft version of this report (consulted in February 2022), the IPCC takes into consideration the conclusions of its *Fifth Assessment Report of the Intergovernmental Panel on Climate Change* (AR5, a synthesis is in IPCC, 2014). According to AR6 Chair's Vision paper some major conclusions of AR5 are:

- "Human influence on the climate system is clear, and recent anthropogenic emissions of greenhouse gases are the highest in history. Recent climate changes have had widespread impacts on human and natural systems.
- Continued emissions of greenhouse gases will cause further warming and long-lasting changes in all components of the climate system, increasing the likelihood of severe, pervasive, and irreversible impacts for people and ecosystems. Limiting climate change would require substantial and sustained reductions in GHG which, together with adaptation, can limit climate change risks.
- Adaptation and mitigation are complementary strategies for reducing and managing the risks of climate change. Substantial

emissions reductions over the next few decades can reduce climate risks in the 21st century and beyond, increase prospects for effective adaptation, reduce the costs and challenges of mitigation in the longer term, and contribute to climate-resilient pathways for sustainable development.
- Many adaptation and mitigation options can help address climate change, but no single option is sufficient by itself. Effective implementation depends on policies and cooperation at all scales and can be enhanced through integrated responses that link adaptation and mitigation with other societal objectives" (IPCC, 2017, p. 7).

The Vision Paper adds: "Some emerging themes and outstanding issues, outlined as "key uncertainties" by AR5 WGI [Working Group I] and as "research and data gaps" by AR5 WGII and WGIII can be identified in the AR5, beyond these major conclusions. As there may be few completely new areas to be explored, efforts should also focus on improving spatial resolution within regions and reducing uncertainties when filling knowledge and data gaps" (*Ibid.*).

2.5 Growing Gap between GHG Emissions Reduction Targets and Needed Actions

Notwithstanding that the Paris Agreement was accorded in 2015, global GHG emissions have not reduced, indicating that commitments of the signing countries have not been fully followed. The scientific-based UNEP's Emissions Gap Report shows that GHG emissions have continuously grown from 2017 to 2019, reaching a record high of 52.4 gigatons of CO_2 equivalent (Gt CO_2e, range: ± 5.2) in 2019 without land-use change (LUC) emissions and 59.1 Gt CO_2e (range: ± 5.9) when including LUC (UNEP, 2021, see Box 2.6).[11]

[11]Emissions gap is measured by the difference between "where we are likely to be and where we need to be." GtCO_2e are gigatons of equivalent carbon dioxide emissions. It is a way to put emissions of various GHGs on a common footing by expressing them in terms of the amount of carbon dioxide that would have the

Box 2.6. United Nations 2019 Emissions Gap Report

Global GHG emissions continued to grow for the third consecutive year in 2019, reaching a record high of 52.4 Gt CO_2e (range: ± 5.2) without land-use change (LUC) emissions and 59.1 Gt CO_2e (range: ± 5.9) when including LUC.

Fossil carbon dioxide (CO_2) emissions (from fossil fuels and carbonates) dominate total GHG emissions including LUC (65%) and consequently the growth in GHG emissions. Preliminary data suggest that fossil CO_2 emissions reached a record 38.0 Gt CO_2 (range: ± 1.9) in 2019.

Since 2010, GHG emissions without LUC have grown at 1.3% per year on average, with preliminary data suggesting a 1.1% increase in 2019. When including the more uncertain and variable LUC emissions, global GHG emissions have grown 1.4% year since 2010 on average, with a more rapid increase of 2.6% in 2019 due to a large increase in vegetation forest fires. LUC emissions account for around 11% of the global total, with the bulk of the emissions occurring in relatively few countries.

- Over the last decade, the top four emitters (China, the United States of America, EU27+UK, and India) have contributed to 55% of the total GHG emissions without LUC. The top seven emitters (including the Russian Federation, Japan, and international transport) have contributed to 65%, with G20 members accounting for 78%. The ranking of countries changes dramatically when considering per capita emissions (Figure ES.2).

There is some indication that the growth in global GHG emissions is slowing. However, GHG emissions are declining in the Organisation of Economic Co-operation and Development (OECD)

same global warming effect. Land use, land-use change, and forestry (LULUCF): A greenhouse gas inventory sector that covers emissions and removals of GHGs resulting from direct human-induced land use, land-use change, and forestry activities.

Box 2.6. (*Continued*)

economies and increasing in the non-OECD economies. Many OECD economies have had a peak in GHG emissions, with efficiency improvements and growth in low-carbon energy sources more than offsetting the growth in economic activity. Despite improving energy efficiency and increasing low-carbon sources, emissions continue to rise in countries with strong growth in energy use to meet development needs.

There is a general tendency that rich countries have higher consumption-based emissions (emissions allocated to the country where goods are purchased and consumed, rather than where they are produced) than territorial-based emissions, as they typically have cleaner production, relatively more services and more imports of primary and secondary products. In the 2000s, the gap between consumption and production was growing in rich countries but stabilized following the 2007–2008 global financial crisis. Even though rich countries have had higher consumption-based emissions than territorial-based emissions over the last decade, both emission types have declined at similar rates (2020 report, measurement of the gap for 2019).

Source: UNEP (2020, pp. XIV–XV).

The AR6 draft of IPCC Assessment Report on global warming concludes that recent changes in the climate are widespread, rapid, intensifying, and unprecedented.

Human activities are causing CC, making extreme climate events — such as heat waves, heavy rainfall, and droughts — more frequent and severe. So, unless immediate, rapid, and large-scale reductions in GHG emissions take place, limiting warming to 1.5°C will be beyond reach. To limit global warming, strong, rapid, and sustained reductions in CO_2, methane (N_2O), and other GHGs are necessary. This would not only reduce the consequences of CC but also improve air quality (IPCC 2021a, see Box 2.7).

Box 2.7. Current State of Climate Change. IPCC 2021 Summary for Policy Makers

Purpose The Summary for Policymakers (SPM) provides a high-level summary of the understanding of the current state of the climate, including how it is changing and the role of human influence, and the state of knowledge about possible climate futures, climate information relevant to regions and sectors, and limiting human-induced climate change (IPCC, 2021a, p. SPM-4).

Headline Statements from the Summary for Policymakers

A. The Current State of the Climate
A.1 It is unequivocal that human influence has warmed the atmosphere, ocean, and land.
Widespread and rapid changes in the atmosphere, ocean, cryosphere, and biosphere have occurred.
A.2 The scale of recent changes across the climate system as a whole and the present state of many aspects of the climate system are unprecedented over many centuries to many thousands of years.
A.3 Human-induced climate change is already affecting many weather and climate extremes in every region across the globe. Evidence of observed changes in extremes such as heatwaves, heavy precipitation, droughts, and tropical cyclones and, in particular, their attribution to human influence, has strengthened since the Fifth Assessment Report (AR5).
A.4 Improved knowledge of climate processes, paleoclimate evidence and the response of the climate system to increasing radiative forcing give a best estimate of equilibrium climate sensitivity of 3°C, with a narrower range compared to AR5.

B. Possible Climate Futures
B.1 Global surface temperature will continue to increase until at least the mid-century under all emissions scenarios considered. Global warming of 1.5°C and 2°C will be exceeded during the 21st century unless deep reductions in carbon dioxide (CO_2) and other GHGs occur in the coming decades.

Box 2.7. (*Continued*)

B.2 Many changes in the climate system become larger in direct relation to increasing global warming. They include increases in the frequency and intensity of hot extremes, marine heatwaves, and heavy precipitation, agricultural and ecological droughts in some regions, and proportion of intense tropical cyclones, as well as reductions in Arctic Sea ice, snow cover, and permafrost.
B.3 Continued global warming is projected to further intensify the global water cycle, including its variability, global monsoon precipitation and the severity of wet and dry events.
B.4 Under scenarios with increasing CO_2 emissions, the ocean and land carbon sinks are projected to be less effective at slowing the accumulation of CO_2 in the atmosphere.
B.5 Many changes due to past and future greenhouse gas emissions are irreversible for centuries to millennia, especially changes in the ocean, ice sheets, and global sea level.

C. Climate Information for Risk Assessment and Regional Adaptation
C.1 Natural drivers and internal variability will modulate human-caused changes, especially at regional scales and in the near term, with little effect on centennial global warming. These modulations are important to consider in planning for the full range of possible changes.
C.2 With further global warming, every region is projected to increasingly experience concurrent and multiple changes in climatic impact-drivers. Changes in several climatic impact-drivers would be more widespread at 2°C compared to 1.5°C global warming and even more widespread and/or pronounced for higher warming levels.
C.3 Low-likelihood outcomes, such as ice sheet collapse, abrupt ocean circulation changes, some compound extreme events and warming substantially larger than the assessed *very likely* range of future warming cannot be ruled out and are part of risk assessment.

(*Continued*)

Box 2.7. (*Continued*)

D. Limiting Future Climate Change

D.1 From a physical science perspective, limiting human-induced global warming to a specific level requires limiting cumulative CO_2 emissions, reaching at least net zero CO_2 emissions, along with strong reductions in other GHGs Strong, rapid, and sustained reductions in CH_4 emissions would also limit the warming effect resulting from declining aerosol pollution and would improve air quality.

D.2 Scenarios with low or very low GHG emissions lead within years to discernible effects on greenhouse gas and aerosol concentrations, and air quality, relative to high, and very high GHG emissions scenarios... Under these contrasting scenarios, discernible differences in trends of global surface temperature would begin to emerge from natural variability within around 20 years, and over longer time periods for many other climatic impact-drivers ...

Source: IPCC (2021b), extracts from various pages.

Based on the observed increase in global emission gap (see Box 2.6), UNEP calls for urgent actions all over the world. Specifically, UNEP concludes that current nationally determined contributions (NDCs) under the Paris Agreement remain insufficient to bridge the emissions gap by 2030.

Neither NDCs nor current policies are adequate to limit warming below the temperature limits included in the Paris Agreement.[12] This inadequacy is even further emphasized when considering the cumulative CO_2 emissions by 2030 as implied by current NDCs. Starting from the 2018 level of global CO_2 emissions of 41.6 Gt CO_2 and assuming a straight trajectory to 2030, the current unconditional NDC scenario implies cumulative emissions of about 510 Gt CO_2 until 2030. Meanwhile, the IPCC SR1.5 estimated that the remaining

[12] Gao *et al.* (2019) evaluate the case of China in regard to the international carbon markets proposed in Paris Agreement.

carbon budget starting from 2018 and consistent with limiting warming to 1.5°C amounts to around 320–480 Gt CO_2, which rises to 700 Gt CO_2 and 1,070 Gt CO_2 for limiting warming to 1.75°C and 2°C, respectively. Current NDCs therefore fully deplete the carbon budget consistent with limiting warming to 1.5°C and strongly reduce the remaining budgets for limiting warming to well below 2°C, without making any progress toward bringing global CO_2 emissions closer to net zero.[13]

In regard to COVID-19, containment measures have resulted in a marked but temporary reduction in global GHG emissions in 2020. However, unless economic recovery is used as an opportunity to foster a low-carbon transition, this temporary blip in global GHG emissions is estimated to result in no more than a 0.01°C reduction of global warming by 2050, which by then is expected to have exceeded 1.5°C. NDCs to date fail to reverse the long-term upward trend in emissions, which leaves no doubt that the current NDCs are completely inadequate to achieve the climate goals of the Paris Agreement. So, COVID-19 is only likely to significantly reduce total GHG emissions if the pandemic is used as an opening for economic recovery that fosters strong decarbonization. Achieving the long-term temperature goals of the Paris Agreement to limit global warming to well below 2°C and pursue 1.5°C depends strongly on implementing mitigation actions by 2030. Taking a longer-term perspective illustrates how the low-carbon transition challenge until 2050 depends critically on this near-term action (UNEP, 2020, pp. 33–35).

A major challenge faced by UN agencies for measuring progress in global and countries' commitments on GHG emissions and to accomplish the SDFs is the data needed to measure advancements. This limitation is exemplified by the case of Mexico's progress reports

[13]The Paris Agreement target is to reach net-zero GHG emissions by the second-half of the 21st century, meaning that any remaining CO_2 and non-CO_2 emissions are balanced with net CO_2 removal or negative emissions. In Chapter 3, we discuss the role of land as a sink of CO_2 emissions as well as the gaps between commitments and tendencies in GHG emissions related to land use.

that limits academic empirical research (Yúnez Naude and Santana Sosa, 2021).

Notwithstanding the challenges, progress has been made in estimating future trends in global warming. In addition to IPCC's, a recent study aimed to evaluate progress in the Paris Agreement target to limit global warming to below 2°C was carried out. Nieto *et al.* (2018) provide results of an analysis of the effectiveness of the Paris Agreement policies by quantifying the variation in GHG emissions that the Intended Nationally Determined Contributions (INDCs) will entail and their financial allocation and policies country-by-country and regionally. The objective is evaluating the Paris Agreement feasibility regarding the 161 INDCs representing 188 countries. The criteria through which the 161 INDCs are analyzed are: socio-economic impact of the transition; to focus on energy management; the substitution of non-renewable sources; the role of technology; equality of the transition; and the compliance with emission reductions.

The findings of Nieto *et al.* (2018) indicate that a best-case scenario would be an annual global emission increase of approximately 19.3% in 2030 compared to the base period (2005–2015). In comparison, if no measures are taken a 31.5% increase in global emissions is projected. These results imply that if the predicted best-case scenario level of emissions is maintained between 2030 and 2050 a temperature increase of at least 3°C would be realized. Furthermore, a 4°C increase is assured should annual emissions continue to increase.

Nieto *et al.* (2018) conclude that their results show that the Paris Agreement excessively relies on external financial support (41.4%). Moreover, its unilateralist approach and the socioeconomic and biophysical constraints could be the underlying cause of the ineffectiveness of the 2°C objective.

Considering IPCC's pathway modeling, the findings of these authors are alarming. Based on the pathway for a 1.5°C warming scenario, a 45% decline in anthropogenic GHG emissions must be reached by 2030 as compared to 2010 levels, and net-zero emissions must be achieved by 2050. To maintain a 2°C global warming level by the end of the century, emissions should decline by approximately 25% in 2030 as compared to 2010 levels and net-zero emissions should be achieved by 2070 (IPCC, 2018).

References

Fawzy, S., Osman, A. I., Doran, J., and Rooney, D. (2020). Strategies for mitigation of climate change: A review. *Environmental Chemistry Letters, 18*, 2069–2094. https://doi.org/10.1007/s10311-020-01059-w.

Gao, S., Meng-Yu, L., Mao-Sheng, D., and Can, W. (2019). International carbon markets under the Paris Agreement: Basic form and development prospects. *Advances in Climate Change Research, 10*(1), 21–29. https://doi.org/10.1016/j.accre.2019.03.001.

Hernández Solano, A. and Yúnez Naude, A. (2016). *Impactos del Cambio Climático en la Economía Rural de México: Un Enfoque de Equilibrio General.* El Colegio de México, Centro de Estudios Económicos. https://ideas.repec.org/p/emx/ceedoc/2016-06.html.

Intergovernmental Panel on Climate Change (IPCC). (2014). *Climate Change 2014: Synthesis Report. Contribution of Working Groups I, II and III to the Fifth Assessment Report of the Intergovernmental Panel on Climate Change* [Core Writing Team, R. K. Pachauri and L. A. Meyer (eds.)]. https://www.ipcc.ch/site/assets/uploads/2018/05/SYR_AR5_FINAL_full_wcover.pdf.

IPCC. (2017). *Chair's Vision Paper. AR6 Scoping Meeting Addis Ababa, Ethiopia*, May 1–5, 2017. https://www.ipcc.ch/site/assets/uploads/2018/09/220520170356-Doc.-2-Chair-Vision-Paper-.pdf.

IPCC. (2018). Summary for Policymakers. In V. Masson-Delmotte, P. Zhai, H.-O. Pörtner, D. Roberts, J. Skea, P. R. Shukla, A. Pirani, W. Moufouma-Okia, C. Péan, R. Pidcock, S. Connors, J. B. R. Matthews, Y. Chen, X. Zhou, M. I. Gomis, E. Lonnoy, T. Maycock, M. Tignor, and T. Waterfield (eds.), *Global Warming of 1.5°C.* An IPCC Special Report on the impacts of global warming of 1.5°C above pre-industrial levels and related global greenhouse gas emission pathways, in the context of strengthening the global response to the threat of climate change, sustainable development, and efforts to eradicate poverty. https://doi.org/10.1017/9781009157940.001.

IPCC. (2021a). Summary for policymakers. In V. Masson-Delmotte, P. Zhai, A. Pirani, S. L. Connors, C. Péan, S. Berger, N. Caud, Y. Chen, L. Goldfarb, M. I. Gomis, M. Huang, K. Leitzell, E. Lonnoy, J. B. R. Matthews, T. K. Maycock, T. Waterfield, O. Yelekçi, R. Yu, and B. Zhou (eds.), *Climate Change 2021: The Physical Science Basis. Contribution of Working Group I to the Sixth Assessment Report of the Intergovernmental Panel on Climate Change.* Cambridge University Press. https://www.ipcc.ch/report/ar6/wg1/downloads/report/IPCC_AR6_WGI_SPM.pdf.

IPCC. (2021b). *Headline Statements from the Summary for Policymakers [working group]*. https://www.ipcc.ch/report/ar6/wg1/downloads/report/IPCC_AR6_WGI_Headline_Statements.pdf.

IRP. (2019). Global Resources Outlook 2019: Natural Resources for the Future We Want. Nairobi: United Nations Environment Programme. https://wedocs.unep.org/handle/20.500.11822/27519.

IRP. (2021). *Building Biodiversity: The Natural Resource Management Approach.* J. Potočnik and I. Teixeira (eds.). A think piece of the International Resource Panel Co-Chairs. https://wedocs.unep.org/bitstream/handle/20.500.11822/35972/BDNR.pdf.

Nieto Vega, J., Carpintero Redondo, O., and Miguel González, L. J. (2018). Less than 2°C? An economic-environmental evaluation of the Paris Agreement. *Ecological Economics, 146*, 69–84. https://doi.org/10.1016/j.ecolecon.2017.10.007.

Taylor, J. E. and Filipski, M. (2014). *Beyond Experiments in Development Economics: Local Economy-wide Impact Evaluation.* Oxford University Press. https://doi.org/10.1093/acprof:oso/9780198707875.001.0001.

United Nations Climate Change (UNCC). (1992). *United Nations Framework Convention on Climate Change.* https://unfccc.int/files/essential_background/background_publications_htmlpdf/application/pdf/conveng.pdf.

UNCC. (2019). *Global Conference on Strengthening Synergies: Between the Paris Agreement and the 2030 Agenda for Sustainable Development.* UN City, Copenhagen, Denmark. April 1–3, 2019. https://sustainabledevelopment.un.org/content/documents/25236un_bookletsynergies_v2.pdf.

United Nations Environment Programme (UNEP). (2020). *Emissions Gap Report 2020.* https://www.unep.org/emissions-gap-report-2020.

UNEP. (2021). *Measuring Progress: Environment and the SDGs.* https://wedocs.unep.org/bitstream/handle/20.500.11822/36607/SDGMP_EN.pdf.

Yúnez Naude, A. and Santana Sosa, M. S. (2021). *El Comercio Agropecuario de México: Implicaciones en el Desarrollo Sustentable y en La Seguridad Alimentaria. Agendas Internacionales y Política Ambiental en México.* El Colegio de México.

Chapter 3

Agriculture and Economic Development

We dedicate this chapter to the introduction of the reader to major economic thinking about the specific features of agriculture and its roles in economic development as well as the evolution of the literature regarding the inclusion of agriculture as part of the rural sector, as a user of natural resources/capital and as a source of greenhouse gas (GHG) emissions. All this under the perspective of development policies.

3.1 Traditional Economic Thinking on Agriculture and Development

Beginning with David Ricardo and Karl Marx's theories of land rent there has been a long tradition in economic thinking about the role of agriculture in economic development. Inspired by this classical tradition in economics, Arthur Lewis wrote an article in the mid-1950s which is considered as one of the foundations of theories on economic development: "Economic Development with Unlimited Supplies of Labour" (Lewis, 1954), which lead to what are called dual (growth) models.

Lewis's model describes the process of growth of an economy characterized by the coexistence of two sectors: traditional and modern that in practical terms are identified by agriculture and industry, respectively. The former being stagnant and much bigger than industry, which is the dynamic sector. Agriculture has surplus labor or disguised unemployment and so, marginal productivity of labor there is zero, and workers receive a fixed institutional wage lower than that paid by the industry, which is higher than the institutional wage. Under this situation labor can be transferred to the industry sector without any loss in agricultural output. The real wages in the industrial sector remain fixed and are equal to the initial level of real income in agriculture.

In Lewis's model agriculture is a passive productive sector providing a given quantity of food and surplus labor to the industrial sector. Ranis and Fei (1961) propose a dual model of an economy with the characteristics defined by Lewis at the beginning of its development process. However, Ranis and Fei improve Lewis's model by considering that apart from providing cheap labor to industry, agricultural production plays an additional role of combining population growth and investment in the industry through the use of the surplus profits obtained in this sector resulting from the difference between the real wages it pays with respect to labor productivity in the sector.

In Ranis and Fei's model the process of development of a surplus labor economy includes three stages:

- The first stage is very similar to Lewis's. Supply of agricultural labor is perfectly elastic and its marginal productivity equals zero, and so, there is disguised unemployment in this sector that is to be transferred to industry at a constant institutional wage.
- The authors add a second stage to Lewis's model called "the take-off," where agricultural workers contribute to agricultural growth but at a labor productivity level below that of the institutional wage they get; i.e., in this phase labor surplus prevails. Therefore, surplus labor prevails and moves to industry. If agricultural labor migration continues a state is eventually reached in which agricultural labor productivity equals the institutional wage (Lewis calls this the "turning point").
- In the third phase, the take-off ends and the era of self-sustained growth begins, where agricultural workers produce more than the institutional wage they get. Hence, in this stage there is no surplus

labor and agriculture becomes modern or fully commercialized, following a pattern similar to that of the industrial sector. In this step, i.e., the economy behaves according to market signals, as proposed by neoclassical economics.

One condition of Ranis and Fei's take-off (second phase) is a simultaneous growth in both agricultural and industrial sectors, implying that the authors propose that there should be a "balanced growth" for the economy to reach the self-sustained growth.[1] In the sphere of development policies and during the second-half of 20th century, the question was whether to promote a balanced or an unbalanced growth process.[2] It is worth mentioning that in his seminal work on international trade between industrialized and developing countries, Prebisch (1959) adopts an unbalanced growth proposal based on the adoption of trade restrictions and an industrial policy to promote production of manufactures at the expense of agriculture in order to replace foreign imports of manufactures with developing economies' domestic production (see Irwin, 2021). The strategy is called "import substitution" and has been adopted by a considerable number of developing countries since the second-half of the 20th century. As discussed below, the issue is relevant in the evaluation of policies to promote sustainable development in agriculture and in rural areas.

Dual models inspired the work of Harris and Todaro (1970) on migration and development (see Chapter 5). In addition, these models are in harmony with the observed tendencies all over the world indicating that as per capita income grows, the proportion of labor dedicated to agriculture declines (figure in https://data.worl

[1]In parallel, Jorgenson (1961) proposed another version of a dual model. One limitation of Ranis and Fei's model is that it fails to consider trade. Yúnez-Naude (1978) evaluates Ranis and Fei's conditions to attain a self-sustainable growth based on the experience of Mexico during 1950–1970.

[2]For example, contrary to Hirschman (1958) contention that measures to accelerate development has to adjust to adopt an unbalanced growth perspective. Rosenstein-Rodan (1961) criticizes Hirschman arguing that the discussion of balanced growth–unbalanced growth is a false problem.

dbank.org/). The Food and Agriculture Organization of the United Nations (FAO) data show that this process has continued: whereas worldwide agriculture employed 1,050 million people in 2000, the figure was 884 million in 2019 (i.e., during the period the proportion of agriculture's workforce dropped from 40% to 27%. In addition, FAO data series indicate that agriculture has had a role to play in economic growth since the share of this sector in global gross domestic production (GDP) has remained in around 4% since 2000. In part, this can be explained by technological change, including the growth of the use of agrochemicals (fertilizers and pesticides) and by growing livestock production which are major GHG emissions coming from agricultural activities: For example, GHG emissions from crops and livestock increased by 16% between 2000 and 2017, and enteric fermentation accounted for around 40% of emissions (FAO, 2020).

During the last decades of the 20th century and the beginning of the 21st century, the role of agriculture in economic development was emphasized in the literature, as well as the specificities of agricultural production that have to be considered in the process of policymaking. Timmer's (1988) proposals regarding agricultural transformation stand out.

Timmer begins by mentioning two facts related to agricultural production in the process of growth: the decline of agricultural participation in total production of a growing economy and that, under certain assumptions, as income rises the demand for agricultural products diminishes in relative terms, i.e., the unitary income elasticity for the products of this sector guarantees that gross value of sales by farmers will grow less rapidly than GDP (in economics this is called Engel's Law). He adds that agriculture is important and requires resources or support policies, taking into account that agriculture is part of the overall economy. So, policy design has to emphasize the sector's interdependence with industry and services.

The latter considerations are similar to Ranis and Fei's model. However, one of Timmer's contributions is his proposal stating that enhancing the role of agriculture in economic development in Less-Developed Countries (LDCs) requires a rise in productivity through technical changes, taking into consideration that agricultural production deeply differs from production in other sectors of the economy, often neglected by development economists. There are three specific features of agricultural production: farming is undertaken by millions of dispersed individuals and households making many decisions; the importance of home consumption of rural households producing food; the intensive use of natural resources by agriculture and its role as a reservoir of these resources (details in Chapter 4, Section 4.2).

According to Timmer, the vast number of agricultural decision-makers implies that there are too many farmers to reach directly. So, he proposes a mix of public policies and market orientation that offers the farmers material rewards for the physical effort they expend in their fields and households and for the risks they face from both nature and markets.

In his reflections about agricultural transformation, Timmer takes into consideration that agriculture is an important component of rural areas and with this, other activities related to the environment and the use of natural resources. However, Timmer does not consider in depth the heterogeneity that characterizes the structure of agriculture in many LDCs (i.e., the coexistence of subsistence farming with commercial farmers). In addition, Timmer does not pay enough attention to the fact that agriculture is mostly located in rural areas where natural resources are mostly located or to the challenges agricultural production faces with regard to global warming and climate change (CC).

3.2 Agriculture, Rural Areas, and Sustainable Development: Contemporary Knowledge

In this section, we present the state-of-the-art as regards the role of agriculture and rural areas in the sustainable development, mainly based on the World Bank Report on agriculture published in 2008 and the more recent FAOs publications.

3.2.1 *Agriculture for development according to the World Bank*

In its 2008 World Development Report (2008), the World Bank (WB) focuses on agriculture.[3] This focus is based on the premise that "In the 21st century, agriculture continues to be a fundamental instrument for sustainable development and poverty reduction" (p. 1).

The report is a major contribution to the understanding of agricultural activities in the world with special attention to developing countries, as the WB considers agriculture as part of rural areas and stresses the heterogeneity of agricultural production between and within countries as well as the positive and negative contributions of agriculture to attain sustainable development.

The WB proposes that a major component of agricultural contribution to growth of LDCs is to pursue a smallholder-driven approach that reconciles the economic, social, and environmental functions of agriculture; an approach that has been generally neglected by governments of many low-and medium-income countries (*Ibid.*, p. 44).

So, the institution covers issues not treated by Timmer such as that of small farmers having the potential to contribute to growth and that agricultural production is mostly done in rural areas where natural resources are located, as well as the relationships between agriculture and the environment.

The Report addresses three main questions:

(1) "What can agriculture do for development? Agriculture has served as a basis for growth and reduced poverty in many countries, but more countries could benefit if governments and donors were to reverse years of policy neglect and remedy their underinvestment and mis-investment in agriculture.
(2) What are the effective instruments in using agriculture for development? Top priorities are to increase the assets of poor

[3]In the Report, agriculture consists of crops, livestock, agroforestry, and aquaculture. It does not include forestry and commercial capture fisheries.

households, make smallholders — and agriculture in general — more productive, and create opportunities in the rural non-farm economy that the rural poor can seize.

(3) How can agriculture-for-development agendas best be implemented? By designing policies and decision-processes best suited to each country's economic and social conditions by mobilizing political support and improving the governance of agriculture" (WB, 2008, pp. 1–2).

To answer these questions, the WB proposes that agriculture's contributions to development depend on the differing characteristics of rural areas and of agriculture in low-and middle-income countries. Accordingly, the institution distinguishes three types of countries defined by the way in which they rely on agriculture as a source of growth and as an instrument for poverty reduction: agriculture-based, transforming, and urbanized (see Box 3.1). The WB recognizes that each agriculture-for-development agenda differs in pursuing sustainable growth and reducing poverty.

Box 3.1. Three Types of Countries According to the World Bank

Agriculture's contributions differ in the three rural worlds. The contribution of agriculture to growth and poverty reduction can be seen by categorizing countries according to the share of agriculture in aggregate growth over the past 15 years, and the current share of total poverty in rural areas, using the $2-a-day poverty line ... This perspective produces three types of countries — three distinct rural worlds ...:

- ***Agriculture-based countries*** — Agriculture is a major source of growth, accounting for 32% of GDP growth on average — mainly because agriculture is a large share of GDP — and most of the poor are in rural areas (70%). This group of countries has 417 million rural inhabitants, mainly in Sub-Saharan countries. Eighty-two percent of the rural Sub-Saharan population lives in agriculture-based countries.

(*Continued*)

Box 3.1. (*Continued*)

- ***Transforming countries*** — Agriculture is no longer a major source of economic growth, contributing on average only 7% to GDP growth, but poverty remains overwhelmingly rural (82% of all poor). This group, typified by China, India, Indonesia, Morocco, and Romania, has more than 2.2 billion rural inhabitants. Ninety-eight percent of the rural population in South Asia, 96% in East Asia and the Pacific, and 92% in the Middle East and North Africa are in transforming countries.
- ***Urbanized countries*** — Agriculture contributes directly even less to economic growth, 5% on average, and poverty is mostly urban. Even so, rural areas still have 45% of the poor, and agribusiness and the food industry and services account for as much as one-third of GDP. Included in this group of 255 million rural inhabitants are most countries in Latin America and the Caribbean and many in Europe and Central Asia. Eighty-eight percent of the rural populations in both regions are in urbanized countries.

Countries follow evolutionary paths that can move them from one country type to another. China and India moved from the agriculture-based to the transforming group over the past 20 years.... In addition, countries have sharp subnational geographical disparities — for example, many transforming and urbanized countries have agriculture-based regions (such as Bihar in India and Chiapas in Mexico).

Source: WB, 2008, p. 4.

With regard to the role of agriculture in development (first question), the WB proposes that agriculture contributes to development in three forms: as an economic activity; as a livelihood; as a provider of environmental services. Notwithstanding that these three specific roles differ among the three types of countries, in general they make agriculture a unique instrument for development (Box 3.2).

Box 3.2. Contributions of Agriculture in Sustainable Development

- **As an economic activity.** Agriculture can be a source of growth for the national economy, a provider of investment opportunities for the private sector, and a prime driver of agriculture-related industries and the rural non-farm economy. Two-thirds of the world's agricultural value added is created in developing countries. In agriculture-based countries, it generates on average 29% of the GDP and employs 65% of the labor force. The industries and services linked to agriculture in value chains often account for more than 30% of GDP in transforming and urbanized countries. Agricultural production is important for food security because it is a source of income for the majority of the rural poor. It is particularly critical in a dozen countries of Sub-Saharan Africa, with a combined population of about 200 million and with highly variable domestic production, limited tradability of food staples, and foreign exchange constraints in meeting their food needs through imports. These countries are exposed to recurrent food emergencies and the uncertainties of food aid, and for them, increasing and stabilizing domestic production is essential for food security.
- **As a livelihood.** Agriculture is a source of livelihood for an estimated 86% of rural people. It provides jobs for 1.3 billion smallholders and landless workers, "farm-financed social welfare" when there are urban shocks, and a foundation for viable rural communities. Of the developing world's 5.5 billion people, 3 billion live in rural areas, nearly half of humanity. Of these rural inhabitants an estimated 2.5 billion are in households involved in agriculture, and 1.5 billion are in smallholder households. The recent decline in the $1-a-day poverty rate in developing countries — from 28% in 1993 to 22% in 2002 — has been mainly the result of falling rural poverty (from 37% to 29%) while the urban poverty rate remained nearly constant (at 13%). More

(*Continued*)

Box 3.2. (*Continued*)

than 80% of the decline in rural poverty is attributable to better conditions in rural areas rather than to out-migration of the poor. So, contrary to common perceptions, migration to cities has not been the main instrument for rural (and world) poverty reduction. But the large decline in the number of rural poor (from 1,036 million in 1993 to 883 million in 2003) has been confined to East Asia and the Pacific. In South Asia and Sub-Saharan Africa, the number of rural poor has continued to rise and will likely exceed the number of urban poor until 2040. In these regions, a high priority is to mobilize agriculture for poverty reduction.

- **As a provider of environmental services.** In using (and frequently misusing) natural resources, agriculture can create good and bad environmental outcomes. It is by far the largest user of water, contributing to water scarcity. It is a major player in underground water depletion, agrochemical pollution, soil exhaustion, and global climate change, accounting for up to 30% of greenhouse gas emissions. But it is also a major provider of environmental services, generally unrecognized and unremunerated, sequestering carbon, managing watersheds, and preserving biodiversity. With rising resource scarcity, climate change, and concern about environmental costs, business as usual in the way agriculture uses natural resources is not an option. Making the farming systems of the rural poor less vulnerable to climate change is imperative. Managing the connections among agriculture, natural resource conservation, and the environment must be an integral part of using agriculture for development."

Source: WB (2008, pp. 2–4).

In regard to food, the WB proposes four reasons why global food production is a challenge that has to be addressed:

(1) The need for agriculture-based countries (mainly in Sub-Saharan Africa where food production is important for food security) to

feed themselves based largely on their own production remains a stark reality. Faster growth of agricultural production is essential for overall growth and poverty reduction.

(2) Poor agricultural performance is the second reason for a continued focus on agricultural production in areas with difficult agroclimatic conditions or inadequate infrastructure that constrain market access. In these regions, livelihoods depend on agricultural production, either as a source of income or for food-for-home consumption. The challenge is to improve the productivity of subsistence agriculture, diversify to new markets and open opportunities for non-farm work and migration as pathways out of poverty.

(3) Even high potential areas that led during the last decades the global increase in food production (such as the transforming countries of Asia) are facing a production challenge. They must sustain productivity and income growth, diversify in high-value horticulture and livestock in response to rapidly growing domestic and international demand at the same time as they reduce the environmental footprint of intensive crop and livestock systems.[4]

(4) The last reason is, according to the WB Report, more speculative, but still important. Even at the global level, future agricultural success may be compromised by greater resource scarcity, heightened risks from climate change, higher energy prices, competition for land between food and biofuels, and underinvestment in technical progress.

The WB adds that for the first time since the world food crisis in the 1970s, global models predict the possibility of rising food prices. The world food supply requires close monitoring and new investments to speed productivity growth, make production systems more sustainable, and adapt to CC (WB, 2008, pp. 68–69).

[4]The Cambridge Dictionary defines environmental or ecological footprint as the effect that a person, company, activity, etc., has on the environment. For example, the amount of natural resources that they use and the amount of harmful gases that they produce.

The WB Report gives attention to rural households in developing countries and considers they do play a role in agricultural development, food production, and in reducing rural and urban poverty as long as appropriate policies are implemented to increase household farms productivity.[5] By including the specific characteristics of these agents and the context in which economic decisions are taken, the WB relates agriculture with rural areas and the specificities of economic behavior of millions of agents living there.

The coverage followed by the WB contrasts with the approach followed by the reviewed authors, as well as with the continued tradition of public policies in some countries to ignore that agriculture is part of rural areas and that rural subsistence households prevail even in many medium-income countries. The disregard of small rural subsistence farmers and the way they take economic decisions may be explained by the view — shared with dual models — that sustained economic growth of developing countries will eventually lead to the disappearance of household farms; that the role of small farmers in development as food providers is negligible; and/or by assuming that their behavior is irrational or similar to that followed by commercial farming.[6] As we discuss in Chapter 4 (Section 4.2), to include the rural sector and rural households in discussing the role of agriculture in sustainable development is fundamental.

In its 2008 Report, the WB rejects these visions by considering both the context where farm rural households take their decisions and their potential to contribute to development. According to the

[5]The WB presents evidence that declining rural poverty has been a key factor in aggregate poverty reduction (WB, 2008, "Focus A," pp. 45–49).

[6]That rural households or the peasantry will eventually disappear as a consequence of development is controversial and has roots in Marxists' writings (Yúnez-Naude, 1988). The assumption that rural households behave as commercial farmers is exemplified by the current Mexican federal government's program that promotes corn production by buying it at a guaranteed price (i.e., higher than its market price) to poor subsistence households producing corn (Yúnez-Naude, 2019). The case of Mexico is relevant since Mexico still is rich in cultivated corn biodiversity due to traditional practices of subsistence farm households (Dyer *et al.*, 2014).

institution, due to high transaction costs in rural areas,[7] markets fail to give rural households the required information to make their economic decisions, leading to inefficient socioeconomic outcomes. Instead, heads of rural households (men and/or women) determine their livelihoods' strategies. When market failures occur, households need to consider their consumption needs when making production decisions, and *vice versa.* This can explain many aspects of rural households' livelihood strategies, including some that might otherwise appear irrational. In rural settings many markets do not function because of high transaction costs, insufficient and unequal access to information, imperfect competition, externalities, and state failures to provide public goods.[8] With such market and state failures, initial asset endowments affect the efficiency of resource use and thus the well-being of households. In addition, the strategies of rural households are conditioned by the agricultural potential and natural resources availability.

So, when market failures coincide, households need to consider their consumption needs when making production decisions, and *vice versa.* The WB provides the following example that illustrates the argument. "Farm households that produce food and cash crops will not always be able to respond to an increase in the price of the cash crop. When transaction costs in food markets are high and labor markets function imperfectly, a household might not be able to employ more labor to increase cash crop production while maintaining the necessary food production for its own food security. It is thus confined to responding to price incentives through technological change or more use of fertilizers, but capital market imperfections can

[7]Transaction costs are the costs that economic agents incur when goods and services are exchanged. Transaction costs are particularly high in rural areas due to the lack or deficiencies in communications such as roads and information. Small farmers in low and middle-income countries are typical agents suffering this situation, to which their lack of bargaining power *vis-á-vis* bigger input sellers and product buyers is added. High transaction costs may prevent exchange to take place, a situation that inhibits markets to function (see Boxes 2.2 and 3.3).
[8]In economics, a public good refers to a good or service available to all members of a society, which are typically administered by governments.

limit these possibilities. As a result, the response to price incentives in cash crops is often limited, shrinking the benefits from price and trade policies that increase producer incentives" (*Ibid.*, p. 82).

In addition to the complexities of small farming behavior, one must take into consideration that a household is not necessary a homogeneous decision-making unit since it is a domain of interactions of cooperation and power between, for example, adult male and female members. With respect to men, women's power has been limited, among others, by their lower access to assets, education, and participation in waged economic activities outside the household. As we will discuss below, the empowerment of women is fundamental for the attainment of rural-agricultural sustainable development.

As for the potential contribution of household farmers to growth and poverty reduction, the WB argues that they can achieve this by increasing their assets and productivity in food production, by changing the plantation of traditional crops to crops with higher value added such as labor-intensive horticultural goods and by increasing their engagement in non-farm activities. In the policy arena, the WB emphasizes measures required to facilitate the transition from subsistence to market-oriented farming.

The WB also maintains that a smallholder-driven approach to agricultural growth has to reconcile the economic, social, and environmental functions of agriculture and define and implement specific agendas to each country type (*Ibid.*, pp. 44, 93). With regard to this aspect, the design of agricultural policies requires considering the economic and social heterogeneity that characterize rural areas in developing countries; in particular, that small commercial farmers coexist with subsistence farming. Commercial smallholders deliver surpluses to food markets and share in the benefits of expanding markets for the new agriculture of high-value activities. In contrast, many others are subsistence farmers, mainly due to low asset endowments and unfavorable contexts such as high transaction costs. Most of the food subsistence farmers produce is for family consumption, they participate in markets as buyers of food and as sellers of labor. Membership in these household farmers is affected not only by asset positions but also by gender, ethnicity, and social status, as they imply differing abilities to use the same assets and resources in responding to opportunities.

The heterogeneity of small farmers requires the designing and implementation of differentiated agricultural policies for favored (small commercial farmers) and less favored (subsistence farmers) farmers — an approach that is one of the toughest policy dilemmas facing poor countries (see Box 3.3).

The WB includes another form of heterogeneity in rural areas related to labor markets where there are many low-skilled, poorly remunerated agricultural jobs and a small number of high-skilled jobs that offer workers pathways out of poverty. In addition, the rural non-farm economy is defined by the coexistence of low productivity self- and wage-employment with dynamic enterprises. A potential way out of poverty of workers from rural households is migration to the urban sector. However, migrants face the risk to live in urban slums and continue to suffer poverty.

Box 3.3. Heterogeneity Defines the Rural World

Economic and social heterogeneity is a defining trait of rural areas. Large commercial farmers coexist with smallholders. This diversity permeates the smallholder population as well. Commercial smallholders deliver surpluses to food markets and share in the benefits of expanding markets for the new agriculture of high-value activities. But many others remain in subsistence farming, mainly due to low asset endowments and unfavorable contexts. Consuming most of the food they produce, they participate in markets as buyers of food and sellers of labor. Membership in these categories is affected not only by asset positions, but also by gender, ethnicity, and social status, as they imply differing abilities to use the same assets and resources in responding to opportunities.

Heterogeneity is found in the rural labor market where there are many low-skilled, poorly remunerated agricultural jobs and a small number of high-skilled jobs that offer workers pathways out of

(*Continued*)

Box 3.3. (*Continued*)

poverty. It is found in the rural non-farm economy where low productivity self- and wage-employment coexists with employment in dynamic enterprises. And it is also found in the outcomes of migration, which lifts some of the rural poor out of poverty but takes others to urban slums and continued poverty (WB, 2008, pp. 5–6).

The potential of agriculture to contribute to growth and poverty reduction depends on the productivity of small farms. The vast majority of farmers in developing countries are smallholders, and an estimated 85% of them are farming less than two hectares.

The literature linking households' asset endowments to agricultural productivity has long emphasized an inverse relationship between farm size and factor productivity. Both theory and empirical evidence have shown that such a relationship is common when imperfections in both land and labor markets are large.

Even if small farmers use their resources more efficiently than larger farmers, there may still be disadvantages in being small. While smallholders have an advantage in overcoming labor supervision problems, other factors can erase their competitive advantage. Yields on land allocated to crops might be higher on larger farms, which tend to apply more fertilizer or other inputs. Yield gaps can arise because imperfections in credit and insurance markets prevent small farmers from adopting more productive capital-intensive techniques or higher-value products. Imperfections in capital and insurance markets, combined with transaction costs, can also prevent markets for land sales and rentals from allocating land to the most efficient users. Moreover, imperfect competition in those markets might favor land concentration in larger farms. These complexities indicate the need to jointly consider policies targeting land, capital, and risk for smallholders.

Box 3.3. (*Continued*)

... while there may be constant returns to scale in production, economies of scale in the "new agriculture" often are the key for obtaining inputs, technology, and information and in getting products to the market ... As agriculture becomes more technology driven and access to consumers is mediated by agro-processors and supermarkets, economies of scale will pose major challenges for the future competitiveness of smallholders.

These different mechanisms can all reverse the small farm labor advantage, or make it irrelevant, leading to a potential decline of the family farm ... But there are many policy instruments to help smallholders increase their competitiveness, as long as governments do not tilt the playing field against them ...

Smallholders can act collectively to overcome high transaction costs by forming producer organizations. Cooperation between larger commercial farmers and smallholders is another possibility. Smallholders sometimes can also benefit from economies of scale in input or output markets by renting out their land and working on the larger farms. Increasing the bargaining power of smallholders in this type of arrangement can help guarantee that benefits are shared by smallholders and the larger farms.

Source: WB (2008, pp. 90–92).

Instead of adopting the traditional view that small or family farming has no potential to contribute to economic growth and development, the WB argues that these agents have this potential as long as appropriate policies are designed and implemented through agricultural policy reform. Policies have to be designed and implemented to speed the transition from subsistence to market-oriented farming and to help increase small-subsistence farmers' asset holdings improving the context that determines the level and volatility of the returns on assets such as investing in transport and communications. The WB adds that policy design to promote the role of agriculture in development has to consider the heterogeneity in agriculture and in rural areas and unsuccessful experiences in LDCs of a pro-commercial agriculture policy bias, as well as the fact that agricultural policy reform is likely to have gainers and losers (*Ibid.*, pp. 92–93).

From Chapters 5 onward we discuss the convenience of promoting indiscriminate profit-seeking market orientation of subsistence farmers by considering that a considerable portion of these agents are in natural-rich areas and that in many regions of low and medium-income countries subsistence farmers and households are indigenous.

Notwithstanding that in Chapter 11 of its 2008 Report the WB includes issues of governance necessary to promote agriculture for development, the institution lightly addresses the challenges corruption poses to attain this goal. As we discuss in Chapter 7, corruption is a major problem for low- and middle-income countries to accomplish their commitments to reduce global warming. Nonetheless, the WB approaches the role of agriculture and rural areas to contribute to sustainable development by taking care of natural resources or natural capital (see Box 3.2).

The WB considers the negative and positive relationships between agriculture and the environment: agriculture's environmental footprint and agriculture as a source of environmental services. The organization also discusses agriculture's vulnerability to CC and its consequences on food production and poverty incidence, as well as measures that can be taken to mitigate CC and adaptation strategies to this phenomenon in agriculture and in rural areas.

Degradation of natural resources caused by agricultural activities undermines the basis for agricultural production and increases vulnerability to risk, imposing high economic losses. So, the success of agricultural role for development requires a sustainable use of natural resources such as water, forests, soil, and the protection of genetically diverse crops and animal varieties and of other ecosystem services. The reason for this is because agriculture is the main user of land and water, a source of GHG emissions and the main cause of conversion of natural ecosystems and loss of biodiversity (*Ibid.*, p. 200).

In its discussion on sustainable agriculture, the WB distinguishes intensive from extensive farming. Based on the experience of the "Green Revolution"[9] and on Nelson and Maredia (2007), the organization argues that intensive agriculture — those farmers adopting improved seed varieties — expanded cultivated area and preserved forests, wetlands, biodiversity, and the ecosystem services they provide. In areas not adopting seeds provided by the Green Revolution, there has been little intensification; instead, agriculture has grown by bringing more land under cultivation, leading to the degradation and loss of forests, wetlands, soils, and pastures.[10] Notwithstanding the latter, farming has also brought environmental problems since intensive cropping systems use excessive and inappropriate agrochemicals that pollute waterways, poison people, and upset ecosystems. In addition, wasteful irrigation that characterizes intensive agriculture has contributed to the growing scarcity of water, the unsustainable pumping of groundwater and the degradation of agricultural land (we discuss the pros and cons of intensive-extensive agriculture in Chapter 4).

Intensive livestock systems using modern technologies have also been known to cause environmental and health problems. High concentrations of livestock in or near urban areas produce waste and can spread animal diseases, such as tuberculosis and avian (bird) flu, with risks for human health (WB, 2008, pp. 189–190).

Livestock and crops release carbon dioxide (CO_2), methane (CH_4), nitrous oxide (N_2O), and other gases, making agriculture a major source of GHG emissions. These negative impacts of agriculture on the environment are two-fold: onsite and offsite and differ

[9] The Green Revolution began in the mid-20th century. Based on the introduction of high-yielding seed varieties, it has conducted an increase in production of food grains where corn, rice and wheat stand out. Two drawbacks are associated with the Green Revolution: to produce high yields (output per cultivated area) the varieties require considerable amounts of agrochemicals (fertilizers and pesticides) that small farmers cannot afford to pay.

[10] According to the Millennium Ecosystem Assessment (MEA) (2005), every year about 13 million hectares of tropical forest are degraded or disappear, mainly because of agriculture. Some 10–20% of drylands may suffer from land degradation or desertification (WB, 2008, p. 180).

between intensive and extensive agriculture (see Table 3.1).[11] The WB provides evidence showing that onsite degradation of natural capital has direct impacts on agricultural productivity because it undermines the basis for future agricultural production through the erosion of soil and depletion of soil nutrients (*Ibid.*, p. 180).

Negative effects of agriculture ask for actions to promote mitigation of CC. In a similar fashion, to avoid negative impacts on agriculture arising from CC requires agriculture to adapt to the phenomenon (*Ibid.*, pp. 200–201).

3.2.2 *Agriculture, food security, and sustainability: FAO's contributions*

More recent knowledge of assessments of agriculture, food production, and sustainable development are FAO's studies, framed in the UN member states commitments under the Paris Agreement and the SDGs (see Chapter 2). FAO's reported findings provide data-based evidence on food security, poverty, and climate change and were used as part of the inputs for COP26 held in Glasgow in November 2021.

During the last years FAO has paid special attention to the consequences of CC on agriculture, food security, and nutrition sustainability. The organization defines sustainable development as: "... the management and conservation of the natural resource base, and the orientation of technological and institutional change in such a manner as to ensure the attainment and continued satisfaction of human needs for present and future generations. Such sustainable development (in the agriculture, forestry, and fisheries sectors) conserves land, water, plant and animal genetic resources, is environmentally non-degrading, technologically appropriate, economically viable and socially acceptable" (http://www.fao.org/3/ai388e/AI38 8E05.htm, other definitions of sustainable development can be found in Box 3.4).

---

[11]Offsite effects are externalities, defined as a side-effect or consequence of economic activities that affects other economic agents without this being reflected in the cost of the goods or services involved; e.g., water contaminated by agrochemical used for human consumption.

Table 3.1. Agriculture's Environmental Problems Onsite and Offsite

	Onsite effects	Offsite effects (Externalities)	Global effects (Externalities)
Intensive agriculture (high-potential areas)	Soil degradation (salinization, loss of organic matter)	Groundwater depletion. Agrochemical pollution. Loss of local biodiversity	Greenhouse gas emissions. Animal diseases. Loss of *in situ* crop genetic diversity
Extensive agriculture (less-favored areas)	Nutrient depletion Soil erosion onsite effects	Soil erosion downstream effects (reservoir siltation) Hydrological change (e.g., loss of water retention in upstream areas) Pasture degradation in common property areas	Reduced carbon sequestration from deforestation and carbon dioxide emissions from forest fires Loss of biodiversity
Level of cooperation typically required	None (individual or household)	Community, watershed, basin, landscape-level, regional, or national	Global

Source: WB (2008, p. 181).

Box 3.4. Definitions of Sustainable Development

Different stakeholders have different definitions of sustainability, or sustainable development. The definitions provided by some of the most authoritative organizations are the following:

FAO defines ***sustainable agriculture and rural development*** as processes that meet the following criteria:

- They ensure that the basic nutritional requirements of present and future generations, qualitatively and quantitatively, are met while providing a number of other agricultural products.
- They provide durable employment, sufficient income, and decent living and working conditions for all those engaged in agricultural production.
- They maintain and, where possible, enhance the productive capacity of the natural resource base as a whole, and the regenerative capacity of renewable resources, without disrupting the functioning of basic ecological cycles and natural balances, destroying the sociocultural attributes of rural communities, or contaminating the environment.
- They reduce the vulnerability of the agriculture sector to adverse natural and socioeconomic factors and other risks, and strengthen self-reliance.

FAO also defines a ***sustainable livelihood*** as a livelihood that can cope with, and recover from, stresses and shocks and maintain or enhance its capabilities and assets both now and in the future, whilst not undermining the natural resource base.

The ***United Nations Environment Programme (UNEP)*** defines ***sustainable development*** as development that ensures that the use of resources and the environment today does not compromise their use in the future.

Box 3.4. (*Continued*)

Sustainable development, or sustainability, is defined by the ***World Wildlife Fund for Nature (WWF)*** as an economic activity that meets the needs of the present generation without compromising the ability of future generations to meet their needs. Sustainability is based upon three components: economic growth, social progress and environmental protection.

The ***World Summit for Sustainable Development (WSSD)*** held in Johannesburg in 2002 states that ***sustainable development*** is built on three interdependent and mutually re-enforcing pillars — economic development, social development and environmental protection — that must be established at local, national, regional and global levels. This establishes linkages among poverty alleviation, human rights, biodiversity, clean water and sanitation, renewable energy and the sustainable use of natural resources.

The aforesaid definitions share some key concepts such as the long-term environmental, social and economic viability of activities and their ability to deliver quantity and quality outputs now and for generations to come.

Applied to the aquaculture sector this means long-term production of safe aquaculture products with respect to natural resources and in such a way as to deliver socioeconomic development not only for local fishery communities, but also for other resource users and globally.

Source: http://www.fao.org/3/ai388e/AI388E05.htm (consulted on July 25, 2021).

Based on evidence, FAO is concerned about current and future trends in food production, poverty, malnutrition, and the environment which represent challenges to achieve the 17 SDGs. In regard to the trends, the organization considers the world's population is expected to grow to almost 10 billion by 2050, boosting demand for agricultural products by around 50% compared to 2013. In addition, income growth in low and medium-income countries will move demand from cereals to meat, fruits, and vegetables, adding pressure on natural resources. These trends require to increase agricultural productivity that, if not accompanied by changes in agricultural systems, will continue to hamper the degradation of natural resources, the loss of biodiversity, and the spread of transboundary pests and diseases of plants and animals.[12] If deterioration of the environment caused by human activities continues, global warming will likely lead to more intense competition for natural resources, increase GHG emissions, and further deforestation and land degradation (FAO, 2017).

Notwithstanding global progress in reducing poverty and malnutrition during the last decades, these trends have reversed since around 2015; so, in a "business-as-usual" scenario without additional efforts to promote pro-poor growth and development, FAO estimates that some 653 million people would still be undernourished in 2030. Furthermore, development policies must promote the reduction of pervasive inequalities (*Ibid.*).

As in the 2008 WB Report, FAO includes in its studies the heterogeneity of agricultural production, particularly in rural areas of the world suffering high rates of poverty incidence. However, an important difference with respect to the WB is that FAO is concerned about the consequences of the tendency of capital intensification in agricultural production. FAO argues that critical parts of food systems[13] are becoming more capital-intensive, vertically integrated, and concentrated in fewer hands and that this is happening in

[12]FAO's notion of "agricultural systems" or "agri-food systems" include fisheries and forestry systems, and other systems include systems that are critical to food systems transformation, including among others: education, energy, the environment, legal, social, economic, finance, trade and marketing systems.

[13]The IPCC defines global food system as "all the elements (environment, people, inputs, processes, infrastructures, institutions, etc.) and activities that relate to the production, processing, distribution, preparation and consumption of food,

all components of the food chain, from input provisioning to food processing and distribution. This process is affecting small producers and landless households whose — mainly male — members are increasingly seeking employment opportunities outside agriculture and migrating out of rural areas. In turn, this is leading to the "feminization" of farming in many parts of the world. FAO's concern about the process of capital intensification of agriculture is because this type of production is resource-intensive, causing massive deforestation, water scarcities, soil depletion, and high levels of GHG emissions.

Notwithstanding the above difference between WB and FAO's views, their contributions to the knowledge of agriculture's role and corresponding challenges are complementary. Among others, the WB 2008 Report analyzes the functioning of heterogeneous agents in agriculture and proposes different channels for rural population to get out of poverty, and FAO provides evidence on recent trends in food production, poverty, and food security and offers explanations of the drivers accounting for current changes in these variables, including those related to the environment.

In one of its latest publications, "The State of Food Security and Nutrition in the World," FAO and associates study the observed increase of extreme negative natural events that are reducing food production and food availability, disrupting healthcare, and undermining social protection systems, pushing many affected people back into poverty and hunger and promoting migration and conflict. FAO adds present concerns about these trends: "Well before the COVID-19 pandemic, we were already not on track to meet our commitments to end world hunger and malnutrition in all its forms by 2030. Now, the pandemic has made this significantly more challenging." (FAO *et al.*, 2021, p. 5 and see Box 3.5).

---

and the output of these activities, including socioeconomic and environmental outcomes at the global level" (IPCC 2019, footnote 22).

Box 3.5. Recent Tendencies in Global Food Security and Nutrition

- After remaining virtually unchanged for 5 years, the prevalence of undernourishment (PoU) increased 1.5 percentage points in 2020 — reaching a level of around 9.9%, heightening the challenge of achieving the Zero Hunger target by 2030.
- Between 720 and 811 million people in the world faced hunger in 2020. Considering the middle of the projected range (768 million), around 118 million more people were facing hunger in 2020 than in 2019.
- Compared with 2019, about 46 million more people in Africa, 57 million more in Asia, and about 14 million more in Latin America and the Caribbean were affected by hunger in 2020.
- Around 660 million people may still face hunger in 2030, in part due to lasting effects of the COVID-19 pandemic on global food security — 30 million more people than in a scenario in which the pandemic had not occurred.
- While the global prevalence of moderate or severe food insecurity has been slowly on the rise since 2014, the estimated increase in 2020 was equal to that of the previous 5 years combined. Nearly one in three people in the world (2.37 billion) did not have access to adequate food in 2020 — an increase of almost 320 million people in just one year.
- Close to 12% of the global population was severely food insecure in 2020, representing 928 million people — 148 million more than in 2019.
- At the global level, the gender gap in the prevalence of moderate or severe food insecurity has grown even larger in the year of the COVID-19 pandemic.
- The high cost of healthy diets coupled with persistent high levels of income inequality put healthy diets out of reach for around 3 billion people, especially the poor, in every region of the world in 2019.

(Continued)

Box 3.5. (*Continued*)

- Globally, malnutrition in all its forms also remains a challenge. Although it is not yet possible to fully account for the impact of the COVID-19 pandemic, in 2020, it is estimated that 22.0% (149.2 million) of children under 5 years of age were affected by stunting, 6.7% (45.4 million) were suffering from wasting and 5.7% (38.9 million) were overweight. The actual figures are expected to be higher due to the effects of the pandemic.
- Africa and Asia account for more than 9 out of 10 of all children with stunting, more than 9 out of 10 children with wasting and more than 7 out of 10 children who are affected by overweight worldwide. An estimated 29.9% of women aged 15–49 years in 2019 around the world are affected by anemia — now a Sustainable Development Goal (SDG) Indicator (2.2.3). Adult obesity is increasing sharply in all regions.
- Globally, the world is not on track to achieve targets for any of the nutrition indicators by 2030. The current rate of progress on child stunting, exclusive breastfeeding and low birthweight is insufficient, and progress on child overweight, child wasting, anemia in women of reproductive age and adult obesity is stalled or the situation is worsening.
- The COVID-19 pandemic has likely impacted the prevalence of multiple forms of malnutrition, and could have lasting effects beyond 2020. These will be compounded through the intergenerational effects of malnutrition and the resulting impacts on productivity.

Source: FAO *et al.* (2021, pp. 5–6).

FAO proposes six major drivers behind the recent changes in food security and nutrition and adopts a holistic approach to feed into a broader analysis of how these drivers interact and lead to combined effects on these two phenomena. This approach allows to move from silo solutions to integrated food systems solutions that specifically address the challenges posed by the major drivers; some knowledge is required to transform food systems for sustainable food security, improved nutrition, and affordable healthy diets.

The six drivers transmitted throughout food systems undermining food security and nutrition are: (1) biophysical and environmental; (climate variability and extremes); (2) technology and innovation; (3) economic and market (slowdowns and downturns); (4) political and institutional (conflict); (5) economic and sociocultural (poverty and inequality); and (6) demographic. These drivers affect food environment, mainly composed by systems supporting food production, food supply chains, and consumer behavior, which affect nutrition and health. In turn, these nutrition and health outcomes affect the food environment.[14]

Based on evidence, previous FAO's studies and its holistic approach, the organization summarizes its diagnosis about the reasons explaining the observed recent negative tendencies regarding food security and nutrition as follows:

- "Conflict, climate variability and extremes, and economic slowdowns and downturns (now exacerbated by the COVID-19 pandemic) are major drivers of food insecurity and malnutrition that continue to increase in both frequency and intensity and are occurring more frequently in combination. The reversal in the prevalence of undernourishment (PoU) trends in 2014 and continuous increase are largely attributed to countries affected by conflict, climate extremes and economic downturns, and to countries with high income inequality.
- Between 2017 and 2019, the PoU increased by 4% in countries affected by one or more of these major drivers while it decreased by 3% in countries not affected by them. High income inequality

[14]See Figure 14 in FAO *et al.* (2021), for a detailed account of how these drivers have disturbed the food environment during the last 6 years. In Chapter 5, we present multisectoral economy-wide models. If data are available, these models can be applied and designed to measure direct and indirect effects of shocks such as those coming from FAO's drivers in the food system and in the rest of the studied economy and society, i.e., how an external shock affects directly and indirectly the structure of the whole socioeconomic system and its components.

magnified this negative impact of the drivers, particularly in middle-income countries. In the same period, countries affected by multiple drivers exhibited the highest increases in the PoU, 12 times larger than those in countries affected by only a single driver.

- Drivers that are external (e.g., conflicts or climate shocks) and internal (e.g., low productivity and inefficient food supply chains) to food systems are pushing up the cost of nutritious foods which, combined with low incomes, are increasing the unaffordability of healthy diets, particularly in countries affected by multiple drivers.
- In 2020, almost all low- and middle-income countries were affected by pandemic-induced economic downturns. When combined with climate-related disasters, conflict, or a combination of these, the largest increase in the PoU were seen in Africa and Asia.
- Because these major drivers are negatively affecting food security and nutrition by creating multiple, compounding impacts throughout our food systems, a food systems lens is essential to better understand their interactions and identify entry points for interventions to address them.
- While 2020 was an immense challenge for the world, it may also be a warning of unwelcome events to come if more resolute actions to change course are not taken because the major drivers have their own trajectory or cyclicality and will continue to occur." (FAO *et al.*, 2021, pp. 6–7).

In regard to the bio-physical and environmental drivers of climate variability and extremes, global climate studies show that not only temperatures are increasing and precipitation levels are becoming more varied but all projections also indicate these trends will continue, upsetting agriculture production and food security. Based on this evidence, FAO published a technical study on the impact of changing climate on agriculture and food security. The research addresses two questions that contribute to understand recent changes in climate over agriculture areas and their impacts on food security: Are these changes already affecting agriculture and hunger, and are they driving or contributing to the observed uptick in hunger? What is the evidence? (Holleman *et al.*, 2020).

The major findings of the study are the following:

- More countries are exposed to increasing climate variability and extremes and the frequency (the number of years exposed in a 5-year period) and intensity (the number of types of climate extremes in a 5-year period) of exposure over agricultural areas have increased.
- Globally, regionally, and sub-regionally climate variability and extremes have a clear role in yield and production variability in major cereal crops. These trends create a high degree of vulnerability of food systems to climate factors.
- Evidence unequivocally shows that the Earth's climate is changing. Not only are temperatures increasing and precipitation levels becoming more varied, but all projections also indicate these trends will continue.
- Agricultural areas in many countries are experiencing increase in the mean temperature, more frequent hot days, and below-normal rainfall levels, resulting in widespread severe droughts conditions.
- Strongest direct impacts from increasing climate variability and extremes are felt in agriculture. These shocks reduce agricultural productivity affecting its primary role as a source of food and livelihoods for the rural poor.
- Increased climate variability and extremes are inflicting economic losses on agriculture and often trigger changes in agricultural trade flows, leading to increased import expenditures and reduced export revenues for several countries.
- The impacts of the studied climate shocks are also affecting food access, which is also significantly undermined. Many people whose livelihoods depend on agriculture and natural resources lose important sources of their livelihoods and hence, their ability to access food.
- Increased climate variability and extremes also cause spikes in food prices and increase food price volatility. These changes go beyond the actual climatic event. Price spikes hit harder net buyers of food, especially the urban and rural poor. Price volatility and the uncertainty it creates negatively affect both food buyers and small-scale food producers.

Notwithstanding the knowledge provided by Holleman and associates on the impacts of recent extreme weather events on food security, their empirical analyses are based on simple correlations between these two variables and its components, a restriction that the authors recognize, to which data limitations are added. So, in order to contribute to our knowledge on how CC is currently impacting and will impact agricultural production and food security, States and academics all over the world need to increase their research efforts and build the data bases necessary to address these challenges.

3.3 Agricultural Development Policies

Since the beginning of systematic thinking about the role of agriculture in economic development the question of "markets versus state intervention" has been discussed extensively. The dual sector neoclassical model of Ranis and Fei that propose that when a surplus labor dual economy reaches the "turning point" this economy behaves according to market signals. Timmer adopts an intermediate position by suggesting that agricultural transformation in LDCs requires a mix of public policies and market orientation. For Timmer, state intervention is necessary to help farmers deal with the risks they face because their production is highly dependent on weather-changing conditions.

During the 21st century, natural capital has been incorporated as an integral part of major studies on agricultural development. These studies also take into consideration that agriculture forms part of rural areas and is formed by heterogeneous producers, including rural household farmers and the transaction costs they face to get involved in markets.

In terms of agricultural policy, the WB argues that heterogeneity in agriculture and rural economies and society has deep implications and that a particular policy reform is likely to have gainers and losers. For example, trade liberalization that raises the price of food will hurt net buyers (the largest group of rural poor in countries like Bolivia and Bangladesh) and benefit net sellers (the largest group of rural poor in Cambodia and Vietnam). So, policies have to be differentiated according to the status and context of households, taking particular account of prevailing gender norms.

The WB adds that differentiated policies are designed not necessarily to favor one group over the other but to serve all households more cost-effectively, tailoring policies to their conditions and needs, particularly those of the poorest. Balancing attention to the favored and less-favored subsectors, regions, and households is one of the toughest policy dilemmas facing poor countries with severe resource constraints.

The WB also argues that "... the state will need greater capacity to coordinate across sectors and to form partnerships with private and civil society actors. Global actors need to deliver on a complex agenda of interrelated agreements and international public goods. Civil society empowerment, particularly of producer organizations, is essential to improving governance at all levels" (WB, 2008, p. 2).

With respect to agriculture's sustainable development, the WB proposes that agriculture's large environmental footprint be reduced, farming systems made less vulnerable to climate change, and agriculture harnessed to deliver more environmental services. The solution is not to slow agricultural development — it is to seek more sustainable production systems. The first step toward this is to get the incentives right by strengthening property rights and removing subsidies that encourage the degradation of natural resources. Also imperative is adapting to climate change, which will hit poor farmers the hardest, and hit them unfairly because they have contributed little to its causes.

Agriculture thus offers great promise for growth, poverty reduction, and environmental services, but realizing this promise also requires the visible hand of the state — providing core public goods, improving the investment climate, regulating natural resource management, and securing desirable social outcomes" (*Ibid.*, p. 200).

With regard to the issue of state intervention in countries where small and subsistence farmers prevail, the WB proposes that governments pay special attention to the promotion of markets access of these agents by, providing public goods such as roads and other types of communications infrastructure, among others (*Ibid.*, pp. 92–93).

As discussed in the previous section, FAO is concerned about recent global tendencies in food security and nutrition (see Box 3.5). FAO proposes six major drivers behind these tendencies and, accordingly, offers six general pathways to follow toward food systems transformation: (1) integrating humanitarian, development and peacebuilding policies in conflict-affected areas; (2) scaling up climate resilience across food systems; (3) strengthening resilience of the most vulnerable to economic adversity; (4) intervening along the food supply chains to lower the cost of nutritious foods; (5) tackling poverty and structural inequalities, ensuring interventions are pro-poor and inclusive; strengthening food environments, and (6) changing consumer behavior to promote dietary patterns with positive impacts on human health and the environment.

FAO adds that most food systems are affected by more than one driver; hence, the formulation of comprehensive portfolios of policies, investments, and legislation may be elaborated along several pathways simultaneously. This will allow for maximizing their combined effects on food systems transformation, exploiting win–win solutions and mitigating undesirable trade-offs. Coherence in the formulation and implementation of policies and investments among food, health, social protection, and environmental systems is also essential to build on synergies toward more efficient and effective food systems solutions. Systems approaches include territorial, ecosystems, and indigenous peoples' food system approaches, as well as interventions that systemically address protracted crisis conditions (FAO *et al.*, 2021).

It is evident that FAO's recent policy proposals give governments' interventions a much more active role than the WB does. This difference is fundamental in the discussion related to the design and application of sustainable development policies in market-oriented economies, an issue that we discuss in Chapters 6 and 7.

References

Dyer, G. A., López-Feldman, A., Yúnez-Naude, A., and Taylor, J. E. (2014). Genetic erosion in maize's center of origin. *Proceedings of the National Academy of Sciences of the United States of America* (PNAS), *111*(39), 14094–14099. https://www.pnas.org/doi/abs/10.1073/pnas.1407033111.

Food and Agriculture Organization of the United Nations (FAO). (2017). *The Future of Food and Agriculture: Trends and Challenges.* FAO. https://www.fao.org/policy-support/tools-and-publications/resources-details/en/c/472484/.

FAO. (2020). *World Food and Agriculture — Statistical Yearbook 2020.* FAO. https://doi.org/10.4060/cb1329en.

FAO, IFAD, UNICEF, WFP and WHO. (2021). *In Brief to the State of Food Security and Nutrition in the World 2021. Transforming Food Systems for Food Security, Improved Nutrition and Affordable Healthy Diets For All.* https://www.fao.org/3/cb5409en/cb5409en.pdf.

Harris, J. R. and Todaro, M. P. (1970). Migration, unemployment and development: A two-sector analysis. *The American Economic Review*, *60*(1), 126–142. https://www.jstor.org/stable/1807860.

Hirschman, A. O. (1958). *The Strategy of Economic Development.* Yale University Press, New Haven Connecticut.

Holleman, C., Rembold, F., Crespo, O. and Conti, V. (2020). *The Impact of Climate Variability and Extremes on Agriculture and Food Security — An Analysis of the Evidence and Case Studies.* Background paper for The State of Food Security and Nutrition in the World 2018. FAO Agricultural Development Economics Technical Study No. 4. https://doi.org/10.4060/cb2415en.

Irwin, D. A. (2021). The rise and fall of import substitution. *World Development*, *139*, 105305. https://doi.org/10.1016/j.worlddev.2020.105306.

Intergovernmental Panel on Climate Change (IPCC). (2019). Summary for policymakers. In P. R. Shukla, J. Skea, E. Calvo Buendia, V. Masson-Delmotte, H.-O. Pörtner, D. C. Roberts, P. Zhai, R. Slade, S. Connors, R. van Diemen, M. Ferrat, E. Haughey, S. Luz, S. Neogi, M. Pathak, J. Petzold, J. Portugal Pereira, P. Vyas, E. Huntley, K. Kissick, M. Belkacemi, J. Malley, (eds.), *Climate Change and Land: And IPCC Special Report on Climate Change, Desertification, Land Degradation, Sustainable Land Management, Food Security, and Greenhouse Gas Fluxes in Terrestrial Ecosystems.* IPCC. https://www.ipcc.ch/srccl/.

Jorgenson D. W. (1961). The development of a dual economy. *The Economic Journal*, *71*(282), 309–334. https://doi.org/10.2307/2228770.

Lewis, W. A. (1954). Economic development with unlimited supplies of labour. *Manchester School*, *22*(2), 139–191. https://doi.org/10.1111/j.1467-9957.1954.tb00021.x.

Nelson, M. and Maredia, M. K. (2007). International agricultural research as a source of environmental impacts: Challenges and possibilities. *Journal of Environmental Assessment Policy and Management*, *9*(1), 103–119. https://doi.org/10.1142/S1464333207002652.

Millennium Ecosystem Assessment (MEA). (2005). *Current State and Trends Assessment*. Island Press, Washington, D.C.
Prebisch, R. (1959). Commercial policy in the underdeveloped countries. The *American Economic Review*, *49*(2), 251–273. https://www.jstor.org/stable/i331502.
Timmer, P. (1988). The agricultural transformation. In H. Chenery and T. N. Srinivasan (eds.), *Handbook of Development Economics* (pp. 275–331). Elsevier Science.
Ranis, G. and Fei, J. (1961). A theory of economic development. *The American Economic Review*, *51*(4), 533–565. https://www.jstor.org/stable/1812785.
Rosenstein-Rodan, P. N. (1961). Notes on the theory of the "Big Push." In H. S. Ellis and H. C. Wallich (eds.), *Economic Development for Latin America* (pp. 57–81). Palgrave Macmillan.
World Bank. (2008). *World Development Report 2008: Agriculture for Development*. https://openknowledge.worldbank.org/handle/10986/5990.
Yúnez-Naude, A. (1978). Una evaluación del modelo de crecimiento dual de Ranis y Fei. *El Trimestre Económico*, *357*, 357–399.
Yúnez-Naude, A. (1988). Theories of the exploited peasantry: A critical review. *The Journal Peasant Studies*, *15*(2), 190–217. https://doi.org/10.1080/03066158808438357.
Yúnez-Naude, A. (2019). ¿Hacia dónde ir? *Nexos*, Agenda, (503), 26–28. https://www.nexos.com.mx/?p=45484.

Chapter 4

Land, Agriculture, Sustainable Development, and Climate Change

Agriculture is the economic sector that uses more land. This implies that the growth of this sector and its provision of food has had a negative effect on other land uses where forests stand out, as forests are one of the major natural resource sinks of greenhouse gas (GHG) emissions. In addition to land use, agriculture is the highest fresh water consuming sector.

So, agriculture's competition for land and water use must be considered in the study of climate change (CC) and sustainability. We do so in this chapter to frame the presentation of actions required in agriculture and rural areas to mitigate global warming. In this chapter, we also address questions related to vulnerability to CC and the necessary actions required to adapt to this phenomenon. We give special attention to rural households, whose economic situation, functioning, and risks to CC are explored in some studies on sustainable development and policies to promote it.

4.1 Agriculture, Forestry, and Other Land Uses

Land/soils are part of natural capital (see Box 1.1). United Nations' Conferences on Climate Change (IPCC) define land as the terrestrial portion of the biosphere that comprises the natural resources (soil, near-surface air, vegetation, and other living organisms or biota (the flora and fauna of a region), as well as water, ecological processes, topography, and human settlements and infrastructure that operate within that system (IPCC, 2019).

Land is both a source and a sink of GHG emissions. It provides the principal basis for human livelihoods and welfare, including the supply of food, freshwater, and other ecosystem services and biodiversity. Land also plays an important role in the climate system. Human use of land directly affects more than 70% of the global, ice-free land surface through population growth and agricultural, food production, and forest activities. However, global population growth and changes in per capita consumption of food, animal feed, fiber, timber, and energy have caused unprecedented rates of land and freshwater use: by the end of the first decade of the 21st century agriculture accounted for around 70% of global fresh-water use. (*Ibid.*, pp. 4–5).

For decades, about half of the carbon dioxide (CO_2) that human activities have emitted to the atmosphere has been taken up by natural carbon sinks in vegetation, soils, and oceans. These natural sinks of CO_2 have thus roughly halved the rate at which atmospheric CO_2 concentrations have increased, and therefore slowed down global warming. However, observations show that the processes underlying this uptake are beginning to respond to increasing CO_2 in the atmosphere and CC in a way that will weaken nature's capacity to take up CO_2 in the future. Direct observations which began in 1958 show that the atmosphere has only retained roughly half of the CO_2 emitted by human activities due to the combustion of fossil fuels and land-use change such as deforestation. Natural carbon cycle processes on land and in the oceans have taken up the remainder of these emissions. These land and ocean removals or "sinks" have grown largely in proportion to the increase in CO_2 emissions, taking up 31% (land) and 23% (ocean) of the emissions in 2010–2019, respectively. Therefore, the average proportion of yearly CO_2 emissions staying in the atmosphere has remained roughly stable at 44% over the last six decades despite continuously increasing CO_2 emissions from human activities (IPCC, 2021, p. 1268).

In regard to forests, during the last decade of the 20th century, deforestation in the tropics and forest regrowth in the temperate zone and parts of the boreal zone remained the major factors responsible for CO_2 emissions and removals, respectively (IPCC, 2007a, p. 67; see there Table TS.12 and Figure TS.21, pp. 67, 68 respectively; details in pp. 551–556).

Sustainable forestry can make a significant contribution to global mitigation actions while also meeting a wide range of social, economic, and ecological objectives. In addition, co-benefits can be gained by considering forestry mitigation options as an element of broader land-use actions.

The following terms and acronyms are used in the UN agencies studies on land use and CC, and in other studies on the matter. Agriculture, Forestry and Other Land Uses (AFOLU), Forestry and Other Land Uses (FOLU), and Land Use, Land-Use Change, and Forestry (LULUCF) formed by the subset of AFOLU emissions and removals of GHGs resulting from direct human-induced land use, land-use change, and forestry activities excluding agricultural emissions (IPCC, 2014a, p. 118). In other words, LULUCF emissions represent the net balance between emissions from land-use change and carbon sequestration from the regeneration of vegetation and soils (IPCC, 2019).

The AFOLU sector accounts for an estimated 12 gigatons of carbon dioxide equivalent per year (12 Gt CO_2-eq yr^{-1}) of net anthropogenic GHG emissions and 23% of total GHG emissions between 2007 and 2016. It is estimated that 80% of nitrous oxide (N_2O) emissions from human activities come from AFOLU globally. While the AFOLU sector generates significant emissions, the residual terrestrial sink (i.e., the accumulation of carbon in the terrestrial biosphere, excluding land sinks from land use, land use change, and forestry (LULUCF), which we cannot explain with bottom up LULUCF accounting), also currently sequesters around 30% of annual anthropogenic emissions. Land is, therefore, vitally important to draw carbon out of the atmosphere (*Ibid.*)

To analyze the global relationships between land uses and CC is extremely complex due to several reasons; among others, the fact that land is simultaneously a source of GHG emissions and a sink of CO_2 coming from both anthropogenic and natural phenomena, making it hard to separate anthropogenic from natural fluxes.

In addition, land use affects and is affected by CC, and so evaluating cause and effect poses a challenge which is further complicated by lack of data at the regional-country level.

Notwithstanding the above, in its 2019 report the IPCC documents contemporary evidence on past and present relationships between population, land use, CC, and global warming. IPCC's findings are based on scientific literature and its previous and current research results, mainly covering the period of 2007–2016 (a summary of IPCC findings is listed below).[1]

4.1.1 *AFOLU GHG emissions*

- An estimated 23% of anthropogenic GHG emissions derived from AFOLU during this period (main anthropogenic drivers in Box 4.1, details in *Ibid.*, Figure SPM.1: Land use and observed climate change, pp. 4–5).
- Other approaches, such as global food system, include agricultural emissions and land use change (i.e., deforestation and peatland degradation), as well as outside farm gate emissions from energy, transport, and industry sectors for food production. Emissions within farm gate and from agricultural land expansion contributing to the global food system represent 16–27% of total anthropogenic emissions.[2] Emissions outside the farm gate represent 5–10% of total anthropogenic emissions. Given the diversity of food systems, there are large regional differences in the contributions from different components of the food system. Emissions from agricultural production are projected to increase, driven by population and income growth and changes in consumption patterns.

[1]The summary is taken from IPCC (2019, pp. 2–18). The technical basis of this report is in Shukla *et al.* (2019). When we refer to references other than IPCC (2019), the reference is provided.

[2]IPCC estimates that between 1970 and 2004 the growth of GHG emissions from LULUCF grew by 40% and the direct GHG emissions from agriculture grew by 27% (IPCC, 2007a).

- AFOLU anthropogenic GHG emissions were globally distributed as follows: around 13% of CO_2, 44% of methane (CH_4), and 82% of nitrous oxide (N_2O).
- Global AFOLU emissions of methane (CH_4) during 2007–2016 were between 162 and 49 Mt CH_4 yr^{-1} (between 4.5 and 1.4 Gt CO_2-eq yr^{-1}). Biogenic sources make up a larger proportion of emissions than they did before 2000. Ruminants and the expansion of rice cultivation are important contributors to the rising concentration of CH_4.
- Anthropogenic AFOLU N_2O emissions are rising and were in the range of 8.3 and 2.5 Mt N_2O yr^{-1} (between 2.3 and 0.7 Gt CO_2-eq yr^{-1}) during the period.
  - Anthropogenic N_2O emissions from soils are primarily due to nitrogen application including inefficiencies (overapplication or poorly synchronized with crop demand timings).
  - There has been a major growth in emissions from managed pastures due to increased manure deposition. Livestock on managed pastures and rangelands accounted for more than one half of total anthropogenic N_2O emissions from agriculture in 2014.

Box 4.1. Main Anthropogenic Drivers of GHG Emissions Derived from AFOLU

- Expansion of areas under agriculture and forestry, including commercial production, and enhanced agriculture and forestry productivity have supported consumption and food availability for a growing population.... With large regional variation, these changes have contributed to increasing net GHG emissions ..., loss of natural ecosystems (e.g., forests, savannahs, natural grasslands and wetlands) and declining biodiversity....
- Data available since 1961 shows the per capita supply of vegetable oils and meat has more than doubled and the supply of food calories per capita has increased by about one third.... Currently, 25–30% of total food produced is lost or wasted.

(*Continued*)

Box 4.1. (*Continued*)

- These factors are associated with additional GHG emissions. . . .
- Changes in consumption patterns have contributed to about 2 billion adults now being overweight or obese. . . .
- An estimated 821 million people are still undernourished.

- About a quarter of the Earth's ice-free land area is subject to human-induced degradation ... Soil erosion from agricultural fields is estimated to be currently 10–20 times (no tillage) to more than 100 times (conventional tillage) higher than the soil formation rate. . . .
- Climate change exacerbates land degradation, particularly in low-lying coastal areas, river deltas, drylands and in permafrost areas. . . .
- Over the period 1961–2013, the annual area of drylands in drought has increased, on average by slightly more than 1% per year, with large inter-annual variability.
- In 2015, about 500 (380–620) million people lived within areas which experienced desertification between the 1980s and 2000s.
- The highest numbers of people affected are in South and East Asia, the circum Sahara region including North Africa, and the Middle East including the Arabian Peninsula ...
- Other dryland regions have also experienced desertification.
- People living in already degraded or desertified areas are increasingly negatively affected by climate change.

Source: IPCC (2019, pp. 4–5).

4.1.2 *Land as a sink of CO_2*

- During 2007–2016 the natural response of land (i.e., of LULUCF) to human-induced environmental change caused a net sink of around 11.2 Gt CO_2 yr^{-1} (gigatons of CO_2 per year), equivalent to 29% of total CO_2 emissions.

- Notwithstanding that the persistence of the sink is uncertain due to climate change, land is vitally important to draw carbon out of the atmosphere (IPCC, 2019, p. 7, details in Table SPM1, pp. 9–10).[3]

4.1.2.1 *Impacts of CC on food production and land*

- "Since the pre-industrial period, the land surface air temperature has risen nearly twice as much as the global average temperature. Climate change, including increases in frequency and intensity of extremes, has adversely impacted food security and terrestrial ecosystems as well as contributed to desertification and land degradation in many regions.
- CC has already affected food security due to warming, changing precipitation patterns, and greater frequency of some extreme events. In many lower-latitude regions, yields of some crops (e.g., maize and wheat) have declined, while in many higher-latitude regions, yields of some crops (e.g., maize, wheat, and sugar beets) have increased over recent decades. Climate change has resulted in lower animal growth rates and productivity in pastoral systems in Africa.
- There is robust evidence that agricultural pests and diseases have already responded to climate change resulting in both increases and decreases of infestations. Based on indigenous and local knowledge, climate change is affecting food security in drylands, particularly those in Africa, and high mountain regions of Asia and South America" (*Ibid.*, pp. 5, 7).

[3]Complex modeling tools are needed to fully consider the climatic effect of changing land surface and to manage carbon stocks in the biosphere. The potential effect of projected CC on the net carbon balance in forests remains uncertain (IPCC, 2007a, p. 67). These models are called "top-down models" which are based on methods on inversion of atmospheric transport.

4.1.2.2 *Effects of changes in land conditions*

- Land conditions are affected by both, land use and CC, and these processes impact global and regional climate (as well as food production).
- At the regional scale, changing land conditions can reduce or accentuate warming and affect the intensity, frequency, and duration of extreme events. The magnitude and direction of these changes vary with location and season.
- The intensity and duration of extreme events can be modified by changes in land conditions including heat-related events such as heat waves and heavy precipitation events. Changes in land conditions can also affect temperature and rainfall in regions as far as hundreds of kilometers away.
- Changes in land conditions caused by CC have feedbacks on regional climate.

    - In boreal regions where the tree line migrates northward and/or the growing season lengthens, winter warming will be enhanced due to decreased snow cover and albedo while warming will be reduced during the growing season because of increased evapotranspiration.[4]
    - In those tropical areas where increased rainfall is projected, increased vegetation growth will reduce regional warming. Drier soil conditions resulting from climate change can increase the severity of heat waves, while wetter soil conditions have the opposite effect.

- Desertification amplifies global warming through the release of CO_2 linked with the decrease in vegetation cover.
- Changes in forest cover (e.g., from afforestation, reforestation, and deforestation) directly affect regional surface temperature through exchanges of water and energy.

[4]Albedo is the proportion of the incident light or radiation that is reflected by the earth surface, typically that of a planet or the moon.

- Where forest cover increases in tropical regions cooling results from enhanced evapotranspiration that can result in cooler days during the growing season and can reduce the amplitude of heat related events.
- In regions with seasonal snow cover, such as the boreal region and some temperate regions, increased tree and shrub cover also has a wintertime warming influence due to reduced surface albedo.

4.1.2.3 *Additional stress on land caused by CC*[5]

- Increases in global mean surface temperature, relative to pre-industrial levels, affect processes involved in desertification (water scarcity), land degradation (soil erosion, vegetation loss, wildfire, permafrost thaw), and food security (crop yield and food supply instabilities).
- Changes in these processes drive risks to food systems, livelihoods, infrastructure, the value of land, and human and ecosystem health. Changes in one process (e.g., wildfire or water scarcity) may result in compound risks.
- Risks are location-specific and differ by region. Some regions will face higher risks, while some regions will face risks previously not anticipated.
- Cascading risks with impacts on multiple systems and sectors also vary across regions.

4.1.2.4 *Risks to humans from changes in land-based processes as a result of CC*

- The level of risk on humans posed by CC depends both on the level of warming and on socioeconomic factors such as how population, consumption, production, technological development, and land management patterns evolve.

[5]Details in IPCC (2019), pp. 15–17 and in "Figure SPM.2 Risks to land-related human systems and ecosystems from global climate change, socioeconomic development and mitigation choices in terrestrial ecosystems" (Panel A, pp. 13–14).

- The main risks are associated with desertification, land degradation, and food security.
  - Increasing risks associated with desertification include population exposed and vulnerable to water scarcity in drylands.
  - Risks related to land degradation include increased habitat degradation, population exposed to wildfire and floods and costs of floods.
  - Risks to food security include availability and access to food, including population at risk of hunger, food price increases and increases in disability adjusted life years attributable due to childhood underweight.

The level of risks humans face related to changes in land-based processes as a result of CC depends on socioeconomic choices that can reduce or exacerbate climate-related events. These choices also influence the rate of temperature increase. In its 2019 Report, the IPCC assesses how two contrasted socioeconomic pathways affect the levels of climate-related risks (see Box 4.2). The first pathway — called SSP1 — illustrates a world with low population growth, high income and reduced inequalities, food produced in low GHG emission systems, effective land use regulation, and high adaptive capacity to CC. The second pathway — called SSP3 — has the opposite trends. As depicted in Figure SPM.2, Panel B (*Ibid.*, p. 13), risks are lower in SSP1 compared with SSP3 given the same level of Global Mean Surface Temperature (GMST) increase. So, pathways with higher demand for food, feed, and water, more resource-intensive consumption and production, and more limited technological improvements in agriculture yields result in higher risks from water scarcity in drylands, land degradation, and food insecurity.[6]

[6]Risks are not indicated beyond 3°C and exclude the effects of targeted mitigation policies.

Box 4.2. IPCC Shared Socioeconomic Pathways (SSPs)

- SSP1 includes a peak and decline in population (~7 billion in 2100), high income and reduced inequalities, effective land-use regulation, less resource intensive consumption, including food produced in low-GHG emission systems and lower food waste, free trade and environmentally friendly technologies and lifestyles. Relative to other pathways, SSP1 has low challenges to mitigation and low challenges to adaptation (i.e., high adaptive capacity).
- SSP2 includes medium population growth (~9 billion in 2100), medium income, technological progress, production and consumption patterns are a continuation of past trends, and only gradual reduction in inequality occurs. Relative to other pathways, SSP2 has medium challenges to mitigation and medium challenges to adaptation (i.e., medium adaptive capacity).
- SSP3 includes high population (~13 billion in 2100), low income and continued inequalities, material-intensive consumption and production, barriers to trade, and slow rates of technological change. Relative to other pathways, SSP3 has high challenges to mitigation and high challenges to adaptation (i.e., low adaptive capacity).
- SSP4 includes medium population growth (~9 billion in 2100), medium income, but significant inequality within and across regions. Relative to other pathways, SSP4 has low challenges to mitigation, but high challenges to adaptation (i.e., low adaptive capacity).
- SSP5 includes a peak and decline in population (~7 billion in 2100), high income, reduced inequalities, and free trade. This pathway includes resource-intensive production, consumption and lifestyles. Relative to other pathways, SSP5 has high challenges to mitigation, but low challenges to adaptation (i.e., high adaptive capacity). The SSPs can be combined with Representative Concentration Pathways (RCPs) which imply different levels of mitigation, with implications for adaptation.

(*Continued*)

Box 4.2. (*Continued*)

Therefore, SSPs can be consistent with different levels of global mean surface temperature rise as projected by different SSP-RCP combinations. However, some SSP-RCP combinations are not possible; for instance, RCP2.6 and lower levels of future global mean surface temperature rise (e.g., 1.5°C) are not possible in SSP3 in modeled pathways.

The IPCC adds that the implications of future socioeconomic development on climate change mitigation, adaptation, and land-use (see below) are explored using Shared Socioeconomic Pathways (SSPs). The SSPs span a range of challenges to climate change mitigation and adaptation.

Source: IPCC (2019, pp. 14–15). BOX SPM.1: Shared Socioeconomic Pathways (SSPs).

If global warming tendencies prevail during the next three decades, CC will affect all societies in the world. However, in the medium term some will be more vulnerable to CC than others. This forecast is based on the facts that some countries and regions within them are more exposed than others because of their geographic location and economic conditions, and because societies have different capacities to cope with the consequences of CC. According to the literature, it is expected that during the next three centuries CC will not be uniform and will have heterogeneous impacts through different regions. Low-income countries are the most likely to suffer the consequences of global warming (Dell *et al.*, 2012; IPCC, 2014b) and some economic sectors that depend on climate could be more affected than others, like agriculture since weather is one of the main determinants of agricultural productivity (Adams *et al.*, 1998; Fischer *et al.*, 2005; Mendelsohn, 2009; Hernández-Solano and Yúnez-Naude, 2016).[7]

[7]It is expected that CC impacts will affect in a disproportionate way the welfare of poor rural households, making the fight against poverty more challenging (IPCC, 2014b). See Section 4.2.

So, countries and regional agricultural vulnerability will depend on their geographic location and the type of crops being produced or that could be produced. Lobell *et al.* (2008) argue that for South Asia and Africa the most vulnerable crops are some corn varieties, wheat, and rice. With regard to Latin America, its high agro-ecologic and demographic diversity will lead to diverse expectations of CC impacts within these regions: forecasts indicate that by mid-century crop productivity in the southeast of South America will either keep steady or increase slightly, while in Central America it could be reduced in the next 15 years, risking food security for the most impoverished populations (IPCC, 2014b).

The literature establishes that developing countries face a greater CC threat than developed countries and suggests that this is the case for developing countries because:

(1) of their higher agricultural dependency; (2) they have less capital available to implement adaptation measures; (3) in many cases these countries are more exposed to extreme climate events and higher temperature levels that are already too high (Fischer *et al.*, 2005, Mendelsohn, 2009). In addition, it is likely that small farmers will be the most affected by CC given their low and/or nil access to technology, inputs, information, insurance, and monetary resources to implement adaptation measures (see Chapter 6, Section 6.2).

The Food, Agriculture, Biodiversity, Land, and Energy (FABLE) Consortium has contributed to the measurement of AFOLU's GHG emissions and removals by calculating global GHG emissions and the contributions of each sector — including AFOLU — to total emissions, as well as by decomposing net GHG emissions from AFOLU by source in 2018 (FABLE, 2020, Figure 13, p. 46).

Based on its models' estimations, FABLE reports that in 2018 AFOLU's contribution to global GHG emissions accounted for 18.7% of total emissions. The main sources of AFOLU emissions from agriculture are soils and enteric fermentation, which together represent 78% of the net AFOLU emissions from agriculture. Changes in forest and other woody biomass stocks, forest land and forest and grassland conversion represent 72% of the sinks in countries that have a negative net balance of GHG emissions from LULUCF. Forest and grassland conversion also acts as a source of GHG emissions in countries with a positive net balance of GHG emissions from LULUCF, accounting for 69% of the net emissions from LULUCF (*Ibid.*, pp. 46–47).

As mentioned, agriculture is a major sector in terms of freshwater use. So, sustainable development requires proper water management in agriculture to avoid water scarcity; i.e., to promote reliable availability and fair distribution of quantity and quality of water for health, livelihoods, production, and also to preserve water-related ecosystems.

Freshwater resources are affected by CC and both vary considerably worldwide, regionally and within countries. The areas suffering and/or most likely to face water insecurity are arid areas with low rainfall rates, high population growth, and unsustainable water use (e.g., in agricultural production). These areas are competing both internally and internationally over water sources and alternative uses that might lead to or are currently leading to domestic and international conflicts and/or tensions such as those between upstream and downstream users of water.

With regard to the actions for a sustainable and efficient use of water in agriculture it is important to consider that typical water sources for agriculture are: surface water from rivers, streams, and irrigation ditches, open canals and impounded water such as ponds, reservoirs, and lakes; groundwater from wells; rainwater; locally collected water such as cisterns and rain barrels, and also from municipal water systems.

4.2 Mitigation and Adaptation to Climate Change

Mitigation of CC by human intervention aims to reduce the sources or enhance the sinks of GHG emissions, whereas adaptation is the process of adjustment to actual or expected climate and its effects. Humans understand adaptation as a means that seeks to moderate or avoid harm or exploit beneficial opportunities. In some natural systems, human intervention may facilitate adjustment to expected climate and its effects (IPCC, 2014a).[8]

The attainment of sustainable development is closely linked to mitigation and adaptation to CC. Sustainable development can make an important contribution to CC mitigation. However, irrespective of the scale of mitigation measures, adaptation to CC is also necessary.

Scientific evidence on trends of global warming — hence of unsustainable development — calls for an urgent need to design and implement mitigation measures and "green" technologies. These actions have been recognized since the 1990s by the countries under the United Nations Framework Convention on Climate Change (UNFCCC).

Until the Cancun Climate Change Conference held in November 2010, multilateral negotiations and agreements under the UNFCCC focused on global warming mitigation actions. Adaptation measures to fight CC were added during the Cancun Conference.

4.2.1 *Mitigation in AFOLU sector*

In general, according to the IPCC the main CC mitigation options within AFOLU involve one or more of three strategies: prevention of emissions to the atmosphere by conserving existing carbon pools in soils or vegetation or by reducing emissions of methane and nitrous oxide; sequestration — increasing the size of existing carbon pools and thereby extracting CO_2 from the atmosphere; and substitution — substituting biological products for fossil fuels or energy-intensive products, thereby reducing CO_2 emissions. Demand-side measures (e.g., reducing losses and wastes of food, changes in human diet, or changes in wood consumption) may also play a role (IPCC, 2014a, p. 118).

So, reducing both loss of natural habitat and deforestation can result in significant biodiversity, soil and water conservation benefits and can be implemented in a socially and economically

[8]Note that in Annex II, pp. 118–128, this Report contains a detailed glossary of terms that the IPCC uses.

sustainable manner. Forestation and bioenergy plantations can lead to restoration of degraded land, manage water runoff, retain soil carbon, and benefit rural economies. However, as will be discussed in Section 4.3, these measures could compete with land for food production and may have a negative impact on biodiversity, if not properly designed.

4.2.1.1 *Agriculture*

Based on technology development, agricultural productivity has grown globally during the last decades and along with it, per capita food availability and a decline in per capita agricultural land area. However, this progress has been uneven across the world and poverty and malnutrition has prevailed in many countries; in addition, the share of animal products consumption in diets has increased progressively in medium and low-income countries and the global average daily availability of calories per capita has increased, with some regional exceptions, though. However, food production has grown at the expense of increasing pressure on the environment and on natural capital, and it is expected that global arable land will continue to expand at the expense of other land uses, especially in Africa and Latin America (IPCC, 2007a).

The IPCC estimates that the net flux of exchanges of CO_2 between the atmosphere and agricultural lands to be approximately balanced, with net CO_2 emissions of near zero Gt CO_2 yr. However, future climate change may eventually release more soil carbon. As regards agricultural N_2O and CH_4 emissions, they are projected to increase by 35–60% and around 60%, respectively, by 2030, thus increasing more rapidly than the 14% increase of non-CO_2 GHG observed during the period from 1990 to 2005 (*Ibid.*).

Both the magnitude of the emissions of agriculture and the relative importance of the different sources vary widely among world regions. These differences are related to the divergent levels of development among countries. To address these differences, the 1997 Kyoto Protocol distinguishes two types of countries under its *Clean Development Mechanisms* or CDM: developed countries of the Organization for Economic Development (OECD) and Economies in Transition (EIT), and the remaining countries (see Box 2.3).[9] Distinctions among Partner countries under the UNDFCC have prevailed since the Kyoto Protocol according to countries' development levels, and therefore, according to their GHG emissions and financial capacity to invest in CC mitigation (and adaptation). For example, whereas most high-income countries are major industrial polluters, low-income countries are responsible for most of the total agricultural emissions. As will be discussed below, these structural differences among countries are reflected in the negotiations and tensions in recent multilateral negotiations under the UNFCCC.

The IPCC proposes the following CC mitigation measures for agriculture:

- **Sink enhancement** through soil carbon sequestration (IPCC, 2007a estimates that about 90% of the total mitigation could come from sink enhancement and about 10% from emission reduction, Box 4.3).
- **Improved agricultural management.** Crop land management based on agronomy, including nutrient management, tillage/residue management, and water management through more efficient irrigation and drainage and set-aside/agro-forestry can reduce net GHG emissions, often affecting more than one GHG. The effectiveness of these practices depends on factors such as climate, soil type, and farming system.
    - Restoration of degraded lands (using erosion control, organic amendments, and nutrient amendments.
    - Livestock management (including improved feeding practices, dietary additives, breeding and other structural changes, and improved manure management (improved storage and handling and anaerobic digestion).
    - Improved grazing land management (including grazing intensity, increased productivity, nutrient management, fire management, and species introduction.

[9]Evaluations of the CDM regarding agriculture and developing countries can be consulted in Larson *et al.* (2011) and Rhaman *et al.* (2016).

- **Energy use.** Improved energy efficiency in agriculture and substitution of fossil fuels by energy production from agricultural feedstocks (e.g., crop residues, dung, energy crops).
- **Technology.** Many of the mitigation strategies for the agriculture sector employ existing technology. For example, reduction in emissions per unit of production can be achieved by increases in crop yields and animal productivity. Such increases in productivity can occur through a wide range of practices, such as:
    - better management, genetically modified crops, improved cultivars, fertilizer-recommendation systems, precision agriculture, improved animal breeds, improved animal nutrition, dietary additives and growth promoters, improved animal fertility, bioenergy feed stocks, anaerobic slurry digestion, and CH_4 capture systems.
- Some strategies involve new uses of existing technologies. For example, oils have been used in animal diets for many years to increase dietary energy content, but their role and feasibility as a CH_4 suppressant is still new and not fully defined. More research and development is needed in the case of some technologies (IPCC, 2007a, pp. 64–65).

Box 4.3. Soil Carbon Sequestration

Soil carbon sequestration is the process of capturing atmospheric CO_2 through changing land management practices to increase soil carbon content. The level of carbon concentration within the soil is determined by the balance of inputs, e.g., residues, roots and manure, and the carbon losses realized through respiration which is mainly influenced by soil disturbance.

Practices that increase inputs and/or reduce losses drive soil carbon sequestration. It is well noted in the literature that soil carbon sequestration promotes enhanced soil fertility and health as well as improves crop yields due to organic carbon accumulation within soils.

Box 4.3. (*Continued*)

Land management practices that promote soil carbon sequestration include cropping system intensity and rotation practices, zero-tillage and conservation tillage practices, nutrient management, mulching and use of crop residues and manure, incorporation of biochar, use of organic fertilizers, and water management. Furthermore, the impact of perennial cropping systems on soil carbon sequestration is well documented in the literature.

The main issues related to this approach revolve around permanence, sink saturation as well as the impact on other GHG emissions. According to Fuss *et al.* (2018) the potential of carbon removal through soil carbon sequestration is time-limited. Once soils reach a level of saturation, further sequestration is no longer achieved. This may take 10–100 years depending on soil type and climatic conditions.

However, the Intergovernmental Panel on Climate Change (IPCC) defined a default saturation period of 20 years.

Once saturation is reached, land management practices need to be maintained indefinitely to mitigate reversal. A disadvantage to this would be the ongoing costs with no further removal benefits. Risks of reversibility are significant and weaken this approach's storage integrity.

Another negative effect is the impact of soil carbon sequestration on other GHG, mainly CH_4 and N_2O; however, this effect is reported to be negligible (Fuss *et al.*, 2018).

While soil carbon sequestration is ready for large-scale deployment, since many of such practices are already being used, lack of knowledge, resistance to change as well as lack of policy and financial incentives are identified as barriers for scalability.

Challenges around monitoring, reporting, and verification, as well as concerns about sink saturation and potential reversibility have been the main reasons behind slow policy action.

(*Continued*)

Box 4.3. (*Continued*)

However, non-climate policies have mainly promoted land management practices to improve soil quality, fertility, and productivity as well as prevent land degradation. While policy and market-based mechanisms are required to push this approach forward, international voluntary carbon removal platforms are emerging.

A US-based platform (Nori) is based on the concept of soil carbon sequestration and operates by linking consumers and businesses that wish to offset their carbon footprint with farmers that offer carbon removal certificates that have been audited through an independent verification party. Using blockchain technology, this company is one step further in fighting the challenges associated with monitoring, reporting and verification systems.

Source: Fawzy *et al.* (2020, pp. 14–15).

In the medium term, much of the mitigation potential is derived from removal of CO_2 from the atmosphere and its conversion to soil carbon, but the magnitude of this process will diminish as soil carbon approaches maximum levels, and long-term mitigation will rely increasingly on reducing emissions of N_2O, CH_4, and CO_2 from energy use, the benefits of which persist indefinitely (IPCC, 2007a, pp. 63–64).

With regard to the long run IPCC argues that global food demand will grow and may double by 2050, leading to intensified production practices (e.g., increasing use of nitrogen fertilizer). In addition, projected increases in the consumption of livestock products will increase CH_4 and N_2O emissions if livestock numbers increase, leading to growing emissions with respect to IPCC's baseline after 2030. Agricultural mitigation measures will help reduce GHG emissions per unit of product, relative to the baseline. However, until 2030 only about 10% of the mitigation potential is related to CH_4 and N_2O. Deployment of new mitigation practices for livestock systems and fertilizer applications will be essential to prevent an increase in emissions from agriculture after 2030 (*Ibid.*, pp. 66–67).

Projecting long-term mitigation potentials is also hampered by other uncertainties. For example, the effects of CC are unclear: future CC may reduce soil carbon-sequestration rates, or could even release soil carbon, though the effect is uncertain as CC may also increase soil carbon inputs through higher plant production (*Ibid.*, see also FABLE, 2020).

Growing evidence confirms that current mitigation efforts, as well as future emissions commitments are not sufficient to achieve the temperature goals set by the Paris Agreement. Further measures and new abatement routes must be explored if an attempt is to be made to achieve such goals (Fawzy *et al.*, 2020, pp. 5–6). In this respect, IPCC considers that some studies have suggested that technological improvements could potentially counteract the negative impacts of CC on cropland and grassland soil carbon stocks, making technological improvement a key factor in future GHG mitigation. Such technologies could, for example, act through increasing production, thereby increasing carbon returns to the soil and reducing the demand for fresh cropland (IPCC, 2007a, pp. 66–67).

New technologies for CC abatement are beginning to be available or in progress. They are related to negative emissions and radiative forcing geoengineering. Whereas conventional CC technologies focus on fossil fuels-based CO_2 emissions, negative emissions technologies are aiming to capture and sequester atmospheric carbon to reduce carbon dioxide levels, and geoengineering techniques of radiative forcing alter the earth's radiative energy budget to stabilize or reduce global temperatures (Fawzy *et al.*, 2020). Based on the evidence that conventional mitigation efforts alone are not sufficient to meet the targets stipulated by the Paris Agreement, the authors argue that the utilization of alternative routes appears inevitable.

However, notwithstanding that the significant role of negative emissions technology in meeting CC targets is understood and appreciated among academics and scientists, there is still a debate on the social, economic, technical feasibility, and risks associated with large-scale deployment of this type of technology (*Ibid.*, p. 11).

In their literature review of major negative emissions technologies and carbon removal methods for meeting UNFCC's targets, Fawzy *et al.* include some related to agriculture and forestry (see Figure 2, p. 11 in *Ibid.*, p. 12).

One of these technologies is called Bioenergy Carbon Capture and Storage or BECCS, based on the integration of biopower and carbon capture and storage.[10] However, in order to be an effective emission abatement strategy, the technology requires a significant amount of biomass feedstocks, and hence, land and water and nutrients. This high demand of resources would directly affect food and feed crops production. So, this resource competition between BECCS technologies and food production requires an integrated sustainable approach to land use.[11]

There are also trade-offs between mitigation efforts in agriculture and food security. According to Frank *et al.* (2017), cost-efficient distribution of mitigation across regions and economic sectors, including agriculture, is typically calculated using a global uniform carbon price in climate stabilization scenarios. The authors argue that in reality such a carbon price would substantially affect food availability. Using an integrated partial equilibrium model (see Chapter 5), Frank and associates assess the implications of CC mitigation in the AFOLU sector for agricultural production and food security. With this approach they explore ways of relaxing the competition between mitigation in agriculture and food availability.

Using a scenario that limits global warming cost-efficiently across sectors to 1.5°C, Frank *et al.* find that global food calorie losses would range from 110 to 285 kcal per capita per day in 2050, a reduction that could translate into a rise in undernourishment of 80–300 million people in that year. Less ambitious GHG mitigation in the land use sector reduces the associated food security impact significantly, however the 1.5°C target would not be achieved without additional reductions outside the land use sector.

[10]The IPCC (2018) assessment proposes this technology as a potential root to meet temperature goals.

[11]In addition, as we discuss below, the implementation of BECCS approach with high coverage would compete with forest land.

4.2.1.2 *Forests*

Forestry can make significant contributions to a low-cost global mitigation portfolio that provides synergies with adaptation and sustainable development. There is growing evidence that reduced deforestation and degradation, afforestation, forest management, agroforestry, and bioenergy are major and low-cost actions to mitigate CC. There is also evidence that CC impacts can constrain the mitigation potential of forests (IPCC, 2007a, p. 67).

Globally, hundreds of millions of households depend on goods and services provided by forests. So, actions on the forest sector are fundamental to mitigate CC in the context of sustainable development and for rural households and their communities. This is specially so for low and medium-income countries located in the tropics, where poverty incidence prevails.

Forest mitigation options include reducing emissions from deforestation and forest degradation, enhancing the sequestration rate in existing and new forests, providing wood fuels as a substitute for fossil fuels, and providing wood products for more energy-intensive materials. Properly designed and implemented, forestry mitigation options will have substantial co-benefits in terms of employment and income generation opportunities, biodiversity and watershed conservation, provision of timber and fiber, and aesthetic and recreational services. Many barriers have been identified that preclude the full use of forests mitigation potential.

The design of a forest sector mitigation portfolio should consider the trade-offs between increasing forest ecosystem carbon stocks and raising the sustainable rate of harvest and transfer of carbon to meet human needs. The selection of forest sector mitigation strategies should minimize net GHG emissions throughout the forest sector and other sectors affected by these mitigation activities. For example, forest expansion reduces agricultural land area and may lead to farming practices with higher emissions (e.g., more fertilizer use), conversion of land for cropland expansion elsewhere, or increased imports of agricultural products.

So, the choice of system boundaries and time horizons affects the ranking of mitigation activities required. In addition, forest mitigation strategies should be assessed within the framework of sustainable forest management, and with consideration of the climate impacts of changes to other processes such as albedo and the hydrological cycle.

The IPCC groups options to reduce emissions by sources and/or increase removals by sinks in the forest sector into four general categories:

- maintaining or increasing the forest area through reduction of deforestation and degradation and through afforestation/reforestation;
- maintaining or increasing the stand-level carbon density (tons of carbon per ha) through the reduction of forest degradation and through planting, site preparation, tree improvement, fertilization, uneven-aged stand management, or other appropriate silviculture techniques;
- maintaining or increasing the landscape-level carbon density using forest conservation, longer forest rotations, fire management, and protection against insects;
- increasing off-site carbon stocks in wood products and enhancing product and fuel substitution using forest-derived biomass to substitute products with high fossil fuel requirements and increasing the use of biomass-derived energy to substitute fossil fuels (*Ibid.*, p. 549, a description of these four mitigation strategies in pp. 550–551).

Each mitigation activity has a characteristic time sequence of actions, carbon benefits, and costs. Relative to a baseline, the largest short-term gains are always achieved through mitigation activities aimed at avoiding emissions (reduced deforestation or degradation, fire protection, slash burning, etc.). All forest-management activities aimed at increasing site-level and landscape-level carbon density are common practices that are technically feasible, but the extent and area over which they can be implemented could be increased considerably. Economic considerations are typically the main constraint, because retaining additional carbon on site delays revenues from harvest. In the long term, a sustainable forest-management strategy aimed at maintaining or increasing forest carbon stocks, while producing an annual yield of timber, fiber or energy from the forest, will generate the largest sustained mitigation benefit (*Ibid.*, p. 549).

Notwithstanding the uncertainties about the magnitude of the mitigation benefits and costs of sustainable forestry, there are available technologies and the knowledge required to implement mitigation activities. These technologies are, among others, the following: improved forests-management systems, forest practices and processing technologies including bioenergy that can improve the economic and social viability of the different mitigation options. National and foreign governments could play a critical role in providing financial and technical support, promoting the participation of communities, institutions, and non-governmental organizations (NGOs).

With regard to new technologies related to forests, Fawzy *et al.* (2020) assessment begins with the fact that during tree growth CO_2 is captured from the atmosphere and stored in living biomass, dead organic matter, and soils. Forestation is thus a biogenic negative emissions technology that plays an important role in CC abatement efforts. Forestation can be deployed by either establishing new forests or afforestation and re-establishing previous forest areas that have undergone deforestation or degradation, which is referred to as reforestation.

Depending on tree species, once forests are established CO_2 uptake may span 20–100 years until trees reach maturity and then sequestration rates slow down significantly. At that stage, forest products can be harvested and utilized. Biogenic storage has a much shorter lifespan than storage in geological formations such as in the case of bioenergy carbon capture and storage.

Advantages and co-benefits of forestation technologies are associated with forest-based mitigation which include biodiversity, flood control as well as quality improvement for soil, water, and air. However, to achieve effective abatement results, forestation requires significant amounts of land and hence, competes with other land uses, specially so with agriculture land requirements. Another issue is related to the albedo effect.[12] Forests in high latitudes would actually be counterproductive, accelerating local warming as well as ice and snow cover loss. So, tropical areas would be the most suitable zones to host forestation projects (Fawzy *et al.*, 2020, pp. 12–13).

Biochar is a new technology that has recently gained recognition as a viable approach for carbon capture and permanent storage, capturing and storing CO_2 from the atmosphere. It is considered as one of the promising negative emissions technologies. Biochar is produced from biomass, e.g., dedicated crops, agricultural residues and forestry residues, through a thermochemical conversion process. It is produced through pyrolysis, a process of heating in the absence of oxygen, as well as through gasification and hydrothermal carbonization. The carbon captured by biomass through CO_2 uptake during plant growth is then processed into a char that can be applied to soils for extended periods. The conversion process stores biomass carbon in a form that is very stable and resistant to decomposition. Stability in soils is perhaps the most important property of biochar that makes it a solid carbon removal technology.

In terms of resource requirements, biochar production would require vast amounts of land to have an effective impact on greenhouse gas concentration levels. Land is required for feedstock cultivation, as well as for biochar dispersal acting as a carbon sink, and this may create competition issues with agriculture and other land-use sectors. However, marginal and degraded lands can potentially be utilized for dedicated plantations, relieving pressure on land for other uses (*Ibid.*, pp. 13–14).

Goldar and Dasgupta (2022) present an assessment of Carbon Capture Utilization and Storage (CCUS) technologies that are being developed in major G20 countries such as the United Kingdom. The authors evaluate the pros and cons of extending the application of

[12]Albedo is the ability of surfaces to reflect sunlight (heat from the sun). Light-colored surfaces return a large part of the sunrays back to the atmosphere (high albedo). Dark surfaces absorb the rays from the sun (low albedo).

CCUS in India, a middle-income country member of G20.[13] Key findings of the study are the following:

- "The use of captured carbon dioxide does not translate into reduced emissions. Prior to ascertaining the climate benefits from CO_2 use, a number of considerations need to be taken into account, i.e., duration of carbon retention in the product, source of carbon, quantity and form of energy used to convert CO_2, scale of project for carbon use, etc.
- Countries such as the United Kingdom and China are spearheading the agenda of Carbon Capture, Utilization and Storage (CCUS). Their experience provides key insights into policies and programs that can be adopted by India should it deem this emission mitigation pathway feasible. Some preliminary work is already under way with pilot projects being conducted by ONGC & IOL at the Koyali Refinery; Dalmia Cement setting up its carbon capture cement plant in Tamil Nadu; an industrial port in Tuticorin capturing CO_2 to produce baking soda and so on.
- There exist a number of technical and logistical barriers to CCUS adoption identified from literature, such as issues of land acquisition, in-depth assessment of storage sites to fulfill relevant criteria such as adequacy of capacity and injectivity rates, cap rock containment capacity to prevent CO_2 from escaping and so on. There is always a threat of CO_2 leakage and possible leakage points need to be scouted beforehand for necessary remediation plans to be prepared.
- There is a dearth of data pertaining to geological storage sites in India, which makes it difficult to undertake exhaustive feasibility assessments for CCUS projects.
- Cooperation between G20 countries on matters of CCUS-related research and development is already underway by means of

[13]The G20 or Group of Twenty was created in 1999. It is an intergovernmental forum comprising 19 countries and the European Union (EU). It works to address major issues related to the global economy, including CC mitigation, and sustainable development.

their engagement in international forums as well as bilateral partnerships. What is perhaps lacking at the moment is some kind of international benchmark for CCUS technologies.
- The Business 20 (B20) platform can help mobilize public acceptance of CCUS technologies and perhaps jointly address some of the apprehensions that fellow participants may have in terms of financing options, investment requirements, level of payoffs and so on.
- National policy options may be designed to provide incentives to the private sector in the form of tax concessions in exchange for investing in CCUS-related projects or being engaged in production processes employing these technologies. Clarity in terms of national laws and regulations pertaining to CCUS is a prerequisite for building investor confidence" (Goldar and Dasgupta, 2022, p. 1).

In regard to the extensive application of CCUS technologies and the high land requirements implied by this process the authors argue that this poses a problem to countries like India because of land scarcity; i.e., land acquisition for CCUS projects will prove to be a contentious matter (*Ibid.*, 2022, p. 11).

4.2.2 *Vulnerability in rural areas and adaptation to Climate Change*[14]

CC makes people and economic agents more vulnerable. The livelihood of many inhabitants is vulnerable to CC, to which human populations are adapting and will have to adapt. Adaptation is not new; throughout history humans living in rural areas have adapted their agricultural practices to respond to changing economic, social, and environmental conditions. The main difference is that today climate conditions are changing rapidly, and it is not clear how quickly farmers will be able to adapt to such changes (Jones *et al.*, 2012). The way in which human populations in general, and

[14]The vulnerability component of this section is mainly based on the literature review made by Lopez-Feldman *et al.* (2017).

farmers in particular will respond to CC is only beginning to be studied (Adams *et al.*, 1998; Lobell and Gourdji, 2012). Being able to properly measure and assess vulnerability and adaptation ability is a precondition for the design and implementation of policies aimed at improving adaptation capabilities and reducing vulnerability.

4.2.2.1 *Vulnerability*

The elements underlying vulnerability are complex and context-specific; vulnerability is a dynamic concept that varies with the social and biophysical processes that individuals and communities face over time (Eriksen and O'Brien, 2007). Hence, the temporal dimension and the outcomes that we are concerned about are key factors behind vulnerability assessments. These phenomena are illustrated by Füssel (2007) in regard to alternative answers to the question; Which of two regions is more vulnerable to CC and variability: Florida or Tibet? If our focus were human livelihoods the answer would probably be Tibet, but if we are concerned about infrastructure and economic impacts then we might answer Florida. If we are concerned about current risks, then Florida might be regarded as more vulnerable, but Tibet might be our answer if we were talking about the end of the 21st century.

As Birkmann (2006) points out, it is hard to find a precise definition of vulnerability and different people interpret it in different ways. Even scholars from the same disciplines or knowledge domains might conceptualize vulnerability in very different ways (Füssel, 2007). According to Birkmann there are more than 25 definitions, concepts, and methods to systematize vulnerability. Vulnerability assessments based on different views not only reflect disciplinary focus but they also have different implications in terms of the types of policy recommendations that will emerge (Kelly and Adger, 2000; O'Brien *et al.*, 2007).

In the next sections, we lay out some of the issues behind the different definitions of vulnerability. In doing so, we focus on approaches that define vulnerability in relation to an external stressor such as CC, but there are also definitions based on an undesirable outcome (e.g., famine).

The term vulnerability comes from the Latin *vulnerabilis*, which was used by the Romans to refer to a wounded soldier lying on the battlefield. This definition is the basis for the starting-point (or contextual) approach, which characterizes vulnerability by the current state of an individual or social group in terms of its inability to cope with a given external pressure rather than by what may or may not happen in the future. In this approach vulnerability is an *a priori* condition determined by socioeconomic factors as well as by political, institutional, and technological structures and processes. The starting-point approach is useful to identify policy recommendations that help reduce vulnerability to long-term CC and are also relevant to the solution of immediate needs of individuals and communities (Kelly and Adger, 2000; Füssel and Klein, 2006; O'Brien *et al.*, 2007).

The end-point approach, on the other hand, characterizes vulnerability as an outcome. The vulnerability of a group to CC is thus a matter of exposure, sensitivity, ability, and opportunity to adapt to change. This is a useful approach when trying to summarize the net effects of CC once adaptation has taken place (Kelly and Adger, 2000; Adger *et al.*, 2003). Originally this was the approach followed by the IPCC, which in its third assessment report defined vulnerability as: "The degree to which a system is susceptible to, or unable to cope with, adverse effects of climate change, including climate variability and extremes. Vulnerability is a function of the character, magnitude, and rate of climate variation to which a system is exposed, its sensitivity, and its adaptive capacity" (IPCC, 2001, p. 995).

Behind the definition of vulnerability, but more importantly behind the effects that CC could have on human populations, there are two clearly defined spheres: external exposure and internal coping (Birkmann, 2006). Definitions of vulnerability usually emphasize one over the other, and by doing so they make it seem as if the two are disconnected when in fact they are interlinked. Arguably as a result of this limitation the IPCC substituted "or" by "and" in the definition of vulnerability included in its fourth assessment: "*The degree to which a system is susceptible to, and unable to cope with ...*" (IPCC, 2007b).

An even more fundamental change in the definition of vulnerability was listed by the IPCC in its fifth assessment. The new definition of vulnerability, although less precise, makes an explicit reference to the concepts of contextual and outcome vulnerability mentioned before: "The propensity or predisposition to be adversely affected. Vulnerability encompasses a variety of concepts and elements including sensitivity or susceptibility to harm and lack of capacity to cope and adapt. See also Contextual vulnerability and Outcome vulnerability" (IPCC, 2014b, p. 1775).

If the purpose is to inquire on the effects that CC can have on rural households as well as on potential adaptation measures that can help to ameliorate such effects, the focus is on internal coping aspects and on contextual ones (or starting-point), we can follow the IPCC's definition of vulnerability as: "A present inability to cope with external pressures or changes, such as changing climate conditions. Contextual vulnerability is a characteristic of social and ecological systems generated by multiple factors and processes" (*Ibid.*, p. 1762).

Of particular relevance are the questions of who is most vulnerable, and why. The answers to these provide a starting point for the design and implementation of actions than can promote and facilitate adaptation. Reducing vulnerability, as seen from a starting-point approach should involve a multidimensional process that in the end leads to a situation in which individuals and groups are better equipped to respond to changing climatic conditions (O'Brien *et al.*, 2007).

In general, studies that attempt to measure vulnerability at national and regional levels propose a conceptual framework with a series of indicators to capture sensitivity, exposure, and adaptation capacity. For example, Brooks *et al.* (2005) estimate vulnerability to CC using several indicators grouped in the following categories: economic variables, health and nutrition status, education, infrastructure, governance, reliance on agriculture, ecosystem variables, and technology availability. The authors estimate an index to classify countries according to their level of vulnerability.

Lobell *et al.* (2008) perform a global analysis of adaptation needs in the agricultural sector in order to secure food production. They classify several regions of the world according to nutritional patterns and identify the most vulnerable crops, concluding that South Asia and Southern Africa would be most affected if the production of such crops decreased. The vulnerability ranking of Brooks *et al.* (2005) is consistent with the results of Lobell *et al.* (2008) since many of the most vulnerable countries found by the former are in the food-insecure regions.

In an effort to homogenize vulnerability measurements in communities subject to very different circumstances, the German Agency for International Development (GIZ) developed a guide to perform vulnerability assessments based on pilot applications in Bolivia, Pakistan, Burundi, and Mozambique (Fritzsche *et al.*, 2014). The GIZ guide can be a useful tool for the monitoring and evaluation of adaptation.

Studies to assess vulnerability to CC in agriculture include that of Borja-Vega and De la Fuente (2013) for Mexico. They consider possible changes in vulnerability up to 2045. The municipality index that they propose uses a statistical methodology called Principal Components Analysis based on indicators of vulnerability in the agricultural sector. These indicators include: exposure (average temperatures, average precipitation, past and future climate scenarios), sensitivity (food poverty, percentage of maize production under irrigation areas, and percent of population in agricultural activities), and adaptive capacity (farmers that belong to organizations, remittances received, distance from roads, and federal disaster assistance per capita).[15] The analysis shows that municipalities with higher poverty levels are subject to higher agricultural vulnerability. The authors find that there is high variance in exposure between regions in Mexico, with the tropical south — the poorest region of Mexico — more exposed to flood risks and the arid north to drought risks. Large-scale producers

[15]Maize or corn is the major cereal produced and consumed all over Mexico. It is cultivated under very different agroecological, economic, and technological conditions by commercial farmers and rural households (Box 2.2. Mexico is a center of origin of wild maize and domestication. Subsistence rural farmers have maintained the genetic diversity in the cultivation of maize (Dyer *et al.*, 2014).

are representative of municipalities with low levels of vulnerability, while subsistence farmers prevail in municipalities with higher levels of vulnerability. The authors explain that although the north of Mexico is not currently highly vulnerable to CC, it might become so in the coming decades. This study is similar to those of Monterroso *et al.* (2014); both show how vulnerability varies widely over space.

4.2.2.2 *Adaptation*

Adaptation to CC is the process of adjustment to actual or expected climate and its effects (IPCC, 2014a). There are different types of adaptation and different ways in which it can be classified. When the measures are reactive, we have *ex-post* adaptation, while adaptation that takes place before the impacts of CC are observed is known as *ex-ante* or anticipatory adaptation.

Adaptation measures might be beneficial only for the individual undertaking them (private adaptation), but they might also benefit a group of individuals beyond those directly involved in the decision-making process (public adaptation). According to their origin, adaptation can be autonomous or planned. Autonomous adaptation refers to voluntary actions or measures that individuals or agent (e.g., agricultural cooperatives) undertake in response to a climatic stimulus. Planned adaptation is a deliberate policy decision aimed at complementing, facilitating or improving agents' responses to CC (Tubiello and Rosenzweig, 2008).

When the depth or degree of measures are considered, adaptation can be classified as incremental or transformational. Incremental adaptation refers to actions whose main objective is to maintain the essence and integrity of a system or process at any given scale. Transformational adaptation aims to change the fundamental characteristics of a system (IPCC, 2014a).

A considerable number of adaptation measures for the agricultural sector have been suggested. These go from modifying planting and harvest times to the construction of major infrastructure works, ranging through migration and the implementation of new production practices. Even though at this time there is not much empirical evidence in relation to the efficiency and success of the different planed adaptation measures, there are some strategies that are recommended. Some of these include increasing farmers' level of knowledge as regards CC; improving the education levels and abilities of the rural populations; creating and introducing temperature resistant varieties; promoting irrigation; generating early alert systems in relation to rain temporality and severity; strengthening formal and informal seed exchange systems; improving physical infrastructure and, solving issues concerning the lack of access to credit and agriculture insurance. Asafu-Adjaye (2014), Di Falco *et al.* (2012), and Kabubo-Mariara and Karanja (2007) present a detailed matrix with adaptation options for the agricultural sector.

In relation to irrigation, it is important to consider the fact that one of the expected effects of CC is the modification of precipitation patterns. In this regard, it is essential that water availability projections be made before promoting major irrigation infrastructure works in a particular region. On the other hand, projects involving more efficient irrigation technologies as opposed to those aimed at saving water might give rise to a bouncing effect, and result in an increase in water use (Ward and Pulido-Velázquez, 2008).

A major drawback to agriculture and its contribution to food security is desertification. Some adaptation options to tackle desertification can become maladaptive due to their environmental impacts, such as irrigation causing soil salinization or over extraction leading also to soil salinization as well as ground-water depletion. Hence, adaptation strategies for agriculture have to include those aimed at combating desertification through water harvesting, micro-irrigation, and restoring degraded lands using drought-resilient and ecologically appropriate plants; agroforestry and other agroecological and ecosystem-based adaptation practices. However, extreme forms of desertification can lead to the complete loss of land productivity and limit adaptation options.

Livestock farming is estimated to be the world's largest land use sector and utilizes around 60% of the global biomass harvest. Over the coming decades, CC will affect the natural resource base of livestock production, especially the productivity of rangeland and feed crops. A cost-effective adaptation option for agricultural production is shifting livestock production toward mixed crop-livestock systems. According to Weindl *et al.* (2015) model estimations, this adaptative strategy would reduce agricultural adaptation costs to 0.3% of total production costs and simultaneously abate deforestation by about 76 million ha globally. These authors add that incomplete transitions in mixed crop-livestock production systems already have a strong adaptive and cost-reducing effect: a 50% shift to mixed systems lowers agricultural adaptation costs to 0.8%. General responses of production costs to system transitions are robust across different global climate and crop models as well as regarding assumptions on CO_2 fertilization, but simulated values show a large variation. In the face of these uncertainties, public policy support for transforming livestock production systems provides an important lever to improve agricultural resource management and lower adaptation costs, possibly even contributing to emission reduction.

Literature with detailed research on adaptation options and strategies for agriculture is scarce. However, there is a review paper on adaptation and mitigation covering agriculture of two large world's regions that are major producers of cereals (maize, rice, and wheat), fruits and vegetables: South Asia and Latin America (Jat *et al.*, 2016). This chapter intends to summarize the available information and results of agronomic models for adaptation strategies and mitigation options for CC to achieve food security in South Asia and Latin America.

Jat *et al.*'s study argues that: "Increase in atmospheric CO_2 promotes growth and productivity of plants with C_3 photosynthetic pathway but the increase in temperature, on the other hand, can reduce crop duration, increase crop respiration rates, affect the survival and distribution of pest populations, and may hasten nutrient mineralization in soils, decrease fertilizer-use efficiency, and increase evapotranspiration. The water resources which are already scarce may come under enhanced stress. Thus, the impact of climate change is likely to have a significant influence on agriculture and eventually on the food security and livelihoods of large sections of the urban and rural populations globally" (*Ibid.*, p. 2).

Like other developing countries, South Asia and Latin America have diverse agroclimatic regions and diverse agricultural production systems and are more vulnerable to the effects of CC due to heavy dependence on agriculture for their livelihood.[16]

Findings in the literature show that to secure durable food and nutritional security at the regional and country level in South Asia and Latin America adaptation and mitigation strategies must be promoted. In particular: Upscaling of modern technologies such as conservation and climate smart agriculture; judicious utilization of available water for agriculture through micro irrigation and water-saving technologies; developing multiple stress-tolerant crop cultivars and biotypes through biotechnological tools; restoration of degraded soils and waters, promoting carbon sequestration through alternate production technologies and land use as agroforestry; and conservation of biodiversity. In addition, improvement of risk management is required through reliable early warning systems of environmental changes, their spatial and temporal magnitude, coupled with the dissemination of this information to help farmers and agriculture-dependent industries interpret these forecasts in terms of their agronomic and economic implications.

It is of the utmost importance that the studied regions adopt these and other measures to address the effects of CC, including capacity-building through international collaboration in order to develop databases and analysis systems aimed at efficient weather forecasting and the preparation of contingency plans for vulnerable areas (*Ibid.*, pp. 2–4).[17]

The findings on adaptation requirements for the agricultural sectors of South Asia and Latin America reported by Jat *et al.* (2016) can be generalized to other southern countries of the world.

[16]See Dinar *et al.* (2008) for a study on adaptation in America.

[17]Details in Section 6, pp. 32–68. In Section 8, pp. 73–77, the authors summarize the impacts of CC on crop production in the studied regions based on simulation models (Chapter 5).

4.3 Rural Households and Sustainable Development[18]

Considerations of the special peculiarities and economic functioning of rural households — mostly located in regions of low and middle-income countries — are insufficient in the so far reviewed literature of this chapter. Rural households persist as socioeconomic agents in many regions of the world and the livelihoods of many of them depend on natural resources. Although globally a considerable proportion of rural households are formed by indigenous populations, this is not the case for all of them.

Rural households that possess and/or have rights or access to natural resources — such as land dedicated to agricultural production and forests — take economic decisions that differ from commercial farmers. This difference has to be considered in any attempt to inquire about CC, natural capital and agricultural sustainability, as well rural development policies.

Basically, rural households use family labor in their production activities and, in regards their production of food, this takes place in small and/or very small plots, hence the need to take production and consumption decisions for the subsistence of their families simultaneously. The literature in economic development that follows this approach proposes that this behavior is not an irrational behavior, but a consequence of high market-participation transaction costs, especially in low and medium-income countries. Another aspect of rural households is the diversification of their production activities and income sources. Based on the case of Mexico, Table 4.1 illustrates these trends (see also Box 2.2 and Singh *et al.*, 1986, Sadoulet and de Janvry, 1995, Taylor and Adelman, 2003, 2006; Taylor and Filipski, 2014).

Table 4.1 shows the extent of diversification of Mexico's households living in communities and/or towns of less than 2,500 inhabitants and particularly, the fact that income from forestry activities is

[18]Details of the content of this Section 4.3 are in the study of Lopez-Feldman *et al.* (2017).

Table 4.1. Mexico: Distribution of Rural Households' Income by Source

Income source	**Weight (%)**
Leasing agricultural plots	1.1
Field crops	5.4
Livestock and products	7.3
Other goods and services	10.2
Forestry	4.8
Government transfers	12.2
Intra households transfers	1.7
Remittances from U.S.A.	3.5
Domestic remittances	2.7
Wage income from the rural sector	19.8
Wage income from rest of Mexico	31.4
Total	**100.0**

Source: National Survey of Rural Households, 2013 (the survey is representative of households in Mexico living in communities between 500 and 2,500 inhabitants). http://www.coneval.org.mx/Evaluacion/ECNCH/Paginas/IEPDS_20141217-3509.aspx

almost as high as that from crop and livestock production. Another important aspect revealed in the table is the significant number of international remittances that Mexican rural households receive from family members working in the U.S.A., as they reflect the existence of Mexico–U.S.A. networks which have proved to be a significant factor that facilitates emigration. Specifically, international networks could ease rural emigration from low and medium-income countries suffering CC shocks (see end of this section). In general, Table 4.1 also shows the degree of income diversification that rural households can have in countries like Mexico (see Taylor and Filipski, 2014).[19]

The economic decision-making of rural households is complex and has been modeled considering market failures. These models show

[19]As we discuss in Chapter 5 and shown in Box 2.2, the specificities of rural households' economy require an applied micro-economy-wide modeling approach to measure the effects of CC in areas where rural households prevail.

that when transaction costs are present, market-based policies may not deliver the expected results that conventional microeconomic theory predicts; e.g., a reduction of the domestic price of a staple arising from agricultural trade liberalization may not reduce household production of the crop when it is destined to family consumption (see Yúnez-Naude and Taylor, 2006; details of household models in Chapter 5). So, some market-based policies for sustainable rural development may not work for these economic agents.

Considering the limitations rural households have to cope with CC, the focus shifts to the potential adaptation measures that can help to ameliorate such effects, and hence, follow the starting-point approach (see Section 4.1.2). Reducing vulnerability, as seen from a starting-point approach, should involve a multidimensional process that in the end leads to a situation where individuals, rural households and/or their communities are better equipped to respond to changing climatic conditions (O'Brien *et al.*, 2007, see also Adger *et al.*, 2003).

There are big challenges to promote adaptation in the rural sector and households. Two stand out: (1) to enhance adaptative capacity in a context of competing development objectives such as poverty reduction (Adger *et al.*, 2003), and (2) the effective use of market-based instruments in a context of deep market failures.

Sound adaptation measures for rural households in low and middle-income countries and their diverse regions and cultures require knowledge of the determinants of adaptation as well as the adaptation needs at a disaggregated level (e.g., for a given community); i.e., to identify what needs to be done and in which way in order to reduce the vulnerability for a given community or groups of rural households (Smith and Wandel, 2006).

Relatively abundant literature that inquires on the potential impacts of CC along with assessments of potential adaptations is available. However, there are few studies that go beyond the availability of some adaptations or look at the capacity and willingness of individuals to actually implement these options. Thus, much adaptation by farmers and other agents will be autonomous and facilitated by their own social capital and resources, whereas preventive and planned adaptation may be required to sustain rural households and agricultural production (Füssel and Klein, 2006; Adger *et al.*, 2003).

As to rural migration and CC, over the past decade, the extent of the impacts of CC on humans' migration has been increasingly addressed in the scholarly literature. Basically, research shows that while human mobility due to environmental changes is not new, anthropogenic CC combined with extreme weather events are exacerbating migration, which is also affected by mismanagement and poor allocation of natural and economic resources (Hunter and Simon, 2022; Hunter *et al.*, 2015). Thus, one of the main impacts of CC could affect human migration, with millions of people being displaced by extreme weather events, shoreline erosion, coastal flooding and disruption of agricultural and rural activities (a more detailed discussion of this literature and of migration models can be found in Chapter 5).

It is evident that vulnerability — hence, adaptation options and strategies — differ across regions as well as across rural households inside the same area. However, more research is still needed to better understand the determinants of vulnerability. An aspect that has not been sufficiently studied is the link between adaptation capacity and vulnerability, specially at the community and type of rural household levels. As we will discuss in Chapter 5, micro-economy-wide rural household models that explicitly include adaptation are one path to fill that void. Equally important is the need to better understand the determinants of adaptation to CC at the household and individual level. This requires the use of household (individual) level datasets that provide detailed information not only on the livelihood strategies that households (individuals) follow but also on how they respond or could respond to weather-related events. Data on how individuals perceive weather-related information as well as CC information is also key to better understand household adaptation strategies (Lopez-Feldman *et al.*, 2017).

4.4 Adaptation and Mitigation Strategies and Policies

As it was pointed out before, there may be trade-offs between development policies and adaptation and mitigation strategies, as well as between these two later types of actions. There can also be synergies among these three purposes.

Major trade-offs are related to competition for land and water between food production and other land and water uses. Some of these trade-offs are related to strategies for CC mitigation involving forests. In addition to land use competition between forests, agriculture and other land uses there is yet another within the forest sector. It refers to trade-offs between forest conservation for carbon storage and other environmental services such as biodiversity and watershed conservation with respect to forest harvesting to provide society with carbon containing fiber, timber and bio-energy resources, and trade-offs among utilization strategies of harvested wood products to storage in long-lived products, recycling, and use for bioenergy.

An example of trade-offs between food security purposes and freshwater use is an electricity subsidy for pumping underground water for irrigation aimed at promoting food staples production and/or exports of fresh fruits and vegetables. This policy would promote an inefficient use of water and its salinization, especially so in arid areas, leading to desertification and biodiversity losses. Under these conditions and without water pricing policies, farmers would adapt by pumping more water (Yúnez-Naude and Hernandez-Solano, 2018). In addition, pumping more underground water will result in the increase of electricity consumption and hence, GHG emissions.

The electricity pumping water is an example that illustrates the separation between development and climate policies. So, among others, decisions about macroeconomic policy, agricultural and forestry policies, as well as multilateral development bank lending, insurance practices and electricity policies must take into consideration trade-offs between development, adaptation, and mitigation strategies.

Intended or unintended synergies between development, mitigation, and adaptation policies can exist. With regard to rural areas, we stress the following general synergies:

- Some rural development policies undertaken to fight poverty, such as water management and agro-forestry, are synergistic with mitigation. For example, agro-forestry aimed to produce fuel wood or to buffer farm incomes against climate variation may also increase carbon sequestration in many regions.
- Agricultural mitigation options are influenced most by non-climate policies, including macro-economic, agricultural, and environmental policies. Such policies may be based on UN conventions and/or agendas; e.g., Biodiversity (Box 2.1) Desertification and the Agenda for Sustainable Development, based on SDGs (Box 2.5), but are often driven by national or regional issues. Among the most beneficial non-climate policies are those that promote sustainable use of soils, water, and other resources in agriculture since this helps increase soil carbon stocks and minimize resource (energy, fertilizer) waste.
- Mitigation policies that encourage efficient use of fertilizers, maintain or increase soil carbon and sustain agricultural production are likely to have the greatest synergy with sustainable development. For example, increasing soil carbon can also improve food security and economic returns.

There is a growing understanding of the possibilities to choose and implement mitigation options in several sectors to realize synergies and avoid conflicts with other dimensions of sustainable development. However, studying and acknowledging trade-offs and synergies in the design of land and food policies is still a pressing matter. Acknowledging co-benefits and trade-offs when designing land and food policies can overcome barriers to implementation. Strengthened multilevel, hybrid, and cross-sectoral governance, as well as policies developed and adopted in an iterative, coherent, adaptive, and flexible manner can maximize co-benefits and minimize trade-offs, given that land management decisions are made from farm level to national scales, and both climate and land policies often range across multiple sectors, departments, and agencies (IPCC, 2019, p. 33).

Overall, making development more sustainable by changing development paths can make a major contribution to climate change adaptation and mitigation, but implementation requires resources to overcome multiple barriers, to consider explicitly the context and behavior of rural households as well as political will at the international, regional, national, and community levels (see following chapters).

Before concluding this section, it is worth adding that some adaptation measures to CC differ from mitigation actions. An important difference is that the former can have more immediate benefits. For example, autonomous CC adaptation actions can reduce risks associated to current climate variability and can be implemented on a local or regional scale without the need for international cooperation.

References

Adams, R. M., Hurd, B. H., Lenhart, S., and Leary, N. (1998). Effects of global climate change on agriculture: An interpretative review. *Climate Research, 11*(1), 19–30. https://www.jstor.org/stable/24865973.

Adger, W. N., Huq, S., Brown, K., Conway, D., and Hulme, M. (2003). Adaptation to climate change in the developing world. *Progress in Development Studies, 3*(3), 179–195. https://doi.org/10.1191/1464993403ps060oa.

Asafu-Adjaye, J. (2014). The economic impacts of climate change on agriculture in Africa. *Journal of African Economies, 23*(suppl 2), ii17–ii49. https://doi.org/10.1093/jae/eju011.

Birkmann, J. (2006). Measuring vulnerability to promote disaster-resilient societies: Conceptual frameworks and definitions. In J. Birkmann (ed.), *Measuring Vulnerability to Natural Hazards: Towards Disaster Resilient Societies* (pp. 9–54). United Nations University Press, Tokyo, Japan.

Borja-Vega, C. and De la Fuente, A. (2013). Municipal vulnerability to climate change and climate related events in Mexico. *World Bank Policy Research Working Paper*, (6417). Washington, D.C, USA. https://papers.ssrn.com/sol3/papers.cfm?abstract_id=2255260.

Brooks, N., Adger, W. N., and Kelly, P. M. (2005). The determinants of vulnerability and adaptive capacity at the national level and the implications for adaptation. *Global Environmental Change, 15*(2), 151–163. https://doi.org/10.1016/j.gloenvcha.2004.12.006.

Dell, M., Jones, B. F., and Olken, B. A. (2012). Temperature shocks and economic growth: Evidence from the last half century. *American Economic Journal: Macroeconomics*, *4*(3), 66–95. https://scholar.harvard.edu/files/dell/files/aej_temperature.pdf.

Di Falco, S., Yesuf, M., Kohlin, G., and Ringler, C. (2012). Estimating the impact of climate change on agriculture in low-income countries: Household level evidence from the Nile Basin, Ethiopia. *Environmental and Resource Economics*, *52*, 457–478. https://doi.org/10.1007/s10640-011-9538-y.

Dinar A., Hassan, R., Mendelsohn, R., Benhin, J., and Al, E. (2008). *Climate Change and Agriculture in Africa. Impact Assessment and Adaptation Strategies.* Routledge. https://doi.org/10.4324/9781849770767.

Dyer, G. A., López-Feldman, A., Yúnez-Naude, A., and Taylor, J. E. (2014). Genetic erosion in maize's center of origin. *Proceedings of the National Academy of Sciences of the United States of America* (PNAS), *111*(39), 14094–14099. https://www.pnas.org/doi/abs/10.1073/pnas.1407033111.

Eriksen, S. H. and O'Brien, K. (2007). Vulnerability, poverty and the need for sustainable adaptation measures. *Climate Policy*, *7*(4), 337–352. https://www.tandfonline.com/doi/abs/10.1080/14693062.2007.9685660.

Fawzy, S., Osman, A. I., Doran, J., and Rooney, D. (2020). Strategies for mitigation of climate change: A review. *Environmental Chemistry Letters*, *18*, 2069–2094. https://doi.org/10.1007/s10311-020-01059-w.

Fischer, G., Shah, M., Tubiello, F. N., and Van Velhuizen, H. (2005). Socio-economic and climate change impacts on agriculture: An integrated assessment, 1990–2080. *Philosophical Transactions of The Royal Society B: Biological Sciences*, *360*(1463), 2067–2083. https://doi.org/10.1098/rstb.2005.1744.

Food, Agriculture, Biodiversity, Land-Use and Energy (FABLE). (2020). *Pathways to Sustainable Land-Use and Food Systems. 2020 Report of the FABLE Consortium.* International Institute for Applied Systems Analysis (IIASA) and Sustainable Development Solutions Network (SDSN). https://doi.org/10.22022/ESM/12-2020.16896.

Frank, S., Havlik, P., Soussana, J. F., Levesque, A., Valin, H., Wollenberg, E., Kleinwechter, U., Fricko, O., Gusti, M., Herrero, M., Smith, P., Hasegawa, T., Kraxner, F., and Obersteiner, M. (2017). Reducing greenhouse gas emissions in agriculture without compromising food security? *Environmental Research Letters*, *12*(10), 105004. https://iopscience.iop.org/article/10.1088/1748-9326/aa8c83/pdf.

Fritzsche, K., Schneiderbauer, S., Bubeck, P., Kienberger, S., Buth, M., Zebisch, M., and Kahlenborn, W. (2014). *The Vulnerability Sourcebook Annex.* Deutsche Gesellschaft für Internationale Zusammenarbeit (GIZ) GmbH.

Fuss, S., Lamb. W. F., Callaghan, M. W., HilaIre, J., Creutzing, F., Amann, T., Beringer, T., De Oliveira García, W., Hasrtmann, J., and Khanna, T. (2018). Negative emissions — Part 2: Costs, potentials and side effects. *Environmental Research Letters*, *13*(6), 063002. https://iopscience.iop.org/article/10.1088/1748-9326/aabf9f/meta.

Füssel, H. M. (2007). Vulnerability: A generally applicable conceptual framework for climate change research. *Global Environmental Change*, *17*(2), 155–167.

Füssel, H. M., and Klein, R. J. (2006). Climate change vulnerability assessments: An evolution of conceptual thinking. *Climatic Change*, *75*(3), 301–329. https://doi.org/10.1007/s10584-006-0329-3.

Goldar, A. and Dasgupta, D. (2022). *Exploring Carbon Capture, Utilization and Storage in the Indian Context: ICRIER G20 Policy Series — Run Up to 2023. Indian Council for Research on International Economic Relations (ICRIER)*. http://icrier.org/pdf/Policy_Brief_11.pdf.

Hernández Solano, A. and Yúnez Naude, A. (2016). *Impactos Del Cambio Climático En La Economía Rural De México: Un Enfoque De Equilibrio General*. El Colegio de México, Centro de Estudios Económicos. https://ideas.repec.org/p/emx/ceedoc/2016-06.html.

IPCC. (2001). *Climate Change 2001: Impacts, Adaptation and Vulnerability. Contribution of Working Group II to the Third Assessment Report of the Intergovernmental Panel on Climate Change*. In J. J. McCarthy, O. F. Canziani, N. A. Leary, D. J. Dokken, and K. S. White (eds.). Cambridge University Press, Cambridge. https://www.ipcc.ch/site/assets/uploads/2018/03/WGII_TAR_full_report-2.pdf.

IPCC. (2007a). *Climate Change 2007: Mitigation of Climate Change. Contribution of Working Group III to the Fourth Assessment Report of the Intergovernmental Panel on Climate Change*. In B. Metz, O. R. Davidson, P. R. Bosch, R. Dave, L. A. Meyer (eds.). Cambridge University Press, Cambridge, United Kingdom. https://www.ipcc.ch/site/assets/uploads/2018/03/ar4_wg3_full_report-1.pdf.

IPCC. (2007b). *Climate Change 2007: Impacts, Adaptation and Vulnerability. Contribution of Working Group II to the Fourth Assessment Report of the Intergovernmental Panel on Climate Change*. In Parry, M. L., O. F. Canziani, J. P. Palutikof, P. J. van der Linden, and C. E. Hanson (eds.). Cambridge University Press, Cambridge, United Kingdom. https://www.ipcc.ch/site/assets/uploads/2018/03/ar4_wg2_full_report.pdf.

IPCC. (2014a). *Climate Change 2014: Synthesis Report. Contribution of Working Groups I, II and III to the Fifth Assessment Report of the Intergovernmental Panel on Climate Change*. Core Writing Team, R. K. Pachauri and L. A. Meyer (eds.). IPCC Geneva, Switzerland. https://www.ipcc.ch/site/assets/uploads/2018/05/SYR_AR5_FINAL_full_wcover.pdf.

IPCC. (2014b). *Climate Change 2014: Impacts, Adaptation, and Vulnerability. Part B: Regional Aspects. Contribution of Working Group II to the Fifth Assessment Report of the Intergovernmental Panel on Climate Change*. In V. R. Barros, C. B. Field, D. J. Dokken, M. D. Mastrandrea, K. J. Mach, T. E. Bilir, M. Chatterjee, K. L. Ebi, Y. O. Estrada, R. C. Genova, B. Girma, E. S. Kissel, A. N. Levy, S. MacCracken, P. R. Mastrandrea, and L. L. White (eds.). Cambridge University Press, New York, NY, USA. https://www.ipcc.ch/site/assets/uploads/2018/02/WGIIAR5-PartB_FINAL.pdf.

IPCC. (2018). Summary for Policymakers. In: *Global Warming of 1.5° C. An IPCC Special Report on the impacts of global warming of 1.5° C above pre-industrial levels and related global greenhouse gas emission pathways, in the context of strengthening the global response to the threat of climate change, sustainable development, and efforts to eradicate poverty.* In Press.

IPCC. (2019). Summary for policymakers. In P. R. Shukla, J. Skea, E. Calvo Buendia, V. Masson-Delmotte, H.-O. Pörtner, D. C. Roberts, P. Zhai, R. Slade, S. Connors, R. van Diemen, M. Ferrat, E. Haughey, S. Luz, S. Neogi, M. Pathak, J. Petzold, J. Portugal Pereira, P. Vyas, E. Huntley, K. Kissick, M. Belkacemi, and J. Malley (eds.), *Climate Change and Land.* An IPCC Special Report on climate change, desertification, land degradation, sustainable land management, food security, and greenhouse gas fluxes in terrestrial ecosystems. Unpublished Draft. https://www.ipcc.ch/srccl/.

IPCC. (2021). Summary for policymakers. In V. Masson-Delmotte, P. Zhai, A. Pirani, S. L. Connors, C. Péan, S. Berger, N. Caud, Y. Chen, L. Goldfarb, M. I. Gomis, M. Huang, K. Leitzell, E. Lonnoy, J. B. R. Matthews, T. K. Maycock, T. Waterfield, O. Yelekçi, R. Yu, and B. Zhou (eds.), *Climate Change 2021: The Physical Science Basis.* Working Group I Contribution to the Sixth Assessment Report of the Intergovernmental Panel on Climate Change. IPCC Geneva, Switzerland. https://www.ipcc.ch/report/ar6/wg1/downloads/report/IPCC_AR6_WGI_SPM_final.pdf.

Jat, M. L., Dagar, J. C., Sapkota, J. T. B., Yavinder-Singh, Govaerts, B., Ridaura, S. L., Saharawat, Y. S., Sharma, R. K., Tetarwal, J. P., Jat, R. K., Hobbs, H., and Stirling, C. (2016). Climate change and agriculture: Adaptation strategies and mitigation opportunities for food security in south Asia and Latin America. *Advances in Agronomy, 137*, 127–235. https://doi.org/10.1016/bs.agron.2015.12.005.

Jones, H. P., Hole, D. G., and Zavaleta, E. S. (2012). Harnessing nature to help people adapt to climate change. *Nature Climate Change, 2*(7), 504–509. https://doi.org/10.1038/nclimate1463.

Kabubo-Mariara, J. and Karanja, F. K. (2007). The economic impact of climate change on Kenyan Crop Agriculture: A Ricardian approach. *Global and Planetary Change, 57*(3), 319–330. https://doi.org/10.1016/j.gloplacha.2007.01.002

Kelly, P. M. and Adger, W. N. (2000). Theory and practice in assessing vulnerability to climate change and facilitating adaptation. *Climatic Change, 47*(4), 325–352. https://doi.org/10.1023/A:1005627828199.

Larson, D. E., Dinar, A., and Frisbie, J. A. (2011). Agriculture and the clean development mechanis. *Policy Research Working Paper Series 5621.* The World Bank. http://www-wds.worldbank.org/external/default/WDSContentServer/WDSP/IB/2011/04/04/000158349_20110404091922/Rendered/PDF/WPS5621.pdf.

Lobell, D. B., Burke, M. B., Tebaldi, C., Mastrandrea, M. D., Di Falcon, W. P., and Naylor, R. L. (2008). Prioritizing climate change adaptation needs for food security in 2030. *Science, 319*(5863), 607–610. https://www.science.org/doi/10.1126/science.1152339

Lobell, D. B. and Gourdji, S. M. (2012). The influence of climate change on global crop productivity. *Plant Physiology, 160*(4), 1686–1697. https://doi.org/10.1104/pp.112.208298.

Lopez-Feldman A., Yúnez-Naude, A., Hernández-Solano, A., Taylor, J. E., and Hernández, D. (2017). Mexican rural households' vulnerability and adaptation to climate change. *White Paper for the Environmental Working Group of the UC-Mexico Initiative.* https://escholarship.org/uc/item/11p2k4v0.

Mendelsohn, R. (2009). The impact of climate change on agriculture in developing countries. *Journal of Natural Resources Policy Research, 1*(1), 5–19. https://doi.org/10.1080/19390450802495882.

Monterroso, A., Conde, C., Gay, C., Gómez, D., and López, J. (2014). Two methods to assess vulnerability to climate change in the Mexican agricultural sector. *Mitigation and Adaptation Strategies for Global Change, 19*(4), 445–461. https://doi.org/10.1007/s11027-012-9442-y.

O'Brien, K., Eriksen, S., Nygaard, L. P., and Schjolden, A. (2007). Why different interpretations of vulnerability matter in climate change discourses. *Climate Policy, 7*(1), 73–88. https://www.tandfonline.com/doi/abs/10.1080/14693062.2007.9685639.

Rhaman, S. A., Dinar, A., and Larson, D. (2016). The incidence and extent of the CDM across developing countries. *Environment and Development Economics, 21*(4), 415–438. https://doi.org/10.1017/S1355770X15000388.

Shukla, P. R., J. Skea, R. Slade, R. van Diemen, E. Haughey, J. Malley, M. Pathak, J. Portugal Pereira (eds.) Technical Summary, 2019. In: *Climate Change and Land: an IPCC special report on climate change, esertification, land degradation, sustainable land management, food security, and greenhouse gas fluxes in terrestrial ecosystems.* In press.

Sadoulet, E. and De Janvry, A. (1995). *Quantitative Development Policy Analysis.* Johns Hopkins University Press, Baltimore, USA.

Singh, I., Squire, L., and Strauss, J. (eds). (1986). An overview of agricultural household models. The basic model: Theory, empirical results, and policy conclusions. In *Agricultural Household Models: Extensions, Applications, and Policy* (pp. 17–47). Johns Hopkins University, Baltimore, USA.

Strauss, J. (1986). Appendix. The theory and comparative statics of agricultural household models: A general approach. In I. Singh, L. Squire, and J. Strauss (eds.), *Agricultural Household Models: Extensions, Applications, and Policy* (pp. 71–91). Johns Hopkins University, Baltimore, USA.

Smith, B. and Wandel, J. (2006). Adaptation, adaptive capacity and vulnerability. *Global Environmental Change, 16*(3), 282–292. https://doi.org/10.1016/j.gloenvcha.2006.03.008.

Taylor, J. E. and Adelman, I. (2003). Agricultural household models: Genesis, evolution and extensions. *Review of Economics of the Household, 1*(1), 33–58. https://doi.org/10.1023/a:1021847430758.

Taylor, J. E. and Adelman, I. (2006). *Village Economies. The Design, Estimation and Use of Villagewide Economic Models.* Cambridge: Cambridge University Press. https://doi.org/10.1017/CBO9781139174572.

Taylor, J. E. and Filipski, M. (2014). *Beyond Experiments in Development Economics: Local Economy-Wide Impact Evaluation*. Oxford University Press. https://doi.org/10.1093/acprof:oso/9780198707875.001.0001.

Tubiello, F. N. and Rosenzweig, C. (2008). Developing climate change impact metrics for agriculture. *The Integrated Assessment*, *8*(1), 165–184.

Ward, F. A. and Pulido-Velazquez, M. (2008). Water conservation in irrigation can increase water use. *Proceedings of the National Academy of Sciences*, *105*(47), 18215–18220. https://doi.org/10.1073/pnas.0805554105.

Weindl, I., Lotze-Campen, H., Popp, A., Müller, C., Petr Havlík, P., Herrero, M., Schmitz, C., and Rolinski, S. (2015). Livestock in a changing climate: Production system transitions as an adaptation strategy for agriculture. *Environmental Research Letters*, *10*(9), 094021. https://iopscience.iop.org/article/10.1088/1748-9326/10/9/094021/pdf.

Yúnez-Naude, A. and Taylor, J. E. (2006). The effects of NAFTA and domestic reforms in the agriculture of Mexico: Predictions and facts. *Region et Development*, *23*, 161–186.

Yúnez-Naude, A. and Hernandez-Solano, A. (2018). The Mexican agricultural sector two decades after NAFTA: Expectations, facts and policy challenges. In A. M. Buainain, M. Rocha de Souza, and Z. Navarro (eds.), *Globalization and Agriculture: Redefining Unequal Development* (pp. 71–92). Lexington Books, Lanham Maryland, USA.

Chapter 5

Economic Development Models for Agriculture, Rural Areas, and Climate Change

In this chapter, we describe the main characteristics of models designed to study economic development, highlighting the effects of climate change (CC) on migration, agriculture, and rural economies. This requires a technical approach, which we have attempted to simplify. We also include a historical account of the evolution of the models presented in this chapter. The models summarized cover migration, the Ricardian-inspired models that explore the impacts of CC on agricultural production, the economy-wide models for impact analyzes and the eco-physical models. Because the range of models presented in this chapter is considerable, we have provided an extensive list of references for readers interested in learning more about all of these.

5.1 Labor Migration Models

In this Section, we review the most representative labor migration models. This summary is by no means exhaustive, but it serves to situate our study in the context of agricultural transformations in both developed and developing countries. There is no single migration model that can broadly explain the economic, social, and environmental factors of international and internal migration. Instead, there is a range of theories, frequently segmented by disciplinary areas, which leads to a better understanding of how

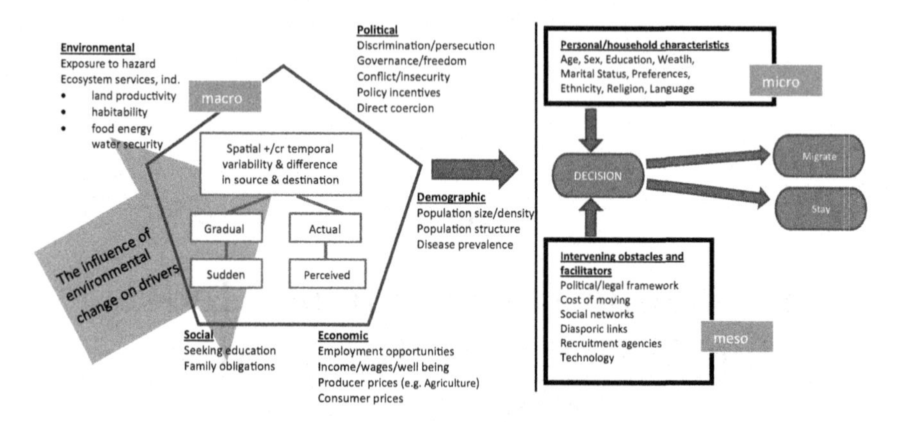

Figure 5.1. Conceptual Framework for the Drivers of Migration
Source: Deheza and Mora (2013).

migration processes influence agriculture and economic development within the context of CC.

The main drivers behind migration decision-making are multiple given that migration is a multicausal process jointly determined by demographic, social, economic, cultural, environmental, psychological, and political aspects (see Figure 5.1; Hunter and Simon, 2022; Massey, 2015; Hunter *et al.*, 2013; De Haas, 2011; Portes and DeWind, 2007; Massey *et al.*, 1993). Beyond doubt, the pioneering research of Ravenstein (1885) paved the way for the theoretical perspectives that explain the underlying motivations individuals consider to join the migration wave.

Among the theoretical perspectives that have contributed to explain the migratory phenomenon, the *neoclassical theory* stands out as it considers migration to be an individual decision that seeks to maximize income under the assumption of perfect markets.

Lewis (1954) attempts to explain the process of economic development within the classical framework which assumes that an unlimited labor supply encourages economic development and how rural migration to cities forms part of this development process, as the surplus labor from the rural sector is the principal input of the urban industrial economy. This idea would later become the basis of theories on the various decisions to migrate from developing to more developed nations. Lewis conceived the model to explain development in the context of dual economies in which migration plays a fundamental role. Dual economies are developing economies where a modern (urban) sector, connected to the outside world, coexists with a traditional (rural) sector that depends on subsistence agriculture for survival. This model considers urban and rural sectors, which have a function of production:

$$X_i = X_i(K_i, N_i) \quad \text{for}\, i = \{a, m\}$$

where:

X_i is the production of sector i

K_i is the capital used in sector i

N_i is the labor used in sector i

a is the amount of agricultural output produced in the rural sector

m is a manufactured product from the urban sector

Lewis (1954) suggests the existence of a considerable difference between the wages of the two sectors, stating that this difference would be a sufficient incentive for workers to move from one sector to another. An unlimited supply of labor allows the advanced sector to expand without increasing its wages and ensures high profitability. In the case of the rural sector, migration is the only means to remove surplus labor and improve capital/production ratios. Migration is therefore the prior condition for a development process that eliminates economic backwardness (Arango, 2003).

The demand for labor in each sector, under optimal conditions, is equal to the value of the marginal product:

$$P_i \partial X_i / \partial N_i = W_i \quad \text{for}\, i = \{a, m\}$$

For the rural sector, it is the following:

$$W_a = X_a\,(P_a / N_a)$$

Based on family evaluations, the assigned rural and urban populations' demand for work considers the value of the mean agricultural production in the rural zone ($N_{\mathrm{a}1}$), which is greater than the optimal distribution (N^*) (Aroca, 2004). Therefore, the difference:

$$(N^* - N_{\mathrm{a1}})$$

corresponds to surplus population in the rural sector. In this scenario, migrations are a crucial development mechanism for the economy as a whole, as they boost the growth potential inherent in economic disparity. Both sectors — rural and urban areas of origin and areas of destination — benefit from migrations (Arango, 2003).

Harris and Todaro contributed to the development of the neoclassical model by incorporating risk and unemployment into their analysis. According to these authors, migration between rural and urban areas occurs when the expected real income differential between both locations is positive (Harris and Todaro, 1970; Todaro, 1969).

Todaro (1969) proposed a model in which migration is a joint function of the wage difference and the probability of finding employment in both the place of origin and destination. The model is based on the premise that paid labor in the modern (urban) sector provides a higher income than rural employment.

These wage differences spark migrations from the countryside to the city, but not all the population that migrates to the cities finds employment immediately. Many individuals are temporarily underemployed in the traditional city sector until an opportunity to obtain paid employment in the modern sector arises.

The greater the number of underemployed workers seeking employment in the modern sector, the longer the individual worker's delay in finding employment and the less attractive the workers' view of migration. Any attempts to reduce urban underemployment, such as the creation of new industrial positions, will be at least partially self-frustrated as it makes rural–urban migration more attractive. Migration will reduce underemployment (as a proportion of the urban workforce) only if the gap between rural and urban incomes is reduced.

Specifically, it is assumed that people migrate if the expected urban–rural income differential exceeds the costs of migration (Taylor and Martin, 2001):

$$\Delta = \int_0^T e^{\delta t}[p_u(t)y_u - y_r(t)]dt - c$$

where:

$p_u(t)$ is the probability of urban employment in time t
y_u is urban income from the job
$y_r(t)$ are expected rural incomes in time t
c is the cost associated with migration
δ is the discount rate

If Δ is positive, the decision will be made to migrate; if it is negative, working at the place of origin is preferable; and if it is zero, the individual is indifferent about migrating or not migrating. The main costs faced by people who decide to migrate are the monetary costs of travel, the costs of obtaining information and seeking a new job, the opportunity costs of quitting during the job search, and the psychological costs of leaving the family behind and moving to an unknown place (Massey *et al.*, 1993).

Todaro's model explains the continuation and often the acceleration of migration from the country to the cities during times of increasing high urban unemployment. Its difference from the neoclassical models is that it does not assume the existence of full employment; therefore, a higher wage in the urban sector than in the rural sector is not a sufficient or even necessary condition for migration. In a setting of high unemployment, the wage or income depends on the migrant's success in finding work (Taylor and Martin, 2001).

Harris and Todaro's model (1970) broaden Todaro's basic framework (1969) of a model of the internal commerce of migration and unemployment in the urban and rural sectors aimed at evaluating the impact of migration on rural income, urban and rural production, and social well-being on the whole (Harris and Todaro, 1970). The model takes production and income into account, in both the urban and rural sectors.

The following assumptions are made:

- The rural sector specializes in agricultural products, some of which are exchanged for the manufactured goods that are the specialty of the urban sector.
- The rural sector has the option of using all available labor to produce agricultural products, some of which are exchanged for urban manufactured products. Its second option is to use only part of its labor to produce food, while exporting its remaining labor to the urban sector (through migration), in exchange for wages paid in the form of manufactured goods.
- Typical migrants preserve their links with the rural sector, and their earned income corresponds to the rural sector.

To prove that individual decisions to migrate are made when growing urban unemployment occurs, the assumption considers that rural–urban migration will continue as long as the expected real urban income (the wage multiplied by the probability of finding a job) exceeds the real agricultural marginal income. In other words, potential rural migrants act as maximizers of expected profit (Todaro, 1969).

The complete model of Harris–Todaro is a mere extension of the traditional neoclassical commercial models of two sectors. There are technologies for agricultural and manufacturing production in variable proportions for the rural and urban sectors, neoclassical rules of behavior for determining the usage levels of factors and production in each sector, and a traditional mechanism of commercial theory to determine the terms of exchange (Harris and Todaro, 1970).

The equations of the Harris–Todaro model are the following: If Si W_R and W_u represent the nominal urban and agricultural wages, E_u the number of urban jobs, and L_u the urban workforce, the expected urban income, $E(W_u)$, is:

$$E(W_u) = W_u \frac{E_u}{L_u}$$

The expected rural income, $E(W_R)$, is simply W_R. Rural–urban migration $M = L_u$ is a function of the expected wage differential in the urban and rural areas. In other words,

$$M = L_u = f(E(W_u) - E(W_R))$$

The expected wage of rural–urban equilibrium is therefore:

$$E(W_u) = E(W_R)$$

which is converted into:

$$W_u \times \frac{E_u}{L_u} = W_R$$

This way, the Harris–Todaro model suggests an urban rate of employment in equilibrium:

$$1 - \frac{E_u}{L_u} = 1 - \frac{W_r}{W_u}$$

This formula shows the inverse relationship between the unemployment rates of equilibrium and the expected wage differences between the urban and rural zones.

Harris and Todaro indicate a series of political implications that their model has for developing nations. In the first place, they evaluate the effects of alternative policies of urban employment on well-being (in terms of production lost or won in each sector); examples would be uniform or specific wage subsidies of the sector, expansion urban demand, and restriction of migration. In second place are the critical importance of the determination of urban wages, the policies of setting prices for basic products, rural development programs at levels of relative production, the terms of exchange, and the intersectoral assignment of labor in the sectors as a result of induced migration. The Harris–Todaro model shows that the accelerated creation of urban employment can truly increase unemployment levels. Lastly, the conditions under which coercive restrictions of migration can reduce the level of rural well-being are described.

Piore (1979) returns to Harris and Todaro's approach and introduces the idea that migration in developed countries is the result of push factors called the structural labor force demand. The demand for migrant labor is the result of a constant increase in primary sector salaries at destination countries. As a result, migrants have incentives to participate in the sector even though they are not considered part of society in those countries. This idea gave way to the *dual labor market theory*, which is based on the premise of a rupture in two broad segments of the labor market: both the primary and secondary. The first is characterized by being intensive in capital and having qualified workers; the second is intensive in manual labor, with unstable employment and low wages. Thus, the constant demand for migrant labor is linked to the economic structures of developed countries (Massey *et al.*, 1993; Arango, 2000).

In addition, Wallerstein (1974) developed the *worldwide system theory*, which views international migration as a phenomenon derived from the world market structure, operating through the penetration of capitalist economic relations into peripheral economies, thereby creating a population prone to migrate. This model sees the migration phenomena as a natural consequence of market penetration and globalization. Consequently, migration follows the dynamics of global economic structures, and does not consider individual motivations. This theory is viewed as a historic and structural generalization that showcases similar migration processes present in various countries during the 1960s and 1970s, in places where migrant labor flows were motivated by the globalizing process of capitalist economies (Arango, 2000; Massey *et al.*, 1993).

The *cumulative causation theory*, attributed to the work of Myrdal (1957), is based on the idea that growth in the networks and institutions supporting migrants leads to a process in which international migration helps itself; in other words, migration is a self-sustaining and self-perpetuating phenomenon (Arango, 2000). Some factors that make these movements possible are associated with global inequalities in human capital, land endowments, and income. This perspective points out that "migration is a selective process that tends, initially at least, to draw relatively well-educated, skilled, productive, and highly motivated people away from sending communities (as pointed out earlier, however, migration tends to become less selective over time as the costs and risks fall because of network formation)" (Massey *et al.*, 1993, p. 453). In addition, they are linked to the organization of agrarian product, social labeling, and the culture of migration. In terms of the culture of migration, it can be said that the migration process leads to changes in cultural values and perceptions on community and individual levels (Massey, 1990). These changes are linked to the social connection between non-migrants and migrants who observe and learn about the countries of destination from relatives and neighbors. This leads to an increase in their likelihood to migrate motivated by the cultural penetration of host countries, which becomes apparent in the patterns of consumption, status aspirations, related deprivations in their place of origin, and the goal of improving their standard of living (Kandel and Massey, 2002). Due to this cultural penetration, individuals living in communities with high rates of international migration and in contact with international labor markets transform the idea of becoming international migrants into an aspiration and a social mobility goal (Kandel and Massey, 2002; Cohen and Sirkeci, 2011).

The *networks theory* can be found within the perspective of knowledge and information exchange among established migrants and future migrants. This approach sees migration as a combination of elements that influence individual decisions and structural aspects in the economies of destination and origin (Massey *et al.*, 1987; McKenzie and Rapoport, 2010). According to this theory, the first migrants from a community will face difficulties during their journey from origin to destination. After migrating, they will share their experiences with the migrants who succeed them, and the transmitted information will facilitate the insertion of newcomers into the migration process (Garip and Asad, 2016; Guilmoto and Sandron, 2001). This perspective highlights how migrant networks perpetuate themselves through institutionalization, and how they are affected by external factors such as changes in labor markets.

From a perspective that unifies migratory flows, transnationalism is a concept that can be understood as "the circular movements of individuals and groups as they travel between two or more destinations in a regular fashion over time" (Cohen and Sirkeci, 2011, p. 7). The core actors involved in this process are the individuals, their networks of social relations, networks of organizations, their communities, and broader institutionalized structures such as local and national governments (Portes and Martinez 2019; Portes *et al.*, 1999). These population movements result in special relations and sociocultural practices specific to the transmigrant lifestyle (Stephen, 2007; Guarnizo, 2003).

More recently, Massey (2015) has argued that a missing element in international migration theories is the role of the State as the institution responsible for formulating and implementing migration policy. Nation-states play a major role in determining the number and characteristics of migratory flows moving from one country to another. This adds a crucial element to the economic and social factors already covered in other migration theories.[1]

5.1.1 *The new economics of labor migration (NELM)*

The new economics of labor migration (NELM) proposed by Stark and Bloom (1985) represented a new direction in theoretical and empirical research on migration. A key idea of this focus is that decisions involving migration are not made in an isolated form by individual actors, but by units of related people (typically families or households) who act collectively not only to maximize the expected income, but also to minimize risks and reduce the restrictions associated with a variety of market flaws, in addition to the flaws of the labor market (Stark and Bloom, 1985).

This theory identifies the source of the migratory decision as the household rather than the maximizing individual agent. It is the family that constructs the migration strategy for its members, with the goal of maximizing income as well as diversifying its sources and reducing economic risks (Stark, 1991). And although the purpose of

[1]Scholars have mentioned additional approaches that explain migration decision-making, which include the brain drain theory (Stark *et al.*, 1997), the institutionalist theory (Massey *et al.*, 1993), and migration as a result of violence (Bucheli *et al.*, 2019; Velásquez, 2019).

migration is to maximize income, it is not exclusively so in terms of the relationship among households in the group of reference, due to the notion of relative deprivation (Stark and Taylor, 1989). In other words, the more unequal the distribution of income in a given community, the more relative deprivation will be felt and the greater the incentives for migration.

In contrast with the neoclassical explanation, the new economics of labor migration are sensitive to income distribution and do not take into account the economic agent proposed by neoclassical economics (De Haas, 2011). An important aspect of the NELM theory is its allusion to migrants who leave households characterized by their poverty: a pertinent consideration in the current study, which explores whether migration becomes, through the sending of remittances, a form of reducing the deprivation of rural households in Mexico (Massey *et al.*, 1993).

Decisions to migrate are a result of volatility or defects in labor markets, which imply the lack of access to credit and the probability of risk. Since imperfect or incomplete markets are typical in rural areas in developing countries, the hypothesis of the NELM is that households use migration as a means to overcome insufficient markets or the flaws in local markets that force households to self-finance their investments in production and protect themselves against risk in income (Stark and Bloom, 1985).

Households send migrants as part of a strategy to diversify their sources of income, to obtain capital for investment, and to provide protection against risks of production and income among non-migrant family members. Taylor (1999) argues that remittances spark a dynamic of development through the relaxation of the restrictions that households face in production and investment. Remittances can be used to encourage production by financing inputs, new technologies, and production activities. They also serve as insurance for households whose income is unrelated, negatively related, or not highly related to agricultural income (Stark and Lucas, 1988).

The theory of the NELM leads to specific hypotheses about the effects of remittances on migrants' households of origin. If credit and risk restrictions are linked and migration helps households in alleviating these restrictions, then migration and remittances must have a positive effect on local production and on the income of migrants' households of origin. The higher the restrictions on household liquidity, the greater the effect of the marginal income of remittances (Taylor, 1999; Massey *et al.*, 1993).

5.1.2 *Migration due to environmental and climatic conditions*

Over the past two decades, the extent of the impacts of CC on migration has received increasing interest in the literature. Contemporary environmental change has reconfigured socioeconomic, political, and ecological systems (Antwi-Agyei and Nyantakyi-Frimpong, 2021). In 1990, the IPCC noted that the greatest single impact of CC could be on human migration, with millions of people being displaced by natural disasters, shoreline erosion, coastal flooding, and disruption of agricultural industries. The Stern Review went further in emphasizing this point, warning that the effects of CC could drive millions of people to migrate.

There is a general agreement in the literature that changes in climate are impacting human mobility and that this process is set to continue and grow in the future. However, the magnitude of such effects is poorly understood, most likely due to the complexity of the process, the lack of reliable and complete datasets, and even the continued debate surrounding basic terminology definitions. In fact, there is no conclusive evidence in the literature supporting the conjecture that CC is a direct or exclusive cause of the movement of people on a large scale. As a consequence of this absence of evidence, factors indirectly linked to CC that are capable of inducing the movement of people must be identified.

In this sense, the work of Hunter and Simon (2022) adds important elements to the previous discussion by reviewing studies that consider the environment as tangible material in physical or natural form. This includes elements such as water, air, or earth, and the catastrophic events caused by these factors. This type of environmental tension can be analyzed within a time interval. For example, over the short term, hurricanes tend to affect coastal zones or zones with deficient drainage systems. In a similar manner, earthquakes reveal fragile physical infrastructure in developing countries. Over the long term, droughts provoke the loss of crops and the interruption of supply chains. CC is related to this type of tension through the systematic increase of greenhouse gases, with growing probabilities of occurrence and intensity over the short and long terms (Seneviratne *et al.*, 2012). In addition, the greatest incidence of catastrophic events has been related empirically to migratory processes. Examples of this type of studies are provided below.

Thiede *et al.* (2021) utilized a focus on macrodata in 31 nations in Africa, Latin America, and Southeast Asia to discover that exposure to stressful environmental factors at a young age provokes lifelong migration, especially among poor women. In a similar manner, Cruz (2021) formulated a dynamic economic model for 287 nations and 6 sectors that includes patterns of structural transformation and heterogenous labor markets. Using census data and population surveys, the study discovered that agricultural productivity in the warmest nations decreases by 6% when the temperature increases by 1°C.

In Latin America, Murray-Tortarolo and Martínez-Salgado (2021) utilized microdata from Mexican municipalities during the period from 1970 to 2009 and found that droughts lead to migration. Specifically, they learned that the migration of poor rural farmers tripled during droughts, representing one-third of total migration. Ibáñez *et al.* (2021) found that high temperatures in El Salvador have negative effects on agricultural production, as well as on the labor market of agricultural workers, sparking migration. Mendes-Delazeri *et al.* (2022) used census data and climate information from Brazil, and through a gravity model discovered that CC contributed to migration from rural households with less economic vulnerability.

In Asia, Choksi *et al.* (2021) utilized data from 500 villages in India from 2013 to 2017 and learned that rich rural households have low rates of migration, but are more sensitive to environmental variability than poor households. Entwisle *et al.* (2020) studied the time and amount of flooding that provoked the return of immigrants from Thailand. In Africa, Mueller *et al.* (2020) researched flooding and extreme temperatures as determinants of urban migration.

In general, it is estimated that the movement of individuals due to environmental stress is more than three times greater than movement caused by wars, armed conflict, and other types of State-induced disturbances (Hunter and Simon, 2022). It is not clear, however, if this relation is unidirectional.

One explanation of this phenomenon is that environmental tensions undermine the life of the most vulnerable populations. This includes individuals and households in low-income and medium-income nations that depend directly on the agricultural sector (Section 4.2, Chapter 4). CC associated with extreme temperatures and flooding encourages survival strategies for adapting and diversifying sources of income (Atuoye *et al.*, 2019). Such strategies involve informal agreement among household members and potential migrants, for sending individuals to work in foreign labor markets where income risks are unrelated to the country of origin.

In the theoretical literature, however, two opposing viewpoints are related to the link between migration and CC. On one hand, in the 1990s, studies proliferated that associated CC with the patterns of global migration. According to Hunter *et al.* (2015), these studies reflected environmental determinism through the so-called climate refugees. This position, nonetheless, was the subject of diverse criticism. For Hulme (2011), for example, the apparent relationship between environmental variables and migratory processes suffers from a methodological reductionism that assigns the main cause of contemporary migration to environmental tension, without considering other types of sociodemographic, economic, political, and cultural variables. In other words, the excessive use of predictive climate models does not recognize the complexity of migration and its relationship with other factors (Meyer and Guss, 2017).

In contrast, various studies have fallen into the fallacy of environmental indeterminism. These studies minimized or suppressed environmental variables in the determination of migratory processes. This led to a bias of an omitted variable and incorrect and incomplete inferences of migratory dynamics in a changing environmental context (Hunter and Simon, 2022). In other words, environmental indeterminism produced poorly specified models that excessively attributed the main causes of migration to economic and social factors.

In any case, the political implications at both extremes have had adverse consequences. Environmental determinism influences the hardening of migratory policies associated with nationalistic, anti-immigrant sentiment (Hagan and Wassink, 2020; Loschmann and Marchand, 2020). On the other hand, the omission of environmental variables does not allow for the formulation and execution of policies that mitigate and reduce the effects associated with CC in the less favored populations (Kuriakose *et al.*, 2013).

For this reason, it is important to consider the inclusion of environmental variables in migration theories. For example, according to a neoclassical model, environmental impacts exert downward pressure on wages and increase the wage gap between countries of origin and destination (Beine and Parsons, 2015). In an approach focused on migratory systems, environmental factors influence the system's appearance, perpetuation, and decline (Hunter and Simon, 2022).

In a push-pull perspective, environmental change produces unexpected catastrophic events that act as relevant push factors (Giannelli and Canessa, 2021), although the dynamics of the environmental context interact with a variety of causes of migration. In the NELM, since environmental stress affects the primary sector, households establish a survival strategy to minimize risks and overcome flaws in credit and insurance markets. Therefore, environmental tension influences the type of households that send migrants abroad (Riosmena *et al.*, 2018). Lastly, from the system/world perspective, CC affects mainly peripheral nations that contribute less to the emission of greenhouse gases (Padilla and Serrano, 2006).

Beyond an analysis framework, CC produces new social configurations. Such factors indirectly affect individual lives. Therefore, including this type of variables in the integral, multidisciplinary analysis of migration can result in a solid holistic comprehension of the interrelationships between migration and the environment.

5.2 Ricardian Partial Equilibrium Model

The Ricardian Model represents a partial equilibrium analysis that uses cross-sectional data to analyze agricultural production. The model's name is linked to the contributions of English economist David Ricardo (1772–1823), who emphasized that land value is determined by its net productivity.

Using this as a central idea, the Ricardian model approach can be used to estimate the net productivity of agricultural land based on climate variables, soil type, and sociodemographic control variables (Mendelsohn *et al.*, 1994). The methodology involves the collection of data from a cross-sectional sample of production units in order to measure the sensitivity of land value or net income per agricultural hectare with respect to changes in climate variables (Mendelsohn *et al.*, 1994, 2009). This approach automatically captures farmers' adaptive responses, assuming that the cross-sectional samples incorporate partial equilibrium decisions with respect to their production choices (Mendelsohn and Dinar, 2009).

Ricardian models have been used worldwide quite regularly; for example, in Africa (Seo *et al.*, 2009), in Asia (Liu *et al.*, 2004, Seo *et al.*, 2005), in America (Seo and Mendelsohn, 2007, Mendelsohn *et al.*, 1994), and in Europe (Jawid, 2020; Van Passel *et al.*, 2017; Lippert *et al.*, 2009).

5.2.1 *Model specification*

The central idea of the Ricardian method states that *Land Value* or *Net Agricultural Income* (π) reflects the *net productivity of the land* (Mendelsohn *et al.*, 1994). This approach assumes that agricultural producers maximize their net income (π), which can be represented by the following equation:

$$\pi = \sum P_i Q_i(\boldsymbol{X},\boldsymbol{F},\ \boldsymbol{Z},\boldsymbol{G}) - \sum \boldsymbol{W}_x \boldsymbol{X}$$

where:

P_i is the price of crop $\boldsymbol{i}$
Q_i is the amount of crop $\boldsymbol{i}$ produced
$\boldsymbol{X}$ is a vector of purchased inputs

$\boldsymbol{F}$ is a vector of climate variables
$\boldsymbol{Z}$ is a vector of other control variables, such as type of soil and distance to markets
$\boldsymbol{G}$ is a vector of sociodemographic variables
$\boldsymbol{W}_x$ is a vector of input prices

The model assumes that each producer chooses $\boldsymbol{Q}$ and $\boldsymbol{X}$ in order to maximize land value, based on certain characteristics of the production unit (temperature, rainfall, soil type) and market prices (Ajetomobi *et al.*, 2011; Mendelsohn and Dinar, 2009). Therefore, the resulting optimal function is the following:

$$\pi^* = \boldsymbol{f}(Pi, \boldsymbol{F}, \ \boldsymbol{Z}, \ \boldsymbol{Wx})$$

The Ricardian model uses the above specification to determine how changes in exogenous variables contained in $\boldsymbol{F}$ and $\boldsymbol{Z}$ affect net land productivity. Thus, land value (LV) reflects the present value of the net income stream:

$$LV = \int_0^\infty \boldsymbol{\pi}_t^* \cdot \boldsymbol{e}^{-rt} \boldsymbol{dt}$$

where $\boldsymbol{r}$ represents the market interest rate.

The results of various studies that implement this type of approach have shown that land value is sensitive to changes in climate variables; hence, its usefulness for studying the effects of CC on agricultural productivity (Mendelsohn *et al.*, 1994, 2001; Mendelsohn, 2009; Dinar *et al.*, 1998; Seo *et al.*, 2005). The empirical implementation of the model can be exemplified by the following equation:

$$LV = \beta_0 + \beta_1 \cdot T + \beta_2 \cdot T^2 + \beta_3 \cdot P + \beta_4 \cdot P^2 + \beta_5 T \cdot P + \sum_j \delta_j z_j + e$$

where LV is the value of cropland per hectare, T is temperature, and P is precipitation. In practice, it is common to make a distinction between temperature and precipitation levels in different seasons of the year. Z represents the set of relevant socioeconomic variables of the production unit, β and δ_j are the parameters to be estimated, and e is the error term (Mora *et al.*, 2010).

The last equation incorporates the linear and quadratic terms for the climate variables (temperature and precipitation) in order to account for the non-linearity of agricultural productivity and climate. For example, laboratory experiments suggest that there tends to be a hill-shaped function between yield and temperature (Mendelsohn and Dinar, 2009), in such a way that at low temperature levels (cool climate), the producer's optimal decision may be to grow a certain type of crop, but as the temperature rises, the marginal profitability of that product decreases until it reaches a negative point.

The producer might then decide to optimize profits by growing a crop better adapted to higher temperatures (warm climate). Similar reasoning applies to crops sensitive to rainfall. Following this line of reasoning, the Ricardian model assumes adaptive behavior among producers throughout the intertemporal production cycle (Mendelsohn *et al.*, 1994; Mendelsohn and Dinar, 2009).

The change in land value due to a marginal change in one of the climate variables (temperature [T], for instance) will be given by the following equation[2]:

$$\frac{\partial LV}{\partial T} = \beta_1 + 2 \cdot \beta_2 \cdot T + \beta_5 \cdot P$$

Once the functional relation between cropland value and the climate variables has been estimated, it is sufficient to evaluate the Ricardian function in both climate scenarios in order to obtain the monetary amount by which the land value or net flow of income has changed. Therefore, it is possible to determine different levels of production units' sensitivity to the CC, with an obvious consideration of the control attributes associated with these production units. Thus, the annual effect of a marginal change in the climate variable is calculated through the sum of the marginal effects of said variable (Mora *et al.*, 2010).

Theoretically, the quadratic formulation can change both the magnitude and sign of the marginal effect (Mendelsohn *et al.*, 2009). When the quadratic term is positive, the function is U-shaped,

[2]The same reasoning can be used with respect to precipitation variables.

whereas when the quadratic term is negative, the function is hill-shaped (Mendelsohn *et al.*, 2009). Each crop has a known temperature at which that crop grows best throughout the seasons. In many crops, there is a broader, flatter hill-shaped relationship. However, the relationship between seasonal climate variables is more complex and may include a mixture of positive and negative squared coefficients among seasons (Mendelsohn *et al.*, 2009).

The change in land value given a specific climate scenario from C_0 to C_1 is given by:

$$\Delta LV = LV(C_1) - LV(C_0)$$

Changes that increase land value are beneficial, while changes that decrease land value are detrimental. In many of the empirical studies, $\Delta LV < 0$ shows a negative effect of CC on agricultural profitability. We can therefore see that this type of approach represents a comparative statistics analysis and that the Ricardian model measures long-term changes rather than the effects of annual changes in climate (Mendelsohn *et al.*, 2009).

In general, to calculate the optimal values of the significant climate variables (temperature and precipitation), the following expression is used (Mendelsohn and Dinar, 2009):

$$\textbf{\textit{Inflection Point}} = \frac{\beta\, Temperature}{2 \times \beta\, Temperature_{Squared}}$$

Since agriculture is one of the main sources of rural income and employment in developing countries and is highly susceptible to climate variability (Falco *et al.*, 2019), studies with this type of Ricardian approach have serious implications for agricultural productivity, rural livelihoods, and food security. As a result, Ricardian economic research is relevant in terms of policymaking and the creation of local strategies and programs that aim to ameliorate CC (IPCC, 2007; Jawid, 2020). However, Ricardian models do not capture general equilibrium effects of CC; i.e., the indirect effects of this phenomenon. As we discuss in the next section, multisectoral models are designed to include both the direct and indirect effects of shocks as those caused by CC.

5.3 Multisectoral Models

As presented in Chapter 3, dual models represent a highly stylized economy with just two sectors: the traditional and the capitalist or modern sector, the former identified with agriculture and the latter with industry. This approach simplifies the role of agriculture and fails to distinguish relevant differences within the sector. For example, Yúnez-Naude (1978) shows that, despite the fact that from the 1950s to early 1970s Mexico followed a growth process as described by Ranis and Fei (1961) model, this country did not reach the "turning point." This was due to the fact that agriculture in Mexico was (and still is as other medium-income countries) heterogeneous and formed by small subsistence household farmers and entrepreneurial farmers: the former offering labor as well as food for family consumption and the latter providing food and other agricultural goods in the market, i.e., functioning as their counterparts in high-income countries.

5.3.1 *Input–Output and SAM-based multisectoral models*

The limitations of dual models as well as the understanding of the various roles of agriculture in economic development began to be addressed using multisectoral approaches. These economy-wide disaggregated models were inspired by the seminal input–output table (IOT) of Wasilly Leontief that led to the development of applied multiplier and general equilibrium empirical analyses.

An IOT relates the inputs used for producing a particular commodity, i.e., the connection between production activities, in monetary terms and for a given period, generally a year. For example, grain production (that in a disaggregated multisectoral approach forms part of the field crops sector and/or agriculture). An IO model includes total final demand of commodities according to the way the latter are disaggregated. On this basis one can calculate the likely effects on production of changes in the final demand — assumed to be exogenous in an IO model — for a specific economy as long as we have the data to build the IOT as wells as final demand and its

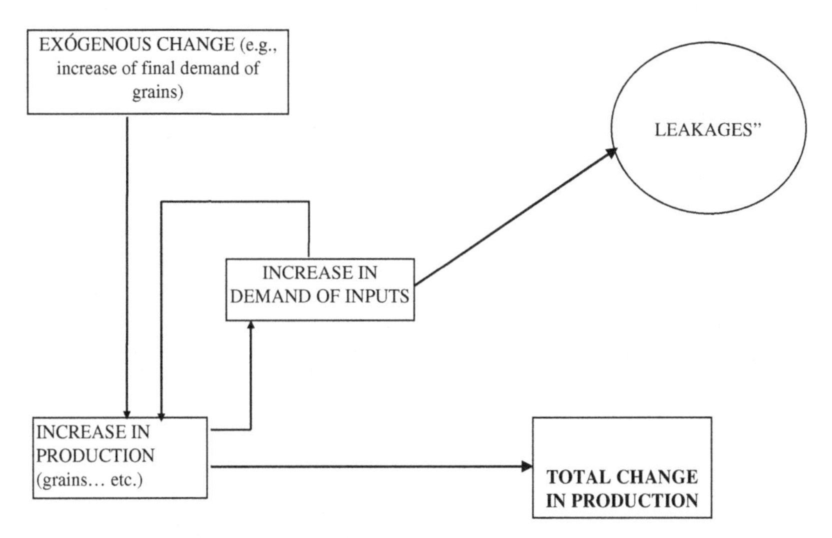

Figure 5.2. Multipliers Based on an Input–Output Table
Source: By authors.

distribution among the activities-commodities for the whole economy in question. Figure 5.2 illustrates this process.

Suppose that there is an exogenous increase in final demand of wheat produced domestically. To meet this demand, farmers require more of inputs such as seeds, machinery, etc. This drives production, which in turn, requires inputs produced by other industries and so on. The final result is that production in the economy increases more than the original demand injection, i.e., a multiplier effect (a decrease in the demand of wheat would have negative multiplier effects).

Suppose that there is an exogenous increase in final demand of wheat produced domestically. To meet this demand, farmers require more of inputs such as seeds, machinery, etc. This drives production, which in turn, requires inputs produced by other industries and so on. The final result is that production in the economy increases more than the original demand injection, i.e., a multiplier effect (a decrease in the demand of wheat would have negative multiplier effects).

An input–output multiplier model (IMOMM) assumes that economic activities use input in fixed proportions to output, that prices are fixed, and that adjustments to exogenous demand changes or shocks are thus made through changes in quantities measured in monetary terms.

An IOMM can be expressed as follows:

$$Y = (I - A)^{-1}X = MX$$

where:

- Y is a vector of sectorial production, $y_i, i = 1, \ldots, n$ (n is the number of sectors or activities)
- X is a vector of final demands, $x_i, i = 1, \ldots, n$, considered as exogenous in the model
- A is the input–output matrix, each cell denoted by aij's, where i and $j = 1, \ldots, n$
- I is a unitary matrix with n × n dimensions
- $(I - A)$ 1 is the inverse of matrix $I - A$
- M is the input–output multiplier matrix.

So, $\Lambda X = M\Lambda F$ expresses the change in output ΛX arising from an exogenous change in final demand ΛF. An IOMM captures both, the direct and indirect effects of the simulated shock — the latter through the input–output linkages within and between activities. A new equilibrium is reached, where the resulting change in production would be greater than the shock as long as the increase in demand is "leaked out" by imports (Figure 5.2).

Based on Leontief contribution to multisectoral input–output analyses, during the 1980s applied multisectoral models have been developed from social accounting matrixes-based multiplier models to computable general equilibrium models. With these models sectorial and economy-wide linkages are studied in detail and depth.

As an IOT, a Social Accounting Matrix or SAM is a representation of the structure and linkages of the components of a complete and particular economy during a period (generally a year), measured in monetary terms. The basic difference is that a SAM adds to inputs factors of production (typically labor and capital); hence, value added and institutions such as the government, enterprises, and households according to their income (the later inclusion is why this matrix is called "social").

The economic system captured in a SAM can be of a country, group of countries or regions of the world or even villages or towns (see Taylor and Adelman, 2006 for the latter). In addition, a SAM is a very flexible accounting system whose contents can be aggregated or disaggregated according to the objectives of a specific applied study and data available to construct the accounting system. A SAM can have as many sectors or activities as those contained in a country's National Accounts and some of its components can be further disaggregated. It is also possible to add additional components such as ecological accounts, natural capital, water, and land as factors of production to a conventional SAM (see below, and for example, Yúnez-Naude and Aguilar-Mendez, 2018; López-López and Yúnez-Naude, 2019).

In Table 5.1 we include a scheme of a SAM. Entries 1 form matrix A of the IOMM (see above, the equation of an IOMM); three in our scheme. Following the conventional reading of matrix cells (mentioning first the row and then the column) and considering that rows in this accounting scheme represent income flows and columns expenditures flow, a_{11} contains the value of the inputs produced in activity 1 and used by itself (e.g., seeds to produce agricultural crops); a_{12} contains the products of the secondary sector used as inputs for primary production (e.g., tractors); and so on.

Entries 2,1 contain value added, i.e., the contribution of factors of production to the economy's output; and the remaining accounts of column 1 capture direct taxes (3b,1) and imports (5,1). As regards column 2, value added is transferred to institutions (3,2), whereas column 3 captures final institutions' demand of goods and services (1,3); transfers between private institutions and direct taxes paid by them to the government (3,3); and savings (4,3). Savings are used for investment in productive activities or gross capital formation (1,4). Finally, the basic SAM has a rest of the world account that includes by column: exports (1,5), transfers to factors of production (e.g., returns to capital located abroad (2,5)), transfers to institutions such as remittances (3,5) and financial capital transfers from abroad (4,5).

As the IOMM, a SAM multiplier model assumes that economic activities use input in fixed proportions to output (input–output

Table 5.1. Scheme of a Social Accounting Matrix

Income	1 Activities	2 Factors	3 Institutions	4 Capital investment	5 Rest of the world	Total
1. Activities primary manufactures services	Input-output table		Final demand	Investment	Exports	Total sales
2. Factors labor, land & capital	Value added				Transfers	Value added (GNP at factor prices)
3. Institutions						
a. Private ... households by ..Income Decil, etc.		Value added transfers	Transfers		Transfers	Total institution's income
b. Public (Government)	Direct taxes	Taxes	Direct taxes			
4. Capital			Savings		Capital transfers	Total savings
5. Rest of the World	Imports					Imports
Total	Total payments	Total payments to factors	Total expenditures	Total investment	Income from abroad	Totals: Income/ Expenditure

Source: By authors.

coefficients are fixed) and also fixed prices. In addition, it assumes that technology and consumer preferences are linear and that factors of production are not fully utilized.[3] As in an IOMM, the working of a SAM-based multiplier model (SAMMM) is through quantities or demand driven.

A SAMMM requires to select which accounts are exogenous and which are endogenous. This is necessary to simulate exogenous shocks and calculate their direct and indirect effects. Typically, domestic (private and public) and foreign demand of goods and services are considered as exogenous, as well as government interventions and other components of the economic relations between the country under study and the rest of the world (e.g., remittances).

Table 5.2 presents the SAM balancing accounts incorporated into a multiplier model. Matrix N is expressed as the product of a square matrix A_n of average propensities of consumption and an endogenous income vector y_n. L represents the "leakages" of the open economy under study (i.e., the transactions it makes with the rest of the world) expressed as the product of a non-square matrix A_l of average propensities of leakages of endogenous income y_n. X is the matrix of exogenous injections to endogenous accounts.

Solving for the total of endogenous accounts we obtain the equilibrium equation, where I_n is the identity matrix nxn.

$$y_n = (I_n - A_n)^{-1}X = M_a X$$

The equation determines the equilibrium of products and incomes consistent with any level of exogenous entries. M_a is the SAM-multiplier matrix relating endogenous income y_n to exogenous variables X. M_a captures the direct and indirect effects of exogenous shock (Round, 2003).

[3]The presence of unemployment means that the economy reacts to a positive shock without bottlenecks. However, there are versions of applied multiplier models imposing restrictions on production. The unemployment assumption is in line with Keynesian economics. In addition, this assumption together with the fixed price context of IOMs and SAMMMs that no substitution between activities takes place under the presence of an exogenous shock is in contrast with the computable equilibrium approach.

Table 5.2. SAM Accounting Balances

	Endogenous accounts	**Exogenous accounts**	**Total**
Endogenous accounts	$N = A_n\hat{y}_n$	X	$y_n = A_n y_n + X$
Exogenous accounts	$L = A_l\hat{y}_n$	R	$y_x = A_l y_n + R_i$
Total	$y_n' = (\acute{\imath}A_n + \acute{\imath}A_l)\hat{y}_n$	$y_x' = \acute{\imath}X + \acute{\imath}R$	

Source: Pyatt and Round (1979).

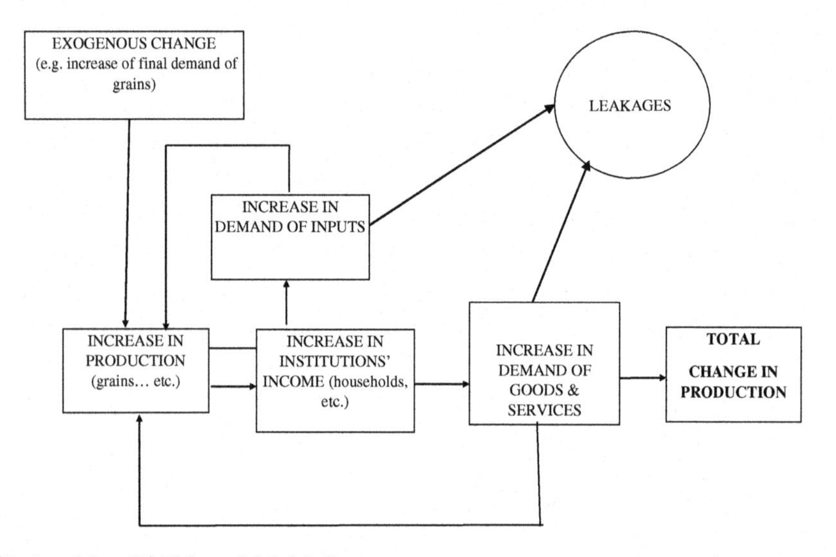

Figure 5.3. SAM-based Multipliers
Source: By authors.

The functioning of a SAMMM when simulating an exogenous shock in Figure 5.3 (it is the same shock as the one used in Figure 5.2).

As in the IOM, the exogenous shock has a direct effect on the production of the affected activity and, indirectly, on the input–demand it uses. The difference is that a SAMMM incorporates factors of production/value added and the income institutions (e.g., households and government) receive these from its ownership of factors (e.g., labor and capital) that in turn affect their demand. The illustration depicted in Figures 5.2 and 5.3 captures these processes and differences. In a SAMMM the rise in the domestic demand of grains adds to its direct effects on the activity producing them and to the rise in the demand for inputs by the activity, the effect on value added and institutions' income. In turn this increased income increases the demand of grains and of other activities. The new equilibrium is characterized by a rise in gross domestic production of the economy in question higher than the shock.

IOM and SAMM have been used extensively for policy impact analyses and for other exogenous shocks (see for example https://www.shaio.es/en/, website of the Spanish and Hispanic America for Input-Output Analysis, SHAIO, Spanish acronym). Recent SAMMM have been applied to estimate the effects of COVID-19 in several countries. A SAM-based multiplier approach is considered to be appropriate to estimate short-term shocks like that caused by COVID-19 since the pandemic was a sudden and unexpected event which led to a significant reduction in economic activity and income (see, for example https://www.ifpri.org/covid-19, accessed on July 20, 2020 and Hernández-Solano *et al.*, 2022).

5.3.2 *Computable general equilibrium models*

Computable General Equilibrium Models (CGEM) can also use SAMs as data base. These models began to be used for policy analyses (e. g., for evaluating empirically the likely impacts of fiscal and trade reforms in several countries) since the late 1980s. The boom of studies based on complex CGEM was in part made possible by advances and access to personal computers by academics. Whereas multiplier models are in line with Keynesian economics, CGEs use the fundamentals of neoclassical economics (Robinson, 1989).

As already stated, multiplier models assume fixed prices and unemployment, whereas in CGEMs, prices are flexible in a context of full employment. In a multiplier model the process of adjustment to a shock is through quantities, whereas in CGEMs it is through relative prices. In addition, multiplier models are linear, whereas

CGEMs are not. One consequence of these differences is that multiplier models overestimate the effects of a shock, whereas CGEMs underestimate it (Adelman and Taylor, 1991; Van Wyk *et al.*, 2015).

As in the neoclassical microeconomic general equilibrium theory, in a CGEM prices based on the functioning of markets are fundamental: economic agents respond to price signals and their changes. In a CGEM product prices and factor prices are relative, typically with respect to either the consumer price index or the exchange rate of the economy in question, called the numeraire. If we select, for example, the consumer price index as the numeraire in the procedures to close the CGEM, the exchange rate will be flexible and will adjust to equilibrate the rest of the world accounts. So, the equilibrium exchange rate will be relative to the consumer price index. This closure of the CGEM (see below) is used for "small" economies that take world prices as given. Alternatively, if we take the exchange rate as the numeraire all prices will be relative to it and the balance of payments will equilibrate through international capital movements (see *Ibid.*).

A CGE usually assumes constant returns to scale and is formulated as a set of simultaneous linear and non-linear equations, which, following neoclassical microeconomics, define the behavior of economic agents, as well as the economic environment in which these agents operate. This environment is described by market equilibrium conditions and macroeconomic balances.[4]

For production and consumption decisions, behavior is captured by linear or nonlinear, first-order optimality conditions. That is, production and consumption decisions are driven by the maximization of profits and utility, respectively, based on prices defined by the markets. The CGEM equations also include a set of constraints that have to be satisfied by the system as a whole but are not necessarily considered by any individual agent. These constraints cover markets

[4]The computational software called General Algebraic Modeling System or GAMS, developed by Brooke, Kendrick, Meeraus, and Raman, is usually used in CGEM models.

(for factors and commodities) and macroeconomic aggregates (balances for the Savings–Investment account, the government account, and the current account with the rest of the world).[5]

Following we describe main characteristics of a CGEM in a non-technical manner aimed at helping to understand how a CGE is built. From a wide range of options, we select a CGEM developed by Lofgren *et al.* (2002) CGE and extended by Thurlow (2004), both from the International Food Policy Research Institute (IFPRI), because this model incorporates land as a factor of production, a procedure that is uncommon in CGEMs that do not focus on agriculture (an extension and adaptation to Mexico of these authors' model is in Yúnez-Naude and Aguilar-Mendez, 2018).

A CGEM consists of several blocks of equations, such as the production and trade block, the price block, the institutions block, and the system constrain blocks and closure (details in Lofgren *et al.*, 2002, and Thurlow, 2004).

As was said earlier, producers and consumers decisions are captured by first-order optimality conditions for profits and utility, respectively. The corresponding equations of the CGEM also include a set of constraints that have to be satisfied by the system as a whole but are not necessarily considered by any individual economic agent. These constraints cover markets (for factors and commodities) and macroeconomic aggregates (balances for the Savings–Investment account, the government, and the current account with the rest of the world.

5.3.2.1 *Activities, production, and factor markets*[6]

Each activity (or producer) is assumed to maximize profits, defined as the difference between revenue earned and the cost of inputs

[5]In contrast to a SAMMM, CGE assume that factors of production are fixed, i.e., they are not unemployed.

[6]The scheme presented in Table 5.1 helps to follow our exposition since it resembles a typical SAM used as the data base of a CGEM. Note that in Table 5.2 no distinction between commodities and activities is made, whereas in the following description of a CGE we separate activities from commodities.

(both intermediate and primary or factors of production). Profits are maximized subject to a production technology, the structure of which is shown in Figure 5.4. The production technology is a nested function of constant elasticity of substitution (CES) and Leontief input–output functions.

At the top level, domestic output is a linear combination of value added and intermediate inputs. This specification allows producers to respond to changes in relative factor returns by smoothly substituting between available factors so as to derive a final value-added composite. As in microeconomic theory, profit maximization implies that the factors receive income where marginal revenue equals marginal cost based on endogenous relative prices.

Value added is a CES function of the primary factors of production (labor, land, and capital), and intermediate input demand is determined according to fixed input–output coefficients, as in an IOM and/or a SAMMMM. In the building of a CGEM and its data base, it is frequent to separate activity accounts from commodity accounts; i.e., to distinguish between activities and the commodities

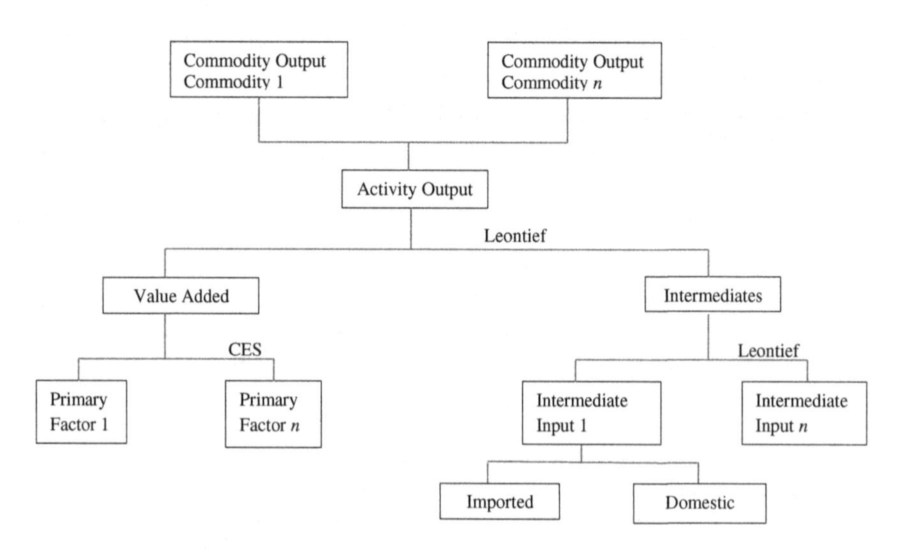

Figure 5.4. Production Technology
Source: Thurlow (2004).

that these activities produce.[7] Among others, this distinction allows for a single commodity to be produced by more than one activity. It also allows to include transaction costs arising from differences in the distance between the origin of production (activities) and final consumption (commodities). This procedure also allows to separate domestic from imported commodities.

As for the factor market, the CGEM assumes that the quantity supplied by each factor is fixed at the observed level (this is a basic difference between standard CGEs and standard multiplier models).

5.3.2.2 *Prices and taxes*

Figure 5.5 shows how producer prices evolve to become the prices of final commodities. Given that more than one activity can produce the same commodity, it is first necessary to combine the prices of the various activities producing a particular commodity (PXAC) into a single producer price for that commodity (PX). The activity price not only includes activity taxes but also factor taxes incurred during the production process. From the producer price of a commodity, it is possible to arrive at a final export price (PE) by including taxes that might be imposed on the exporting of commodities. The interaction of producer and export prices determines the final supply price for the domestic market (PDS).

As regards consumption, the domestic supply price is converted into the domestic demand price (PDD). This is done by including the relevant domestic transaction costs. The price of imports (PM) is calculated considering all tariffs that might be placed on foreign commodities entering the domestic market. The interaction of the import and domestic prices determines the price of the composite commodity (PQ). Sales taxes are then added to the composite price to arrive at a final market price.

[7]This procedure captures the fact that usually consumers are indifferent to commodities produced by different technologies since the use value of similar commodities is the same for them.

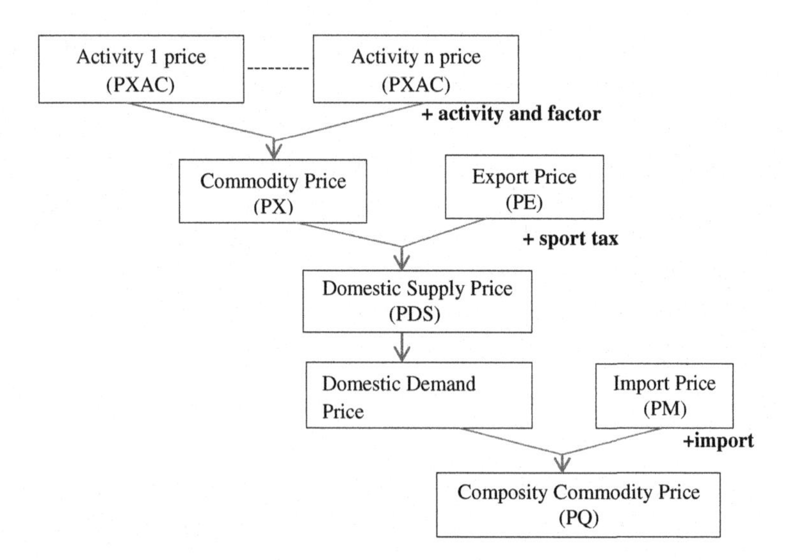

Figure 5.5. Prices and Taxes
Source: Lofgren *et al.* (2002).

5.3.2.3 *Institutional incomes*

Institutions are represented by households, enterprises, the government, and the rest of the world. Households and enterprises mainly receive their incomes from factor returns generated during the production process.

Since enterprises do not consume, their income is allocated to direct taxes, savings, and transfers to other institutions. Apart from this, the payments to and from enterprises are modeled in the same way as the payments to and from households. The government collects taxes and receives transfers from other institutions. The government uses this income to purchase commodities for its consumption and for transfers to other institutions. Government savings (the difference between government income and spending) is, for the closure of the model, a flexible residual. Government income and spending is, for the closure of the model, a flexible residual.

Enterprises are the sole recipient of capital income, which they transfer to households after having paid corporate taxes (based on fixed tax rates), after their savings (based on fixed savings rates), and after their remitted profits to the rest of the world. Households also receive transfers from the government, other domestic institutions, and the rest of the world), e.g., remittances from family members working abroad). Households' disposable income is net of personal income tax (based on fixed rates), savings (based on fixed marginal propensities), and remittances to or from the rest of the world. A simple model considers just a "representative" household for each income group; so, it assumes that households within each income bracket have identical preferences.

The supply of factors of production is fixed within a given time-period and they are fully employed. Capital is assumed to be immobile across sectors, implying that capital earns sector-specific returns. Labor and land supply are mobile across sectors and labor is assumed to be perfectly elastic at a given real wage.

Government income is the sum of all taxes: direct taxes on households and enterprises, value-added taxes, producer taxes, import tariffs, export taxes, social security taxes, and sales taxes. The government consumes commodities according to fixed shares (given in the SAM) and also spends money on transfers to domestic institutions and for its programs related to support activities. In the closure, real government expenditure, real investment, and foreign savings are all held fixed. To give the model a medium-term time horizon labor is allowed to be mobile between sectors, while capital is fixed.

The remaining institution is the rest of the world. As noted, transfer payments between the rest of the world and domestic institutions and factors are all fixed in foreign currency. Foreign savings (or the current account deficit) is the difference between foreign currency spending and receipts.

5.3.2.4 *Commodity markets*

Commodities (domestic output and imports) enter to the market system. The model generates the aggregated domestic output from the output of different activities of a given commodity. These outputs are considered imperfectly substitutable as a result of, for example, differences in timing, quality, and distance between the locations of activities. A CES function is used as the aggregation function.

An addition of Yúnez-Naude and Aguilar-Mendez (2018) to the IFPRI, CGE is the inclusion of substitution possibilities between production for the domestic and the foreign markets. This decision of producers is governed by a constant elasticity of transformation (CET) function which distinguishes between goods for the domestic and foreign markets. As of this specification, it is possible to capture any time or quality differences between the two products. Profit maximization drives producers to sell in those markets where they can achieve the highest returns. These returns are based on domestic and export prices.

5.3.2.5 *System constraints and macroeconomic closures*

In order to calibrate the CGEM, i.e., to reproduce the SAM using the CGEM specifications, there are different strategies to close the model. One option is the following:

Equilibrium in the goods market requires that the demand for commodities equals the supply. Aggregate demand for each commodity comprises household and government consumption spending, investment spending, and export and transaction services demand. Supply includes both domestic production and imported commodities. In the CGEM, equilibrium is attained through the endogenous interaction of domestic and foreign prices, and the effect that shifts in relative prices have on sectoral production and employment, and hence institutional incomes and demand.

The model includes three broad macroeconomic accounts: the current account, the government balance, and the savings and investment account. In order to get equilibrium in the various macro accounts it is necessary to specify a set of "macro-closure" rules which provide a mechanism through which adjustment is assumed to take place.

Finally, the consumer price index is the numeraire. So, prices and the equilibrium exchange rate are defined in relation to this index.

Multisectoral models can be applied to the global economy, group of countries, a specific country and its regions, to cities, and even to villages and towns. CGEMs have been used extensively to estimate the likely effects of policy reform and other exogenous shocks: from fiscal and trade reforms to measures to reduce pollution.[8]

A world-wide CGEM comes from the Global Trade Analysis Project (GTAP), developed at the Department of Agricultural Economics of the Purdue University in the early 1990s. GTAP is a multiregion, multisector CGEM based on neoclassical economics; i.e., no market failures and/or perfect competition and constant returns to scale. The GTAP was originally designed to quantify the effects of trade reforms and has been extended to cover the impacts of other shocks such as those coming from CC. The project has provided two major contributions for the study of the global economy and its regions/countries: the design and extensions of the basic CGEM and the delivery of world-wide data to researchers to perform impact analyses. The GTAP CGEM and data link the regions of the world through their economic relations and are used to simulate external shocks (https://www.gtap.agecon.purdue.edu/about/histor y.aspx., consulted on April 4, 2022).

The study of Hertel and de Lima (2020) that estimates the effects of CC on global and regional agriculture exemplifies the contributions of the GTAP model and data to the findings on global warming and food security. The authors argue that previous research on the issue had only focused on four staple crops (maize, rice, soybeans, and wheat) and largely centered on yields (output per unit of cropped land); hence, neglecting other important food crops and primary inputs (labor and capital) other than land, and so did not consider the effects of CC on total factor productivity (TFP). Previous studies also ignore other inputs used for agricultural production that form a considerable part of its costs.[9] Using the GTAP modeling and data,

[8]Acemoglu (2010) presents convincing arguments to include CGEMs in the study of economic development, as well as economic theory and political economy.

[9]According to the authors, the four staple crops that previous literature has focused on accounts for only around one-quarter of the total value of worldwide agricultural output, and the sole focus on yields means that former studies account for only about 16% of total production costs. This means researchers have covered just 4% ($0.25 \times 0.16 \times 100\%$) of the economic value of global field crops production (*Ibid.*, p. 31).

the authors present numerical simulations showing that limited input and output coverage of the impact of increasing CO_2 concentrations in the atmosphere, higher temperatures and changing precipitation can lead to biased results of the consequences for food security and economic welfare globally and between different regions of the world.

To illustrate Hertel and de Lima (2020) findings on the relevance of considering the effects of CC on land and labor, their estimated impacts on output by region for rice and wheat are: "Estimated yield losses under global warming are concentrated in South and Southeast Asia, while Europe, Japan, South America and Australia are projected to experience higher yields under +3C warming ... This contrasts sharply with the labor impacts. While rice thrives in a warm, humid environment, the combination of heat and humidity is deadly for humans who can no longer dissipate their internally generated body heat under such conditions. Thus, the impacts of climate change on rice production through labor input are much larger than those that take place through the agronomic channels. Despite the fact that all regions of the world experience diminished labor productivity in rice production, those experiencing the more modest impacts (North America, Europe, Australia) increase rice production in order to make up for the large declines in rice output in Central America, Asia and Africa.... The differential impact of climate change on wheat vs. labor employed in cultivating wheat is quite different from rice.... Wheat has a much lower optimal agronomic temperature.

Furthermore, it is often grown in dry, cooler regions of the world. As a consequence, the labor impacts are more modest than for rice. Therefore, the wheat output impacts of a changing climate are much more dramatic in the agronomic-based scenarios. Southeast Asia and SSA are exceptions, but these are not major wheat producing regions" (*Ibid.*, pp. 27–28).

There are numerous CGEMs to estimate the likely effects of policy reforms and other shocks in agriculture at global, regional and country levels.[10] Notwithstanding the efforts made to disaggregate these CGEMs to single out major crops and the livestock sector production, technologies (e.g., type of water access), demand, trade, etc., the data required in doing so is generally not available (specially so for low and medium-income countries).[11] Furthermore and to our knowledge, these CGEMs disregard the specific features of millions of rural households that face transaction costs and/or market failures (see Chapter 3).

5.3.3 *From rural household models to local economy-wide computable general equilibrium models*

During the second half of the 1980s a systematic analysis of rural household farmers' economic behavior begun. The rural household model proposed by Singh and colleagues (Chapter 4) was used then to develop disaggregated rural economy-wide models (DREM) that capture the conditions under which certain rural households and/or small farmers make their economic decisions, as well as their linkages with the rest of the economy. As CGEM, this modeling approach is used to estimate the likely effects of exogenous shocks, but now in a rural economy in a context of high transaction costs (Taylor and Adelman, 2003, 2006; Sadoulet and de Janvry, 1995).

Rural household models and DREMs include transaction costs in output and factors of production or primary inputs (land labor and capital) markets, hence affecting production and consumption decisions of these agents. This situation forces rural household farmers to produce for their family's own consumption using family

[10]Examples are those built at the IFPRI (https://www.ifpri.org/search?query=cge) and by Sherman Robinson ((https://www.piie.com/experts/senior-research-staff/sherman-robinson and https://www.ifpri.org/profile/sherman-robinson).
[11]Table 5.1 illustrates the considerable amount of data required to build a SAM. An example is the data required to transfer value added as income of the owners of factors of production.

labor: i.e., these are non-tradables. With this approach these models consider features that characterize the rural economy of many low and medium-income countries not incorporated in CGEMs (an in agricultural policy designs), and explain why small farmers react to exogenous shocks in unexpected ways.

It is frequent that economic research on rural economies involves the microeconomic modeling of individual or agricultural households' economic behavior. This approach is partial since it misses the linkages among economic agents that indirectly integrate rural people into local, regional, domestic, and global economies. While DREMs incorporate rural household models, they also model the complex linkages among rural households within the economy, and the linkages between the rural economy and the outside world.

Whereas a household-farm model captures the behavior of a single-representative household, a DREM includes economic linkages between groups of rural households. That is, among others, the notion that a DREM considers that household farms hire labor and purchase other inputs from one another in order to carry out their various production activities, spending the income from these activities on goods and services that may be provided by other rural households. As regards simulating exogenous shocks (e.g., agricultural policy reform or global warming), the linkages identified by a DREM capture the fact that households not directly affected by the shock may be affected indirectly.

Following Taylor *et al.* (1999), we describe the differences between household-farm models and DREM by considering what these two models capture to evaluate the effects of a change in an exogenous variable Z (e.g., a rise in the price of an agricultural good that households sell in the market, or tradable), and on an endogenous variable Y (e.g., production, income of a household group, or migration). Let P_{nt} denote a vector of prices of rural non-tradables caused by high transaction costs (e.g., some staple foods and/or labor). The full impact of the change in Z on Y is given by:

$$dY/dZ = \partial Y/\partial Z + \partial Y/\partial P_{\mathrm{nt}} dP_{\mathrm{nt}}/dZ$$

The first term represents direct income effects analogous to the partial effects in a neoclassical household-farm model in which all prices are exogenous. The second term of the equation accounts for interhousehold income linkages created, for example, by factor/ land and labor) demands. So, this term represents the indirect, rural economy general-equilibrium effects of the exogenous shock through its influence on endogenous rural and household group prices. If all goods and factors are tradable at both levels (that is, all prices are exogenous), the second term vanishes. Otherwise, the second term can magnify, dampen, or even reverse the direct effects represented by the first term. Box 5.1 discusses these differences using as an example a village-rural household economy.

Box 5.1. Differences between Household-farm Models and a Disaggregated Rural Economy-wide Models

Consider an economy in which at least some household-farms produce a tradable good (e.g., staple), and suppose that the price of this crop increases. In a neoclassical household farm model, where all markets are assumed to be perfect, production of the crop will unambiguously increase (unless supply is perfectly inelastic). This raises incomes in producer households. Assuming leisure is a normal good, producers will hire workers as (perfect) substitutes for their own labor to produce the crop. Marketed surplus of the crop generally will increase, although it may be dampened by an increased consumption demand by producers whose full incomes have increased. The change in marketed surplus of the crop equals the difference between the change in production and the change in consumption by representative producer household farms.

In a neoclassical village, however, the demand for hired labor transmits part of the benefit of higher crop prices to wage labor households. If these households have a positive propensity to spend income on the crop, the village marketed surplus of the crop may decrease. Given village resource constraints (on non-tradable factors), land and labor will be withdrawn from competing sectors and channeled into staple production. This may produce adverse income effects for households that supply factors to the competing

(Continued)

Box 5.1. (*Continued*)

activities. It also may exert upward pressure on some factor prices, rewarding owners of factors in which staple production is relatively intensive.

Finally, higher incomes from staple production may drive up the price of village non-tradables, including family time and agricultural commodities for which transactions costs are high. This may encourage suppliers of the non-tradables (who may or may not be the same as the producers of the staple) to increase their production, competing with staple production for scarce village resources and dampening the staple response to the price increase. These interhousehold linkages and general-equilibrium feedbacks are outside the scope of micro household-farm models, but they can be captured in a village-wide CGE model.
Source: Taylor *et al.* (1999)

Both CGEMs and DREMs can distinguish rural households by group according, for example, to their plot size. However, one major difference is that in a DREM "subsistence" household farmers can be modeled as a group that differs from other households because they produce food for their own consumption. CGEMs ignore subsistence households by assuming that all agricultural household groups sell their production to the market.[12]

In the design of a DREM each household type producing agricultural goods can also be distinguished in terms of the technologies among each group; e.g., subsistence farmers producing food staples under rainfed conditions and and/or using ox-and-plow technology and relatively capital-intensive commercial farmers using water to irrigate their crops. A DREM also captures the fact that typically, rural households are also engaged in production activities other than

[12]In aggregate CGEMs, households receive income by selling their labor and other factors to production activities, and they spend this income on consumption goods.

agriculture and have also diversified income sources as producing bricks and selling part of their family labor to the corresponding market (Table 5.1 shows this for rural Mexico).[13]

An example of rural households grouping in a DREM is in Box 2.2. In their research (quoted in this Box), Hernández-Solano and Yúnez-Naude (2016) distinguish landless households from households owning agricultural land. The first category is formed by two household types: landless households not involved in agricultural production and households leasing land for cultivation. The second category is formed by three farming household groups according to their plot size and access to markets: subsistence households cultivating in plots with less than 2 hectares (ha); producing in plots whose size is between 2 and 5 ha, and household farmers with plots of more than 5 has subsistence households produce staples for own consumption, whereas the remaining household groups participate in agricultural goods markets.[14]

In a DREM each household group has its own production technology, expenditure demands, and access to (local, regional and international) markets. As for household-farm models, households are assumed to maximize their utility from consumption goods, both home-produced and purchased, subject to cash income, technologies, time, and self-sufficiency constraints that set consumption equal to production for subsistence households.

The difference between a household-farm model and a DREM is that in the latter individual micro models of rural household groups are "nested" into a general equilibrium model of the whole rural economy.

Based on the application of households' utility maximization, the solution of the DREM generates a set of demands for labor and land

[13]In addition, migration of some family members can be included as a household activity, receiving remittances as income. See Taylor and Dyer (2009) — the following presentation of DREMs draws from this paper.

[14]Hernández-Solano and Yúnez-Naude (2016) also distinguish crop production under rainfed from production under irrigation. This disaggregation as well as the distinction of household types resembles rural Mexico since they are based on surveys statistically representative of Mexican rural households.

Including feedbacks allow us to determine their role in controlling patch size and pattern formation at the landscape scale under different environmental conditions. The model does not consider erosion processes, nutrient dynamics, or feedback between vegetation and the atmosphere.

The model equations are as follows:

$$\partial_T B = \Psi_B B \left(1 - \frac{B}{K}\right) - MB + D_B \nabla^2 B$$

$$\partial_T W = \Omega H - \Phi W - \Psi_W W + D_W \nabla^2 W$$

$$\partial_T H = P - \Omega H + D_H \nabla^2 H^2$$

where $B(\boldsymbol{X}, T)$ represents the biomass per unit area; $W(\boldsymbol{X}, T)$ describes the water content of the soil per unit area; and $H(\boldsymbol{X}, T)$ is the height of a thin layer of water above the soil ground. Here, $\boldsymbol{X} = (X, Y)$ are the spatial coordinates, T is the time, and $\nabla^2 = \partial_X^2 + \partial_Y^2$ is the Laplacian operator.[18] In this case, we focus on the quantities and terms that are most relevant in this type of modeling.

We first note that the biomass growth rate, Ψ_B; the water absorption (transpiration) rate, Ψ_W; the infiltration rate, Ω; and the evaporation rate, Φ, are all functions of dynamic variables that model various feedbacks. Two types of feedback, which we refer to as infiltration and root enhancement, are particularly relevant. Both are positive in the sense that they accelerate the growth of local biomass and involve water transport processes that induce long-term competition.

The most relevant parameters are the precipitation rate, P, which serves as a control parameter; the soil-water diffusion coefficient, D_W; and the surface water transport coefficient, D_H, which is inversely related to the soil-surface friction coefficient. Other parameters include the local seed dispersal coefficient, D_B; the maximum biomass, K; and the biomass decomposition rate, M.

Infiltration feedback is associated with higher rates of surface water infiltration into vegetated soil relative to bare soil. Physical or

[18]For a more detailed version of this model, see Gilad *et al.* (2007).

biogenic crusts in arid areas can significantly reduce the infiltration rate into bare soil, increasing the flow of surface water into patches of vegetation (von Hardenberg *et al.*, 2010). This process favors the growth of newly formed patches of vegetation (short-range facilitation), but reduces the availability of water resources over greater distances, introducing competition between different patches (long-range competition).

The feedback is captured by a monotonically increasing dependence of the infiltration rate on the aboveground biomass, $\Omega = A(B+Qf)/(B+Q)$ (Gilad *et al.*, 2007). This dependency is controlled by a parameter $0 \leq f \leq 1$ that quantifies the infiltration contrast between the soil with and without vegetation. When $f = 1$, the infiltration rate becomes independent of biomass, $\Omega = A$, and there is no infiltration contrast. When $f < 1$, the infiltration rate is very low in unvegetated soil ($\Omega = fA$) but increases to $\Omega \approx A$ in vegetated patches.

The feedback in root growth is positive between the aboveground biomass and the belowground root system. As plants grow, their root systems increase in size and explore new regions of the soil. This expansion increases the amount of water available to plants and speeds up their growth. As in the case of infiltration feedback, the accelerated growth of a patch of vegetation occurs at the expense of the growth of vegetation in its vicinity, which introduces long-range competition.

The feedback is modeled by the following non-local biomass growth rate and water absorption rate equations:

$$\Psi_B(\boldsymbol{X},T) = \Lambda \int G(\boldsymbol{X},\boldsymbol{X}',T)W(\boldsymbol{X}',T)d\boldsymbol{X}'$$

$$\Psi_W(\boldsymbol{X},T) = \Gamma \int G(\boldsymbol{X}',\boldsymbol{X},T)B(\boldsymbol{X}',T)dX'$$

where the kernel $G(\boldsymbol{X},\boldsymbol{X}',T) \propto \exp\{-|\boldsymbol{X} - \boldsymbol{X}'|^2/[2(\boldsymbol{X})^2]\}$ represents the spatial extent of the root system. The root increase is captured by assuming a monotonically increasing dependence on the Gaussian width S of the aboveground biomass. Specifically, $S(\boldsymbol{X}) = S_0[1 + EB(\boldsymbol{X})]$, where S_0 represents the root size of a seedling, and the parameter E provides a measure for root-to-shoot allocation; the larger E is the more the roots spread per given aerial biomass. The long-range competition that feedback induces is explained by the form of Ψ_W; plants at $\boldsymbol{X}'$ deplete the water content of the soil at $\boldsymbol{X}$ if their roots extend that far.

Less important is the positive feedback between biomass and water due to shade and reduced evaporation, which is modeled as $\Phi = N/(1 + \frac{RB}{K})$ (Gilad *et al.*, 2007). This feedback does not involve water transport and therefore does not induce long-range competition as do infiltration and root augmentation feedbacks.

This basic model has been successfully applied to a wide range of self-organization problems in the context of water-limited vegetation. Such applications include vegetation patterns and pattern transitions along environmental strain gradients (Gilad *et al.*, 2007), trade-offs between productivity and resilience in vegetation on hill slopes (Yizhaq *et al.*, 2005), mechanisms of vegetation-ring formation (Sheffer *et al.*, 2007), plants as ecosystems (Meron *et al.*, 2007), and effects of stochastic rainfall on vegetation production and ground cover (Kletter *et al.*, 2009), among others.

An extension of the eco-physical models are the so-called "socioecological models." A socioecological model analyzes the environmental factors that impact a population's characteristics (Crook and Gartlan, 1966). According to Koenig *et al.* (2013), socioecological models can have the structure depicted in Figure 5.6.

We present a model developed by Figueiredo and Pereira (2011), to identify balances of rural migration, the abandonment of farmland, and the regeneration/eradication of forests.

(a) Ecological Model: The ecological model has one state variable: the forested area, F. We assume that the total potential arable area is a constant T, and therefore the agricultural area A is equal to $T - F$. The forest system is subject to two processes of interest: growth and deforestation. We assume that the forest cover grows logistically since after an initial exponential increase, the growth will be limited by the total area available; ε is the forest growth rate, and T is the maximum area available. We also assume that deforestation depends on each resident's ability to deforest (remove

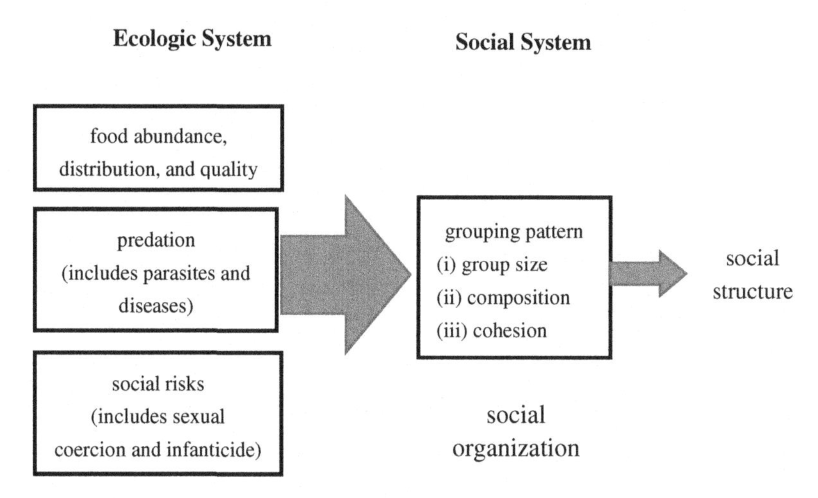

Figure 5.6. Ecologic and Social Systems
Source: By authors based on Koenig *et al.* (2013).

vegetation for agricultural purposes), λ; the number of residents is R; and the existing forest area, F; that is, residents tend to deforest more if there is a larger area available for deforestation. Therefore, the forest dynamics are given by:

$$\frac{dF}{dt} = \varepsilon F\left(1 - \frac{F}{T}\right) - \lambda RF$$

Balance and Stability Analysis: The last equation has two equilibria, $\hat{F} = 0$ y $\hat{F} = \frac{T}{\varepsilon}(\varepsilon - R\lambda)$. Stability analysis reveals that if $> \varepsilon$, $\hat{F} = 0$ is a stable equilibrium (and the other equilibrium is unstable); that is, when the deforestation rate exceeds the forest growth rate, the forest disappears. If $R\lambda < \varepsilon$, $\hat{F} = \frac{T}{\varepsilon}(\varepsilon - R\lambda)$ is the stable equilibrium (and the other equilibrium becomes unstable), when the intrinsic rate of forest growth exceeds the rate of deforestation, the area of equilibrium forest increases with the rate of forest growth, ε, and decreases with increased deforestation capacity of residents, λ, or with an increasing number of residents.

(b) Social Model: The social model has one state variable: the number of migrants, M. We assume that the size of the population is a constant, P, and therefore the number of residents, R, is equal to $P - M$. Individuals migrate at a rate:

$$\frac{dM}{dt} = f\left(\frac{M}{P}\right)$$

where f is the function that describes how the migration rate depends on the proportion of individuals who have already migrated, M/P. This reflects that migration is a collective behavior and the decision of an individual is frequently affected by the decision of others (Fischbacher *et al.*, 2001). Furthermore, in a population, every person has a certain threshold, and only when this threshold is reached will individuals change their decision and choose the other alternative.

Therefore, we assume that at a given moment, the probability of an individual migrating depends on the proportion of individuals in the population who have already migrated M/P; that is, an individual will migrate only if the proportion of migrants equals or exceeds a threshold. In this case, the thresholds are assumed to have a bell-shaped distribution and to follow a logistic distribution.

In other words, everyone has a probability per unit of time, w, of making the decision to migrate. The proportion of individuals who will decide to migrate will be the proportion that has a threshold lower than M/P, which is given by the function of cumulative distribution of the logistic distribution, minus the proportion of individuals in the population who have already migrated. Therefore, the number of individuals who migrate is equal to this proportion multiplied by the size of the population, P. That is:

$$f\left(\frac{M}{P}\right) = w * \left[CDF\left(\frac{M}{P}\right) - \frac{M}{P}\right] * P$$

where

$$CDF\left(\frac{M}{P}\right) = \frac{1}{1 + e^{\frac{(\mu - \frac{M}{P})}{s}}}$$

The dynamics of the number of migrants are:

$$\frac{dM}{dt} = w\left[\frac{1}{1+e^{\frac{(\mu-\frac{M}{P})}{s}}} - \frac{M}{P}\right]P$$

The parameters of the logistic distribution μ and s determine the probability of migration. The parameter μ represents the average threshold in the population, that is, the average proportion of migrants who cause the others to migrate. In addition, an economic sub-model was developed to determine this parameter and link it to the ecological component of the system. The parameter s is proportional to the variance of the thresholds in the population and will therefore be used to characterize the strength of personal connections (social ties that lead to higher levels of conformity) in the population. In other words, a smaller s represents a population where individuals have similar thresholds, and therefore a greater migration synchronism.

Balance and Stability Analysis: Depending on the combination of μ and s the number of migrants can have different equilibria. For high values of s (that is, individuals in the population who have different thresholds), the number of migrants in equilibrium, $\hat{M}$, decreases with increasing μ. For small values of s (that is, individuals with similar thresholds), the social system may have one of three equilibria: (i) when μ is small, there is a stable equilibrium, $\hat{M} \approx P$, and all or most of the individuals will abandon farmland; (ii) when μ is high, there is a stable equilibrium, $\hat{M} \approx 0$ that will cause all or most migrants to return to farmland; (iii) when μ has an intermediate value, there are three equilibria, one of the equilibria is unstable and the other two are stable ($\hat{M} \approx 0 \, \mathrm{y} \hat{M} \approx P$). In the last case, the social dynamic is partially irreversible because there is a hysteresis. For example, a population of 100 individuals with a similar threshold (small s corresponding to high social bonding, e.g., $s = 0.1$) will initiate a migration process if the mean threshold μ is less than 0.3; however, for these individuals to return, it would be insufficient to increase μ to 0.3 since μ would need to be increased to 0.7.

Economics of Migration: Migration has its roots in socioeconomic conditions (Gellrich and Zimmermann, 2007). Therefore, we shall use μ (average threshold in the population) to characterize the socioeconomic dynamics. We assume the utility of agricultural land as Ah; that is, the satisfaction that an individual derives from being a farmer, including income and other non-financial benefits, the product of the area of agricultural land, A, and the profit per unit of agricultural area per year, h. The utility of agricultural land per resident is defined as $Ah/(P-M)$, where P is the total population.

We define the utility per capita of the city as δ. When the utility of agricultural land is equal to the utility of the city, the economic reasons for migrating are irrelevant; in this case, the reasons for migrating would be strictly social and motivated by social bonding. In other words, we assume that individuals migrate only if more than half of the population has already done so.

Therefore, when $\frac{Ah}{P-M} = \delta$, the mean threshold must be $\mu = 0.5$ and the mean threshold in the population is:

$$\mu = \frac{\frac{Ah}{P-M}}{2}\delta$$

The final equation of the social model that represents the dynamics of migrants is the following:

$$\frac{dM}{dt} = w * \left[\frac{P}{1 + e^{\frac{\left(\frac{\frac{Ah}{P-M}}{2\delta} - \frac{M}{P}\right)}{s}}} - M \right]$$

(c) Socioecological Model: The equations of the socioecological model for the agricultural/forest ecosystem results from the combination of the equations of the ecological and social models. Given that the number of residents R used in the ecological model is equal to $P - M$, and the area under cultivation, A, is given by $T - F$, the equations of the socioecological model are as follows:

$$\frac{dF}{dt} = \varepsilon F\left(1 - \frac{F}{T}\right) - \lambda(P - M)F$$

$$\frac{dM}{dt} = w * \left[\frac{P}{1 + e^{\frac{\left(\frac{\frac{(T-F)h}{P-M}}{2\delta} - \frac{M}{P}\right)}{s}}} - M \right]$$

In this socioecological model the number of residents, R, from the ecological model equation and the area of farmland, A (or $T - F$), from the social equation are state variables rather than parameters. The two variables can now change over time and affect both social and ecological dynamics, creating a reciprocal influence between ecological and social systems.

Balance and Stability Analysis: The equilibria of the socioecological model can be determined by plotting the zero isoclines of the ecological and social models on the same graph. The intersection points of the zero isoclines of the social and ecological models represent the equilibria of the socioecological model. The stability of these equilibria is determined by the sum of the vectors of change in the social and ecological models. For example, if the sum of the vectors points to equilibrium, the model will be stable; if the vectors point in opposite directions, the balance will be unstable. For a given combination of parameters, the socioecological model can have from one to four equilibria. Both the number and the position of the equilibria vary with the parameters.

The socioecological model has five types of stable equilibria:

(1) $\mathrm{M}^\wedge \approx \mathrm{P\,y\,F}^\wedge \approx T$; that is, all individuals migrate, and the forest area grows to occupy the entire area previously occupied by farmland (a situation with high urban utility and a medium-high forest growth rate).
(2) $\hat{M} \approx 0$ y $\hat{F} \approx 0$; that is, individuals do not migrate, and the entire area is cultivated, and the forest is decimated (a situation with high social bonding, a slow rate of forest growth, and low utility of the city).
(3) $\hat{M} \approx 0 \mathrm{y} \hat{F} = \frac{T}{\varepsilon}(\varepsilon - P\lambda)$; that is, individuals do not migrate and do not have the capacity to deforest the entire cultivable area, leaving an area to be occupied by forests (a situation with high social bonding, a high forest growth rate, and low utility of the city).
(4) $\hat{M} \in]\,0, 100\,[y\ \hat{F} \approx 0$; that is, part of the population migrates, and the entire cultivable area is occupied by agricultural activities (situations of low social bonding and a low rate of forest growth).

(5) $\hat{M} \in]0, 100[$ y $\hat{F} \in]0, 100[$; that is, part of the population migrates, and part of the cultivable area is occupied by forests (a situation with low social ties, low city utility, and average forest growth rate).

Lastly, the system can show an intermediate stable equilibrium where only part of the population migrates and the arable area is divided into farmland and forest, as well as extreme cases (no migration or mass migration in the social system and a decrease in the population) or the complete regeneration of the forest in the ecological system.

The above situations are examples of the relevance of this kind of model to analyze the impacts of CC on the primary sector of the economy, which is highly sensitive to changes in temperature patterns and water cycles. At a cultural level, changes are seen in the types of production and consumption, as well as in employment and local income. Other studies that show these effects can be consulted in Tubiello and Fischer (2007), Fischer *et al.* (2005), and Kirchner *et al.* (2015). In short, eco-physical and socioecological models are fundamental to understanding the natural and cultural interrelationships that shape a systemic view of reality. In this sense, policymakers can benefit from scientific evidence and implement corrective measures for CC in national development processes.

5.5 Summary

By presenting the evolution and state-of-the-arts in empirical inquires on the effects of CC and other shocks on migration, agricultural production and incomes, this chapter shows the progress in modeling economic agents' behavior to measure the likely socioeconomic impacts of global warming and state policies. However, much more academic research is still needed to fully understand the complexities of these phenomena. And this effort has to be accompanied with data gathering.

These pending tasks are reflected in the following chapters which discuss why the commitments of countries under the United Nations conventions on CC have not been fully addressed (Chapter 6), as well as issues related to valuation of priceless resources, institutions, democracy, and governance (Chapter 7).

References

Acemoglu, D. (2010). Theory, general equilibrium, political economy and empirics in development economics. *Journal of Economic Perspectives*, *24*(3), 17–32. https://doi.org/10.1257/jep.24.3.17.

Adelman, I. and Taylor, J. (1991). Multisectoral models and structural adjustment: New evidence from Mexico. *Journal of Development Studies*, *28*(1), 154–163. https://doi.org/10.1080/00220389108422228.

Ajetomobi, J., Abiodun, A., and Hassan, R. (2011). Impacts of climate change on rice agriculture in Nigeria. *Tropical and Subtropical Agroecosystems*, *14*(2), 613–622. https://www.revista.ccba.uady.mx/ojs/index.php/TSA/article/view/689.

Antwi-Agyei, P. and Nyantakyi-Frimpong, H. (2021). Evidence of climate change coping and adaptation practices by smallholder farmers in Northern Ghana. *Sustainability*, *13*(3), 1308. https://www.mdpi.com/2071-1050/13/3/1308.

Arango, J. (2000). Explaining migration: A critical view. *International Social Science Journal*, *52*(165), 283–296. https://doi.org/10.1111/1468-2451.00259.

Arango, J. (2003). La explicación teórica de las migraciones: Luz y sombra. *Migración y Desarrollo*, (1), 1–31. http://www.redalyc.org/articulo.oa?id=66000102.

Aroca, P. (2004). Migración interregional en Chile. Modelos y resultados 1987–2002. *Notas de Población*, *21*(78), 97–154. https://repositorio.cepal.org/handle/11362/12762?show=full.

Atuoye, K. N., Antabe, R., Sano, Y., Luginaah, I., and Bayne, J. (2019). Household income diversification and food insecurity in the Upper West Region of Ghana. *Social Indicators Research*, *144*(2), 899–920. https://doi.org/10.1007/s11205-019-02062-7.

Beine, M. and Parsons, C. (2015). Climatic factors as determinants of international migration. *The Scandinavian Journal of Economics*, *117*(2), 723–767. https://doi.org/10.1111/sjoe.12098.

Brewer, D. T., Flynn, A., Skewes, T. D., Corfield, J., Pearson, B., Alowa, J., and Young, J. W. (2007). *Ecosystems of the East Marine Planning Region. Report to Department of Environment and Water Resources.* CSIRO. https://parksaustralia.gov.au/marine/pub/scientific-publications/archive/ecosystems.pdf.

Bucheli, J. R., Fontenla, M., and Waddell, B. J. (2019). Return migration and violence. *World Development*, *116*, 113–124. https://doi.org/10.1016/j.worlddev.2018.12.010.

Choksi, P., Singh, D., Singh, J., Mondal, P., Nagendra, H., Urpelainen, J., and DeFries, R. (2021). Sensitivity of seasonal migration to climatic variability in central India. *Environmental Research Letters, 16*(6), 064074. https://doi.org/10.1088/1748-9326/ac046f.

Cohen, J. H. and Sirkeci, I. (2011). *Cultures of Migration: The Global Nature of Contemporary Mobility.* University of Texas Press, Texas, USA.

Coulson, R. N., Birt, A., and Tchakerian, M. D. (2014). Landscapes forest landscape management in response to change: The practicality. In J. C. Azevedo, A. H. Perera, and M. A. Pinto (eds.), *Forest and Global Change. Challenges for Research and Management* (pp. 227–248). Springer. https:// doi.org/10.1007/978-1-4939-0953-7.

Crook, J. H. and Gartlan, J. S. (1966). Evolution of Primate Societies. *Nature, 210*, 1200–1203. https://doi.org/10.1038/2101200a0.

Cruz, J. L. (2021). *Global Warming and Labor Market Reallocation.* International Trade Seminar. Princeton University. https://ies.princeton.edu/events/jose-luis-cruz-alvarez-3/.

De Haas, H. (2011). *The Determinants of International Migration: Conceptualizing Policy, Origin and Destination Effects.* Working Paper 32. Oxford: International Migration Institute.

Dinar, A., Mendelsohn, R., Evenson, R., Parikh, J., Sanghi, A., McKinsey, J., and Lonergen, S. (1998). *Measuring the Impact of Climate Change on Indian Agriculture.* World Bank Group. http://documents.worldbank.org/curated/en/793381468756570727/Measuring-the-impact-of-climate-change-on-Indian-agriculture.

Deheza, E. and Mora, J. (2013). *Climate Change Migration and Security: Best-practice Policy and Operational Options for Mexico* (Whitehall Report, pp. 1–13). London: The Royal United Services Institute for Defense and Security Studies. London, UK.

Entwisle, B., Verdery, A., and Williams, N. (2020). Climate change migration: New insights from a dynamic model of out-migration and return migration. *American Journal of Sociology, 125*(6), 1469–1512. https://doi.org/10.1086/ 709463.

Falco, C., Galeotti, M., and Olper, A. (2019). Climate change and migration: Is agriculture the main channel? *Global Environmental Change, 59*, 101995. https://doi.org/10.1016/j.gloenvcha.2019.101995.

Figueiredo, J. and Pereira, H. M. (2011). Regime shifts in a socio-ecological model of farmland abandonment. *Landscape Ecology, 26*, 737–749. https://doi.org/10.1007/s10980-011-9605-3.

Fischbacher U., Gachter S., and Fehr, E. (2001). Are people conditionally cooperative? Evidence from a public goods experiment. *Economic Letters, 71*, 397–404. https://doi.org/10.1016/S0165-1765(01)00394-9.

Fischer, G., Shah, M., Tubiello, F. N., and van Velhuizen, H. (2005). Socio-economic and climate change impacts on agriculture: An integrated assessment, 1990–2080. *Philosophical Transactions of The Royal Society B, Biological Sciences. 360*(1463), 2067–2083. https://doi.org/10.1098/rstb.2005.1744.

Garip, F. and Asad, A. L. (2016). Network effects in Mexico–U.S. migration: Disentangling the underlying social mechanisms. *American Behavioral Scientist*, *60*(10), 1168–1193. https://doi.org/10.1177/0002764216643131.

Gellrich, M. and Zimmermann, N. E. (2007). Investigating the regional-scale pattern of agricultural land abandonment in the Swiss mountains: A spatial statistical modelling approach. *Landscape and Urban Planning*, 79, 65–76. https://doi.org/10.1016/j.landurbplan.2006.03.004.

Giannelli, G. C. and Canessa, E. (2021). After the flood: Migration and remittances as coping strategies of rural Bangladeshi households. *Economic Development and Cultural Change*, *70*(3), 1159–1195. https://doi.org/10.1086/713939.

Gilad, E., Hardenberg, J. V., Provenzale, A., Shachak, M., and Meron, E. (2007). A mathematical model for plants as ecosystem engineers. *Journal of Theoretical Biology*, *244*(4), 680–691. https://doi.org/10.1016/j.jtbi.2006.08.006.

Guarnizo, L. E. (2003). The economics of transnational living. *International Migration Review*, *37*(3), 666–699. https://doi.org/10.1111/j.1747-7379.2003.tb00154.x.

Guilmoto, C. and Sandron, F. (2001). The internal dynamics of migration networks in developing countries. *Population: An English Selection*, *13*(2), 135–164.

Hagan J. M. and Wassink, J. T. (2020). Return migration around the world: An integrated agenda for future research. *Annual Review of Sociology*, *46*, 533–552. https://doi.org/10.1146/annurev-soc-120319-015855.

Harris, J. R. and Todaro, M. P. (1970). Migration, unemployment and development: A two-sector analysis. *The American Economic Review*, *60*(1), 126–142. https://www.jstor.org/stable/1807860.

Hulme, M. (2011). Reducing the future to climate: A story of climate determinism and reductionism. *Osiris*, *26*(1), 245–266. https://doi.org/10.1086/661274.

Hernández-Solano, A., López-López, J., Yúnez-Naude, A., and Govea-Vargas, Y. (2022). Socioeconomic effects of COVID-19 in Mexico: A multisectoral approach and policy options. *Latin American Economic Review*, *31*(1), 1–20. http://mobile.repositorio-digital.cide.edu/handle/11651/4786.

Hernández-Solano, A. and Yúnez-Naude, A. (2016). *Impactos Del Cambio Climático En La Economía Rural De México: Un Enfoque De Equilibrio General.* El Colegio de México, Centro de Estudios Económicos. https://ideas.repec.org/p/emx/ceedoc/2016-06.html.

Hertel Thomas W. and de Lima, C. Z. (2020). Climate Impacts on Agriculture: Searching for Keys under the Streetlight. *GTAP Research Memorandum* No. 86, April 2020.

Hunter, L., Murray, S., and Riosmena, F. (2013). Rainfall patterns and U.S. migration from rural Mexico. *International Migration Review*, *47*(4), 874–909. https://doi.org/10.1111/imre.12051.

Hunter, L. M., Luna, K. J., and Norton, R. M. (2015). Environmental dimensions of migration. *Annual Review of Sociology*, *41*(1), 377–397. https://www.annualreviews.org/doi/10.1146/annurev-soc-073014-112223.

Hunter, L. M. and Simon, D. H. (2022). Time to mainstream the environment into migration theory? *International Migration Review*. https://doi.org/10.1177/01979183221074343.

Ibáñez, A. M., Romero, J., and Velásquez, A. (2021). Temperature shocks, labor markets and migratory decisions in El Salvador. *IDB migration seminar*. Working paper. https://conference.iza.org/conference_files/ClimateChange_2021/velasquez_a26669.pdf.

Intergovernmental Panel Climate Change (IPCC). (2007). Informe de síntesis. Contribución de los grupos de trabajo I, II y III al cuarto informe de evaluación del grupo intergubernamental de expertos sobre el cambio climático. Equipo de redacción principal: Pachauri, R.K. y Reisinger, A. (directores de la publicación). IPCC. https://www.ipcc.ch/site/assets/uploads/2018/02/ar4_syr_sp.pdf.

Jawid, A. (2020). A Ricardian analysis of the economic impact of climatic change on agriculture: Evidence from the farms in the central highlands of Afghanistan. *Journal of Asian Economics*, *67*, 101177. https://doi.org/10.1016/j.asieco.2020.101177.

Kandel, W. and Massey, D. S. (2002). The culture of Mexican migration: A theoretical and empirical analysis. *Social Forces*, *80*(3), 981–1004. https://doi.org/10.1353/sof.2002.0009.

Kassahun, A., Snyman, H. A., and Smit, G. N. (2008). Impact of rangeland degradation on the pastoral production systems, livelihoods and perceptions of the Somali pastoralists in Eastern Ethiopia. *Journal of Arid Environments*, *72*(7), 1265–1281. https://doi.org/10.1016/j.jaridenv.2008.01.002.

Kirchner, M., Schmidt, J., Kindermann, G., Kulmer, V., Mitter, H., Prettenthaler, F., Rüdisser, J., Schauppenlehner, T., Schönhart, M., Strauss, F., Tappeiner, U., Tasser, E., and Schmid, E. (2015). Ecosystem services and economic development in Austrian agricultural landscapes — The impact of policy and climate change scenarios on trade-offs and synergies. *Ecological Economics*, *109*, 161–174. http://dx.doi.org/10.1016/j.ecolecon.2014.11.005.

Kletter, A., Hardenberg, J. von, Meron, E., and Provenzale, A. (2009). Patterned vegetation and rainfall intermittency. *Journal of Theoretical Biology*, *256*(4), 574–583. https://hal.archives-ouvertes.fr/hal-00554522/document.

Koenig, A., Scarry, C. J., Wheeler, B. C., and Borries, C. (2013). Variation in grouping patterns, mating systems and social structure: What socioecological models attempt to explain. *Philosophical Transactions of the Royal Society B*, 368. http://dx.doi. org/10.1098/rstb.2012.0348.

Kuriakose, A. T., Heltberg, R., Wiseman, W., Costella, C., Cipryk, R., and Cornelius S. (2013). Climate-responsive social protection. *Development Policy Review*, *31*(2), o19–o34. https://doi.org/10.1111/dpr.12037.

Lemke, J. L. (1993). Discourse, dynamics, and social change. *Cultural Dynamics*, *6*(1–2), 243–275. https://doi.org/10.1177/092137409300600107.

Levy, S. and van Wijnbergen, S. (1994). Labor markets, migration and welfare: Agriculture in the North-American Free Trade Agreement. *Journal of*

Development Economics, 43(2), 263–278. https://doi.org/10.1016/0304-3878(94)90007-8.

Lewis, A. (1954). Economic development with unlimited supplies of labor. *The Manchester School of Economic and Social Studies, 22*(2), 139–191. https://doi.org/10.1111/j.1467-9957.1954.tb00021.x.

Littell, J. S., McKenzie, D., Kerns, B. C., Cushman, S., and Shaw, C. G. (2011). Managing uncertainty in climate driven ecological models to inform adaptation to climate change. *Ecosphere, 2*(9), 102. https://doi.org/10.1890/ES11-00114.1.

Lippert, C., Krimly, T., and Aurbacher, J. (2009). A Ricardian analysis of the impact of climate change on agriculture in Germany. *Climatic Change, 97*(3), 593. https://doi.org/10.1007/s10584-009-9652-9.

Liu, H., Li, X., Fischer, G., and Sun, L. (2004). Study on the impact of climate change on China's agriculture. *Climatic Change, 65*, 125–148. https://doi.org/10.1023/B:CLIM.0000037490.17099.97.

Lofgren, H., Lee Harris, R., and Robinson, S. (2002). *A Standard Computable General Equilibrium (CGE) Model in GAMS*. International Food Policy Research Institute. Washington, D.C, USA.

López-López, J. and Yúnez-Naude, A. (2019). *Hacia la incorporación de los recursos naturales de México en estudios multisectoriales*. El Colegio de México, Centro de Estudios Económicos. https://cee.colmex.mx/documentos-de-trabajo/2019.

Loschmann, C. and Marchand, K. (2021). The labor market reintegration of returned refugees in Afghanistan. *Small Business Economics, 56*(1), 1033–1045. https://link.springer.com/article/10.1007/s11187-019-0 0315-w.

Luck, G. W., Daily, G. C., and Ehrlich, P. R. (2003). Population diversity and ecosystem services. *Trends in Ecology & Evolution, 18*(7), 331–336. https://doi.org/10.1016/S0169-5347(03)00100-9.

McKenzie, D. and Rapoport, H. (2010). Self-selection patterns in Mexico–U.S. migration: The role of migration networks. *The Review of Economics and Statistics, 92*(4), 811–821. https://doi.org/10.1162/REST_a_00032.

Martin, S. A. and Assenov, I. (2015). Measuring the conservation aptitude of surf beaches in Phuket, Thailand: An application of the surf resource sustainability index. *International Journal of Tourism Research, 17*(2), 105–117. https://doi.org/10.1002/jtr.1961.

Massey, D. (1990). Social structure, household strategies and the cumulative causation of migration. *Population Index, 56*(1), 3–26. https://doi.org/10.2307/3644186.

Massey, D. (2015). A missing element in migration theories. *Migration Letters, 12*(3), 279–299.

Massey, D., Alarcón, R., Durand, J., and González, H. (1987). *Return to Aztlan: The Social Process of International Migration from Western Mexico*. University of California Press.

Massey, D., Arango, J., Graeme, H., Kouaouci, A., Pellegrino, A., and Taylor, E. (1993). Theories of international migration: A review and appraisal. *Population and Development Review, 19*(3), 431–466. https://www.jstor.org/stable/2938462.

Mendelsohn, R. (2009). The impact of climate change on agriculture in developing countries. *Journal of Natural Resources Policy Research, 1*(1), 5–19. https://doi.org/10.1080/19390450802495882.

Mendelsohn, R. and Dinar, A. (2009). *Climate Change and Agriculture: An Economic Analysis of Global Impacts, Adaptation and Distributional Effects.* World Bank. https://doi.org/10.4337/9781849802239.

Mendelsohn, R., Arellano-Gonzalez, J., and Christensen, P. (2009). A Ricardian analysis of Mexican farms. *Environment and Development Economics, 15*(2), 153–171. https://doi.org/10.1017/S1355770X09990143.

Mendelsohn, R., Dinar, A., and Sanghi, A. (2001). The effect of development on the climate sensitivity of agriculture. *Environment and Development Economics, 6*(1), 85–101. https://doi.org/10.1017/S1355770X01000055.

Mendelsohn, R., Nordhaus, W., and Shaw, D. (1994). The impact of global warming on agriculture: A Ricardian analysis. *The American Economic Review, 84*(4), 753–771. http://www.jstor.org/stable/2118029.

Mendes-Delazeri, L. M., Da Cunha, D. A., and Oliveira, L. R. (2022). Climate change and rural–urban migration in the Brazilian Northeast region. *GeoJournal, 87*, 1–21. https://doi.org/10.1007/s10708-020-10349-3.

Meron, E., Yizhaq, H., and Gilad, E. (2007). Localized structures in dryland vegetation: Forms and functions. *Chaos: An Interdisciplinary Journal of Nonlinear Science, 17*(3), 037109. https://doi.org/10.1063/1.2767246.

Meyer, W. B. and Guss, D. M. (2017). *Neo-environmental Determinism. In Neo-Environmental Determinism* (pp. 39–96). Palgrave Macmillan. https://doi.org/10.1007/978-3-319-54232-4_5.

Mora, J., Ordaz, J., Ramírez, Acosta, A., Serna Hidalgo, B., and Ramírez, D. (2010). Panamá: Efectos del cambio climático sobre la agricultura. *Sede Subregional de la CEPAL en México.* LC/MEX/L.971. http://hdl.handle.net/11362/25926.

Mueller, V., Sheriff, G., Dou, X., and Gray, C. (2020). Temporary migration and climate variation in eastern Africa. *World Development, 126*, 104704. https://doi.org/10.1016/j.worlddev.2019.104704.

Murray-Tortarolo, G. N. and Martínez-Salgado, M. (2021). Drought as a driver of Mexico–US migration. *Climate Change, 164*(48), 1–11. https://doi.org/10.1007/s10584-021-03030-2.

Myrdal, G. (1957). *Rich Lands and Poor. The Road to World Prosperity.* Harper and Row. New York, NY, USA.

Nassauer, J. I. (1995). Messy ecosystems, orderly frames. *Landscape Journal, 14*(2), 161–170. http://www.jstor.org/stable/43324192.

Opdam, P., Verboom, J., and Pouwels, P. (2003). Landscape cohesion: An index for the conservation potential of landscapes for biodiversity. *Landscape Ecology, 18*(2), 113–126. https://doi.org/10.1023/A:1024429715253.

Padilla, E. and Serrano, A. (2006). Inequality in CO2 emissions across countries and its relationship with income inequality: A distributive approach. *Energy Policy, 34*(14), 1762–1772. https://doi.org/10.1016/j.enpol.2004.12.014.

Piore, M. (1979). *Birds of Passage: Migrant Labor and Industrial Societies.* Cambridge University Press. https://doi.org/10.1017/CBO9780511572210.

Portes, A. and DeWind, J. (2007). *Rethinking Migration: New Theoretical and Empirical Perspectives.* Berghahn Books. New York, NY, USA.

Portes, A. and Martinez, B. P. (2019). They are not all the same: Immigrant enterprises, transnationalism, and development. *Journal of Ethnic Migration Studies, 46*(10), 1991–2007. https://doi.org/10.1080/1369183X.2018.1559995.

Portes, A., Guarnizo, L. E., and Landolt, P. (1999). The study of transnationalism: Pitfalls and promise of an emergent research field. *Ethnic and Racial Studies, 22*(2), 217–237. https://doi.org/10.1080/014198799329468.

Pyatt, G. and Round, J. I. (1979). Accounting and fixed price multipliers in a social accounting matrix framework. *The Economic Journal, 89*(356), 850–873. https://doi.org/10.2307/2231503.

Rahnama, M. R. and Lyth, A. (2005). Accessibility and urban environment sustainability in Sydney (1991–2001). *WIT Transactions on Biomedicine and Health, 9*, 471–480. https://www.witpress.com/Secure/elibrary/papers/EHR05/EHR05047FU.pdf.

Ranis, G. and Fei, J. (1961). A theory of economic development. *The American Economic Review, 51*(4), 533–565. https://www.jstor.org/stable/1812785.

Ravenstein, E. G. (1885). The laws of migration. *Journal of the Statistical Society of London, 48*(2), 167–227. https://doi.org/10.2307/2979181.

Riosmena, F., Nawrotzki, R., and Hunter, L. (2018). Climate migration at the height and end of the great Mexican emigration era. *Population and Development Review, 44*(3), 455–488. https://doi.org/10.1111/padr.12158.

Robinson, S. (1989). Multisectoral models. In H. Chenery and T. N. Srinivasan (eds.), *Handbook of Development Economics* (pp. 885–947). Elsevier Science Publishing. https://doi.org/10.1016/S1573-4471(89)02005-X.

Robinson, S., Burfisher, M. E., Hinojosa-Ojeda, R., and Thierfelder, K. E. (1993). Agricultural policies and migration in a U.S.–Mexico free trade area: A computable general equilibrium analysis. *Journal of Policy Modeling, 15*(5–6), 673–701. https://doi.org/10.1016/0161-8938(93)90009-F.

Round, J. (2003). Social accounting matrices and SAM-based multiplier analysis. In F. Bourguignon and L. A. P. da Silva (eds.), *Techniques and Tools for Evaluating the Poverty Impact of Economic Policies* (pp. 301–324). World Bank and Oxford University Press. http://dx.doi.org/10.2499/9780896297838fsp5.

Sadoulet, E. and De Janvry, A. (1995). *Quantitative Development Policy Analysis.* Johns Hopkins University Press, Baltimore, USA.

Seneviratne, S. I., Nicholls, N., Easterling, D., Goodess, C. M., Kanae, S., Kossin, J., Luo, Y., Marengo, J., Mclnnes, K., Reichstein, M.,

Sorteberg, A., Vera, C., and Zhang, X. (2012). Changes in climate extremes and their impacts on the natural physical environment. In C. B. Field, V. Barros, T. F. Stocker, D. Qin, D. J. Dokken, K. L. Ebi, M. D. Mastrandrea (eds.), *Managing the Risks of Extreme Events and Disasters to Advance Climate Change Adaptation: A Special Report of Working Groups I and II of the Intergovernmental Panel on Climate Change (IPCC)* (pp. 109–230). Cambridge University Press, New York, NY, USA.

Seo, S. N. and Mendelsohn, R. (2007). A Ricardian analysis of the impact of climate change on South American farms. *Chilean Journal of Agricultural Research, 68* (1), 69–79. https://doi.org/10.4067/S0718-58392008000100007.

Seo, S. N., Mendelsohn, R., and Munasinghe, M. (2005). Climate change and agriculture in Sri Lanka: A Ricardian valuation. *Environment and Development Economics, 10*(5), 581–596. https://www.jstor.org/stable/44379347.

Seo, S. N., Mendelsohn, R., Dinar, A., Hassan, R., and Kurukulasuriya, P. (2009). A Ricardian analysis of the distribution of climate change impacts on agriculture across agro-ecological zones in Africa. *Environmental and Resource Economics, 43*(3), 313–332. https://doi.org/10.1007/s10640-009-9270-z.

Sheffer, E., Yizhaq, H., Gilad, E., Shachak, M., and Meron, E. (2007). Why do plants in resource deprived environments form rings? *Ecological Complexity, 4*(4), 192–200. https://doi.org/10.1016/j.ecocom.2007.06.008.

Stark, O. (1991). *The Migration of Labor.* Basil Blackwell.

Stark, O. and Bloom, D. (1985). The new economics of labor migration. *The American Economic Review, 75*(2), 173–178. https://www.jstor.org/stable/1805591.

Stark, O. and Lucas, R. E. (1988). Migration, remittances, and the family. *Economic Development and Cultural Change, 36*(3), 465–481. https://doi.org/10.1086/451670.

Stark, O. and Taylor, E. (1989). Relative deprivation and international migration. *Demography, 26*(1), 1–14. https://doi.org/10.2307/2061490.

Stark, O., Helmenstein, C., and Prskawetz, A. (1997). A brain gain with a brain drain. *Economics Letters, 55*(2), 227–234. https://doi.org/10.1016/S0165-1765(97)00085-2.

Stephen, L. (2007). *Transborder Lives: Indigenous Oaxacans in Mexico, California, and Oregon.* Duke University Press, Durham, USA.

Taylor, E. (1999). The new economics of labour migration and the role of remittances in the migration process. *International Migration, 37*(1), 63–88. https://doi.org/10.1111/1468-2435.00066.

Taylor, J. E. and Adelman, I. (2003). Agricultural household models: Genesis, evolution and extensions. *Review of Economics of the Household, 1*(1), 33–58. https://doi.org/10.1023/A:1021847430758.

Taylor, J. E. and Adelman, I. (2006). *Village Economies. The Design, Estimation and Use of Villagewide Economic Models.* Cambridge University Press. https://doi.org/10.1017/CBO9781139174572.

Taylor J. E. and Dyer, G. A. (2009). Migration and the sending economy: A disaggregated rural economy-wide analysis. *Journal of Development Studies, 46*(1), 68–90. http://www.tandfonline.com/doi/abs/10.1080/00220380802265553#.V2XJ_qLurgQ.

Taylor, J. E. and Filipski, M. (2014). *Beyond Experiments in Development Economics: Local Economy-Wide Impact Evaluation.* Oxford University Press. https://doi.org/10.1093/acprof:oso/9780198707875.001.0001.

Taylor, J. E. and Martin, P. L. (2001). Human capital: Migration and rural population change. In B. L. Gardner and G. C. Rausser (eds.), *Handbook of Agricultural Economics* (pp. 457–511). Elsevier Science. https://doi.org/10.1016/S1574-0072(01)10012-5.

Taylor, J. E., Dyer, G. A., and Yúnez-Naude, A. (2005). Disaggregated rural economy-wide models for policy analysis. *World Development, 33*(10), 1671–1688. https://doi.org/10.1016/j.worlddev.2005.05.003.

Taylor, J. E., Yúnez-Naude, A., and Hampton, S. (1999). Agricultural policy reforms and village economies: A computable general equilibrium analysis from Mexico. *Journal of Policy Modeling, 21*(4), 453–480.

Termorshuizen, J. W., Opdam, P., and Van den Brink, A. (2007). Incorporating ecological sustainability into landscape planning. *Landscape and Urban Planning, 79*(3–4), 374–384. https://doi.org/10.1016/j.landurbplan.2006.04.005.

Thiede, B. C., Randell, H., and Gray, C. (2021). The childhood origins of climate-induced mobility and immobility. *Population and Development Review, 48*(3), 767–793. https://doi.org/10.1111/padr.12482.

Thurlow, J. (2004). *A Dynamic Computable General Equilibrium (CGE) Model for South Africa: Extending the Static IFPRI Model.* Working Paper.

Todaro, M. (1969). A model of labor migration and urban unemployment in less developed countries. *The American Economic Review, 59*(1), 138–148. https://www.jstor.org/stable/1811100.

Tubiello, F. N. and Fischer, G. (2007). Reducing climate change impacts on agriculture: Global and regional effects of mitigation, 2000–2080. *Technological Forecasting & Social Change, 74*(7), 1030–1056. https://doi.org/10.1016/j.techfore.2006.05.027.

Von Hardenberg, J., Kletter, A. Y., Yizhaq, H., Nathan, J. and Meron, E. (2010). Periodic versus scale-free patterns in dryland vegetation. *Proceeding of the Royal Society B, 277*, 1771–1776. https://doi.org/10.1098/rspb.2009.2208.

Van Passel, S., Massetti, E., and Mendelsohn, R. (2017). A Ricardian analysis of the impact of climate change on European agriculture. *Environmental and Resource Economics, 67*(4), 725–760. https://doi.org/10.1007/s10640-016-0001-y.

Velásquez, A. (2019). The economic burden of crime: Evidence from Mexico. *The Journal of Human Resources, 54*(2), 1–30.

Wallerstein, I. (1974). *The Modern World-System I: Capitalist Agriculture and the Origins of the European World-Economy in the Sixteenth Century.* Academic Press, California, USA.

Wang, B. (2013). Comprehensive evaluation method study of urban pavement ecological physical environment (UPEPE). *Applied Mechanics and Materials, 278–280*, 2304–2307. https://doi.org/10.4028/www.scientific.net/AMM.278-280.2304.

Wu, J. (2013). Landscape sustainability science: Ecosystem services and human well-being in changing landscapes. *Landscape Ecology, 28*, 999–1023. https://doi.org/10.1007/s10980-013-9894-9.

Van Wyk, L., Saayman, M., and Rossouw, R. (2015). CGE or SAM? Ensuring quality information for decision-making. *African Journal of Hospitality, Tourism And Leisure, 4*, 1–20. https://dspace.nwu.ac.za/handle/10394/20781?show=full.

Yizhaq, H., Gilad, E., and Meron, E. (2005). Banded vegetation: Biological productivity and resilience. *Physica A: Statistical Mechanics and its Applications, 356*(1), 139–144. https://doi.org/10.1016/j.physa.2005.05.026.

Yúnez-Naude, A. (1978). Una evaluación del modelo de crecimiento dual de Ranis y Fei. *El Trimestre Económico, 45*(2), 357–399.

Yúnez-Naude, A. and Aguilar-Mendez, P. (2018). Effects of water availability and policy changes for irrigated agriculture. In H. Guerrero (ed.), *Water Policy in Mexico* (pp. 55–74). Springer. https://link.springer.com/chapter/10.1007%2F978-3-319-76115-2_3.

Chapter 6

Trends and Perspectives: Global Warming, Land, Rural Areas, and Agriculture

This chapter presents an overview of the main international agreements signed to reduce global warming with special focus on rural areas and agriculture (Section 6.1). The review includes some issues previously examined in Chapter 2, addressed in the Kyoto Protocol and the most recent Conference of the Parties (COP26) held in Glasgow at the end of 2021. Likewise, we present global trends in GHG emissions in the last three decades and we make an attempt to contrast the commitments acquired by Parties against the real trends. The topics addressed in Section 6.2 include a reflection on the importance of considering rural households and their heterogeneity in the design of policy proposals aimed at achieving sustainability in rural areas, agriculture, and food production.

6.1 Commitments to Reduce vs. Trends

Global warming is currently an unquestionable phenomenon. Scientific consensus is overwhelming: earth's global average surface temperature has risen in the last decades (Intergovernmental Panel on Climate Change (IPCC) 2018). Indeed, in 2021, the IPCC pointed out that we have a 50% chance of overtaking a 1.5°C temperature threshold within the next few decades, since in the last 20 years there has been a substantial increase in global temperature compared to the years before the industrial revolution. Figures indicate that between 2001 and 2020 the global average temperature on the surface was 0.99°C higher than that during the period 1850–1900. Furthermore, this temperature was higher over the period 2011–2020 (1.09°C) compared to the same period, with greater increases in land, 1.59°C (in an interval of 1.34–1.83°C), than in the ocean, 0.88°C (in a range of 0.68–1.1°C) (IPCC, 2021).

The foregoing reveals that concerns about climate change (CC) which worried the world a few years ago have materialized into the most compelling threat to humanity. Consensus on the negative impacts of CC on human and natural systems exists. A large part of these effects are due to human activities, such as the destruction of ecosystems and GHG emissions resulting from burning fossil fuels, industrial processes, and agriculture activities, among others (see Figure 6.1). In this section, we place special emphasis on human activities that contribute significantly to GHG emissions, since these

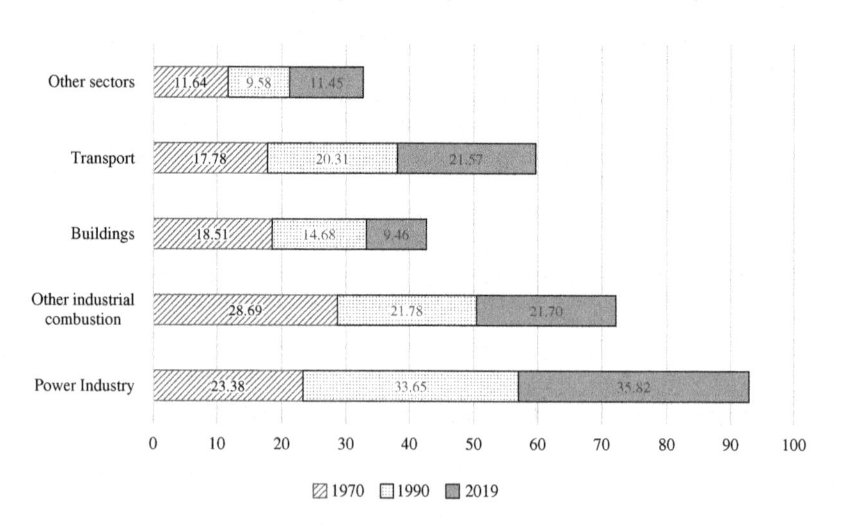

Figure 6.1. Distribution of GHG Emissions by Sector*

Note: *Other sectors include power and heat generation plants (public and auto producers). Transport includes combustion for industrial manufacturing and fuel production. Buildings include small-scale non-industrial stationary combustion. Other industrial combustion includes road, rail, ship, and aviation. Power industry includes industrial process emissions, agriculture, and waste.

Source: By the authors based on Crippa *et al.* (2020).

activities have added pressure on terrestrial systems beyond natural dynamics.

From the last quarter of the last century to the present, governments have committed to fight CC by limiting global warming. Examples of these are the efforts and agreements reached prior to the Kyoto Protocol and even the most recent UN Climate Conference (COP26) held in November 2021. Despite the commitments undertaken and the intensification of diplomacy, the results achieved are far from achieving the goals established in Kyoto and reaffirmed in Paris. Therefore, we could already be facing the consequences of CC without the possibility of reversing them.

6.1.1 *Main efforts (agreements and reports) to reduce GHG emissions with emphasis on agriculture and land*

In this subsection, we present some of the main international agreements aimed at reducing GHG emissions which also consider aspects related to land and agriculture as part of the topics addressed.

6.1.1.1 *Kyoto Protocol*

Although various initiatives preceded the Kyoto Protocol (see Box 6.1), there is no doubt that this agreement is a turning point for all those real initiatives aimed at combating CC. As we previously mentioned in Chapter 2, the Kyoto Protocol was adopted at the third Conference of the Parties to the United Nations Framework Convention on Climate Change (UNFCCC) in Kyoto in 1997; however, it came into effect in 2005 (see Box 2.3). Its main objective was that 37 industrialized countries and the European Union reduce their emissions by an average of 5% against 1990s levels over the 5-year period, 2008–2012 (UNFCCC, 2011).

This Protocol covers aspects related to agriculture and land issues. In Article 2, the Kyoto Protocol set up the promotion of sustainable forms of agriculture in light of CC considerations. Article 10 is about preparing, implementing, publishing, and updating national and regional programs to mitigate CC. These programs must

Box 6.1. Main Climate Change's Initiatives that Preceded the Kyoto Protocol

First World Climate Conference (1979): The First World Climate Conference identified climate change as an urgent world problem and issued a declaration calling on governments to anticipate and guard against potential climate hazards. A World Climate Programme was set up, steered by the World Meteorological Organization (WMO), the United Nations Environment Programme (UNEP), and the International Council of Scientific Unions (ICSU). Several intergovernmental conferences on climate change followed.

Montreal Protocol (1987): International attention was drawn to the urgency of the need for appropriate measures in 1984 when it was confirmed that the ozone layer over Antarctica was disappearing, resulting in the apparition of an ozone hole. The Montreal Protocol on Substances that Deplete the Ozone Layer, the first global legally binding environmental treaty, was signed in 1987. Its aim was to protect the ozone layer by phasing out the production and consumption of substances responsible for its depletion. With the financial support of the Multilateral Fund for the Implementation of the Montreal Protocol, the Global Environment Facility, and various bilateral donors, the United Nations Development Programme has been working with a broad range of partners, including governments, industry, and representative organizations, such as technical associations, agricultural institutes, academia, and civil society, to help developing countries and countries with economies in transition adopt and implement strategies that target the preservation of the ozone layer and sustainable development.

Intergovernmental Panel on Climate Change (1988): The Intergovernmental Panel on Climate Change (IPCC) was created in 1988 jointly by the World Meteorological Organization (WMO) and the United Nations Environmental Programme (UNEP) in

Box 6.1. (*Continued*)

response to the appeal by the United Nations General Assembly (UNGA) in December 1987 to address the issue of a possible future, human-induced climate change. The purpose is to provide a scientific assessment of (i) the factors which may affect climate change during the next century, especially those which are due to human activity; (ii) the responses of the atmosphere–ocean–land–ice system; (iii) current capabilities of modeling global and regional climate changes and their predictability; and (iv) the past climate record and presently observed climate anomalies.

IPCC First Assessment Report (1990): The IPCC published the First Assessment Report on the state of the global climate. It became the main basis for negotiations under the United Nations General Assembly on a climate change convention, beginning in late 1990. The main points were that mean surface air temperature has increased by 0.3–0.6°C over the last 100 years, with the five global-average warmest years being in the 1980s. Over the same period, global sea level has increased by 10–20 cm. These increases have not been smooth with time nor uniform over the globe. The size of this warming is broadly consistent with predictions of climate models, but it is also of the same magnitude as natural climate variability. Thus, the observed increase could be largely due to this natural variability. Alternatively, this variability and other human factors could have offset a still larger human-induced greenhouse warming. Finally, ecosystems will be affected by a changing climate and by increasing carbon dioxide concentrations.

United Nations Framework Convention on Climate Change (1992): The objective of the Convention and any related legal instruments that the Conference of the Parties may adopt is to achieve, in accordance with the relevant provisions of the Convention, stabilization of GHG concentrations in the atmosphere at a level that would prevent dangerous anthropogenic interference with the climate system. Such a level should be achieved within a

(*Continued*)

Box 6.1. (*Continued*)

time frame sufficient to allow ecosystems to adapt naturally to climate change, to ensure that food production is not threatened, and to enable economic development to proceed in a sustainable manner.

IPCC Second Assessment Report (1995): The main points were that the atmospheric concentrations of the GHG, and among them, carbon dioxide (CO_2), methane (CH_4), and nitrous oxide (N_2O), have grown significantly since pre-industrial times. These trends can be attributed largely to human activities, mostly fossil-fuel use, land-use change, and agriculture. Concentrations of other anthropogenic greenhouse gases have also increased. Many greenhouse gases remain in the atmosphere for a long time. Tropospheric aerosols resulting from the combustion of fossil fuels, biomass burning, and other sources have led to a negative direct forcing and possibly also to a negative indirect forcing of a similar magnitude. Finally, evidence from changes in global mean surface air temperature and from changes in geographical, seasonal, and vertical patterns of atmospheric temperature suggests a discernible human influence on global climate.

Source: By the authors based on IPCC (1990, 1995, 2001) and UNFCCC (1992, 1998).

take the energy, transport, industry sectors, agriculture, forestry, and waste management into consideration.

As for land issues, these are mentioned in the Land Use, Land-Use Change, and Forestry (LULUCF) activities. According to the UNFCCC, human activities impact terrestrial *sinks*[1] through LULUCF activities. The role these activities play is important if we think about the mitigation of CC. The LULUCF activities were introduced in the Kyoto Protocol in Article 3, which states that

[1]A *sink* is any process, activity, or mechanism which removes a greenhouse gas from the atmosphere.

mitigation can be achieved through activities in the LULUCF sector aimed at increasing the removal of greenhouse gasses from the atmosphere or decreasing emissions by halting the loss of carbon stocks.

The Kyoto Protocol includes two amendment periods: 2008–2012 and 2013–2020. The target of the first amendment period covers emissions from the six main greenhouse gases: carbon dioxide (CO_2), methane (CH_4), nitrous oxide (N_2O), and the F-gases [hydrofluorocarbons (HFCs), perfluorocarbons (PFCs), and sulfur hexafluoride (SF_6)]. The individual targets for Parties are listed in Annex B of the Protocol. The second amendment is also known as the Doha Amendment. It was established in the COP18 which was held in Doha, Qatar. For this amendment to enter into force, it is required that 144 Parties endorse it. As of 28 October 2020, 147 Parties have deposited their instrument of acceptance. The amendment entered into force on 31 December 2020. It was adopted to assist developing countries with low or insignificant greenhouse gas emissions experiencing problems to access financial assistance to support efforts to adapt to the impacts of CC. The main goal of the Doha Amendment is to reduce GHG emissions by 18% compared to 1990s levels in countries that are participating in this second commitment period. The quantified emission limitation or reduction commitment for this period (2013–2020) has been included in Annex B of the Doha Amendment of the Kyoto Protocol.

6.1.1.2 *Paris Agreement*

The Paris Agreement was adopted in 2016 at the COP21 (see Box 2.4). Today, 192 countries and the European Union (193 Parties) have endorsed this Agreement. It aims to address CC in the context of sustainable development and efforts to eradicate poverty (UNFCCC, 2015).

The Agreement's main goals are the following:

- substantially reduce global greenhouse gas emissions to limit the global temperature increase in this century to 2°C while pursuing efforts to limit the increase even further to 1.5°C;

- review countries' commitments every 5 years;
- provide financing to developing countries to mitigate CC, strengthen resilience, and enhance their abilities to adapt to climate impacts.

The second point establishes that each country must submit a Nationally Determined Contribution (NDC) every 5 years, which is an updated national climate action plan. One important concept that was mentioned throughout the report is net-zero emissions target. According to the United Nations, it means cutting greenhouse gas emissions to as close to zero as possible, with any remaining emissions re-absorbed from the atmosphere, by oceans and forests, for instance. This is important as scientific research shows clearly that in order to avert the worst impacts of CC and preserve a livable planet, global temperature increase needs to be limited to 1.5°C above pre-industrial levels. Emissions must be reduced by 45% by 2030 and reach net zero by 2050. However, no country today has implemented the necessary actions and policies to reduce GHG emissions and reach this goal.

The Paris Agreement does not explicitly mention agriculture; however, it addresses food security, hunger, and food production. In Article 2, we can see the Paris Agreement's objectives. Among them is "increasing the ability to adapt to the adverse impacts of CC and foster climate resilience and low greenhouse gas emissions development in a manner that does not threaten food production." Additionally, the agreement stresses that the Parties must recognize "the fundamental priority of safeguarding food security and ending hunger, and the particular vulnerabilities of food production systems to the adverse impacts of climate change" (UNFCCC, 2015).

Despite the fact that the Paris Agreement does not mention agriculture, countries are aware that it is necessary to set up mitigation strategies for agriculture. The Consultative Group for International Agricultural Research (CGIAR) (2015) points out that "reducing emissions from agriculture will be imperative as it will be impossible to stay within either a 1.5°C or 2°C target if agriculture does not contribute to emissions reductions."

According to Climate Focus (2015), one of the reasons why explicit mention of agriculture was left out of the Paris Agreement was that many developing countries consider that reducing GHG emissions from agriculture would compromise their ability to generate sufficient food for their people. The reference to food production assuages this concern, as well as concerns which may arise in countries with large agroindustrial sectors and powerful industry interests.

Another issue that is not addressed in the Paris Agreement is land, but Article 5 does mention deforestation and forest degradation, as well as land use activities. Article 5.1 states that "Parties should take action to conserve and enhance, as appropriate, sinks and reservoirs of greenhouse gases as referred to in Article 4, paragraph 1(d), of the Convention, including forests." Article 5.2 of the Paris Agreement states that "Parties are encouraged to take action to implement and support, including through results-based payments, the existing framework as set out in related guidance and decisions already agreed under the Convention for policy approaches and positive incentives for activities relating to reducing emissions from deforestation and forest degradation, the role of conservation, sustainable management of forests and enhancement of forest carbon stocks in developing countries, as well as alternative policy approaches, such as joint mitigation and adaptation approaches for the integral and sustainable management of forests, while reaffirming the importance of incentivizing, as appropriate, non-carbon benefits associated with such approaches."

The second paragraph of Article 5 focuses on reducing forest-related emissions in developing country Parties. It recognizes the existing REDD+[2] framework and calls on Parties to take action and move to implementation of REDD+ in accordance with existing

[2]REDD+ is a framework created by the UNFCCC Conference of the Parties (COP) to guide activities in the forest sector that reduces emissions from deforestation and forest degradation and also addresses the sustainable management of forests and the conservation and enhancement of forest carbon stocks in developing countries (UNFCCC, 2015).

UNFCCC decisions, which by reference are integrated into the Paris Agreement. The paragraph explicitly mentions results-based payments as a possible modality of supporting REDD+, in reference to the countries that actively pioneer results-based finance. But it also endorses the concept of joint mitigation and adaptation approaches. This paragraph concludes by stressing the importance of the non-carbon benefits of REDD+ actions (Climate Focus, 2015).

In addition, Article 4.1(d) UNFCCC includes the following paragraph: "Promote sustainable management, and promote and cooperate in the conservation and enhancement, as appropriate, of sinks and reservoirs of all greenhouse gases not controlled by the Montreal Protocol, including biomass, forests, and oceans as well as other terrestrial, coastal and marine ecosystems."

6.1.1.3 *Climate change and land — IPCC Report*

In 2019, the IPCC published a Special Report on Climate Change and Land to respond to the Panel decision in 2016. This report addresses greenhouse gas fluxes in land-based ecosystems, land use, and sustainable land management in relation to CC adaptation and mitigation, desertification, land degradation, and food security. This report mentions relevant data about agriculture, land, and water. According to information from 1961, global population growth and changes in the per capita consumption of food, feed, fiber, timber, and energy have caused unprecedented rates of land and freshwater use.

Moreover, land is both a source and a *sink* of GHGs and plays a key role in the exchange of energy, water, and aerosols between the land surface and the atmosphere. Agriculture, Forestry, and Other Land Use (AFOLU) activities are a significant net source of GHG emissions because an estimated 23% of total anthropogenic GHG emissions derive from AFOLU. In the same way, AFOLU plays a relevant role in food security and sustainable development (IPCC, 2019).

IPCC's Special Report contains Panel A and Panel B, which address the potential global contribution of response options to mitigation, adaptation, combating desertification and land degradation, as well as enhancing food security. In Panel A, we see response options that can be implemented without any or very limited competition for land. In response options based on land management, agriculture-related items such as the increase of food production, agroforestry, improvement of cropland management, improvement of livestock management, agricultural diversification, improvement of grazing land management, integration of water management, and reduction of grassland conversion to cropland are examined. Panel B contains response options that rely on additional land-use change and could have implications across three or more land challenges under different implementation contexts. It also addresses reforestation.

Water stress is also a major concern since vegetation browning has been observed in some regions largely as a result of global warming. In addition, changes in forest cover (i.e., from afforestation, reforestation, and deforestation) affect regional surface temperature through exchanges of water and energy. In addition, current levels of global warming are associated with moderate risks from increased dryland water scarcity, soil erosion, vegetation loss, wildfire damage, permafrost thawing, coastal degradation, and tropical crop yield decline.

Humans and ecosystems seem to be affected by changes in land-based processes. One of the main issues is the growth of global mean surface temperature (GMST). As a result of this, processes that involve desertification (water scarcity, land degradation, and food security) have been affected. Changes in these processes drive risks to food systems, livelihoods, infrastructure, the value of land, and human and ecosystem health.

The IPCC Special Report offers some solutions to help adapt to and mitigate CC while contributing to combating desertification. Some are water harvesting and micro-irrigation, restoring degraded lands using drought-resilient ecologically appropriate plants, agroforestry, and other agroecological and ecosystem-based adaptation practices.

This report takes into consideration that CC is affecting food security in drylands, particularly those in Africa, and in high mountain regions of Asia and South America. It follows methodologies that include interviews and surveys with indigenous peoples and local communities. Moreover, it recognizes that policies that enable and promote sustainable land management for CC adaptation and mitigation include improving access to markets for inputs, outputs, and financial services, empowering women and indigenous peoples, enhancing local and community collective actions, reforming subsidies, and promoting and enabling trade systems.

The IPCC argues that the effectiveness of decision-making and governance is enhanced by the involvement of local stakeholders (particularly those most vulnerable to CC — including indigenous peoples and local communities, women, and the poor and marginalized — in the selection, evaluation, implementation, and monitoring of policy instruments for land-based CC adaptation and mitigation). Coordinated actions across a range of actors such as businesses, producers, consumers, land managers, and policymakers in partnership with indigenous peoples and local communities enable conditions for the adoption of response options (*Ibid.*).

6.1.1.4 *Conference of the Parties*

The UNFCCC was adopted in New York in May 1992 by the Intergovernmental Negotiating Committee (INC) and was opened for signature in Rio in June. Both events were held in 1992. On March 21, 1994, the UNFCCC entered into force.

The UNFCCC was established as a result of concerns about CC since the concentrations of GHG in the atmosphere had been increasing affecting natural ecosystems and humanity. The Conference of the Parties (COP) is the body in charge of supervising the UNFCCC. Currently, a total of 197 parties and territories are part of the COP. The first COP took place in Berlin in 1995. After this date, the COP met annually to discuss CC.

COP17, held in Durban in 2011, was the first time the UNFCCC included agriculture in its agenda; however, no decision was made in this respect. The same happened at COP18. It was not until COP19 (2013) was held in Warsaw when a decision was made that all countries must include agriculture in their National Inventory Report. It is worth mentioning that at COP15 and COP16, agriculture was also included in the negotiations. However, the issue was so controversial that no agreement was reached. In 2014, the Subsidiary Body for Scientific and Technological Advice (SBSTA) declared that for the following 2 years, it would organize workshops, where two of the four topics to be discussed would be about agriculture and address risk assessment and vulnerability of agricultural systems, and the identification and evaluation of agricultural practices and technologies to improve productivity sustainably. An agreement was finally reached on agriculture to address CC and food security during COP23. The Koronivia Joint Work on Agriculture (KJWA) was established at this Conference to develop and implement new adaptation and mitigation strategies within the agricultural sector and reduce the sector's emissions as well as to strengthen its resilience to the effects of CC. The KJWA takes into consideration the vulnerabilities of agriculture to CC and the different approaches to addressing food security.

The adoption of the KJWA represents a major step forward in the negotiations on agriculture under the UNFCCC. Its implementation will require the combination of efforts from both subsidiary bodies and constituted bodies under the Convention and other relevant stakeholders (UNFCCC, 2018). Like FAO, the KJWA's objective is to "eliminate hunger, food insecurity and malnutrition, reduce rural poverty, and make agriculture, forestry and fisheries more productive and sustainable" (UNFCCC, 2018).

Forest and agriculture topics were also addressed during COP26. One of the most important agreements reached was the Glasgow Climate Pact. With regard to forests, 137 countries took a landmark step forward by committing to halt and reverse forest loss and land degradation by 2030. The pledge is backed by the USA with $12bn in public funding and $7.2bn in private funding. In addition, Chief Executive Officers (CEOs) from more than 30 financial institutions with over $8.7 trillion of global assets agreed to cancel all investments intended for activities linked to deforestation (UNFCCC, 2021a).

Prior to COP26, some scholars indicated that while half of the world's land and 80% of its biodiversity is managed and cared for by indigenous and local communities, they only receive 1% of official climate funding (Dupraz, 2021). For the first time in the history of the UNFCCC, 28 indigenous people were nominated from each of the seven UN indigenous sociocultural regions to engage directly as knowledge holders and share experiences as indigenous experts with governments, since indigenous people steward over 80% of the planet's remaining biodiversity (UNFCCC, 2021a). Indigenous people contribute to tackling CC; however, they are some of the most vulnerable victims. Therefore, we can't solve the climate crisis without including indigenous peoples and without protecting their territories.

6.1.1.5 *Fifth Assessment Report (AR5)*

In 2014, the IPCC published the complete version of the AR5, which addresses land, agriculture, and water topics. It is the first report that considers in a single chapter the terrestrial land surface, comprising AFOLU. With regard to agriculture, it discusses the most cost-effective mitigation options, such as cropland management, grazing land management, and restoration of organic soils. The Assessment also discusses some direct options in AFOLU to reduce CO_2 emissions, such as reducing deforestation, forest degradation, and forest fires.

AFOLU activities were examined throughout the report. It was suggested that a combination of supply-side and demand-side options could reduce emissions from the sector by 2030. Moreover, good governance is central for reducing mitigation barriers in this sector. As mentioned earlier, AFOLU accounts for 20–24% of total emissions. Worldwide, it is the largest emitting sector after energy and plays an even major role in developing countries.

Water issues are also important. Evidence of observed CC impacts is strongest and most comprehensive for natural systems. In many regions, changing precipitation or melting snow and ice are altering hydrological systems, affecting water resources in terms of quantity and quality.

The AR5 also addresses urban and rural areas. Concerning the former, CC will affect people, assets, economies, and ecosystems (heat stress, water scarcity, sea level rise, and coastal flooding); whereas rural areas are expected to experience major impacts on water availability and supply, food security, infrastructure, and agricultural incomes, including shifts in the production areas of food and non-food crops around the world. Rural areas are expected to experience major impacts on water availability and supply, food security, infrastructure, and agricultural incomes, including shifts in the production areas of food and non-food crops around the world. As discussed in Chapter 4, Section 4.4, adaptation options for agriculture include technological responses, enhancing smallholders' access to credit and other critical production resources, strengthening institutions at local and regional levels, and improving market access through trade reform.

6.1.2 *Global GHG emissions: Status and trends*

Even though GHG emissions should be drastically decreasing to reach the proposed goals for 2030 and prevent increasing global warming, the emissions continue to increase at an alarming rate. If we look at total accumulated GHG emissions across the world during 1990–2018, carbon dioxide was the top contributor, accounting for almost three-quarters (72.8%) of total emissions, while methane (CH_4) followed with 18.8%. This indicates that, in the last three decades, only these two gases accumulate almost 92% of total GHG emissions (see Figure 6.2).

Likewise, the figures indicate that since 1990, GHG emissions have increased by nearly 50% globally. The top five GHG emitters are China, the USA, and the European Union, followed by India and Russia (see Figure 6.3).

When considering the accumulated emissions since 1990, once again China and the USA stand out as the main GHG emitters. Historical data indicate that, when adding the emissions from both countries, their global contribution is close to 33%; i.e., in the last 30 years, these two countries alone have contributed a third of

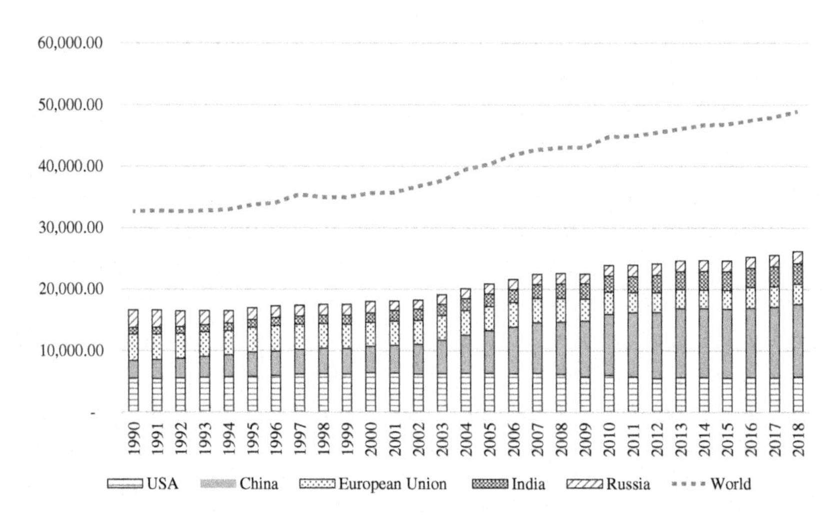

Figure 6.2. Total GHG Emissions by Gas Since 1990 (in $MtCO_2e$)
Source: By the authors based on CAIT Climate Data Explorer via Climate Watch (https://www.climatewatchdata.org/, consulted on April 21st, 2022).

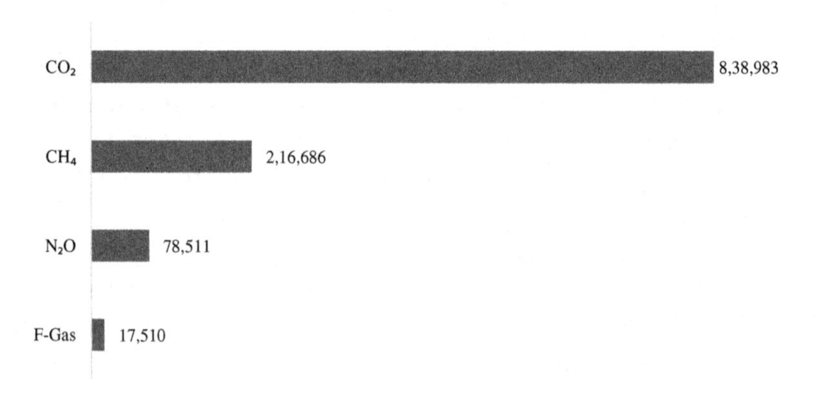

Figure 6.3. Top 5 GHG Emitters Including LUCF (in $MtCO_2e$)
Source: By the authors based on CAIT Climate Data Explorer via Climate Watch (https://www.climatewatchdata.org/, consulted on April 21st, 2022).

GHG emissions. However, the trend in both countries has been very different, while in the period 1990–2018 the emissions from the USA only increased by 5%, those of China did so by an amount greater than 300%. In 2018, China alone contributed 24% of total emissions worldwide (Figure 6.4).

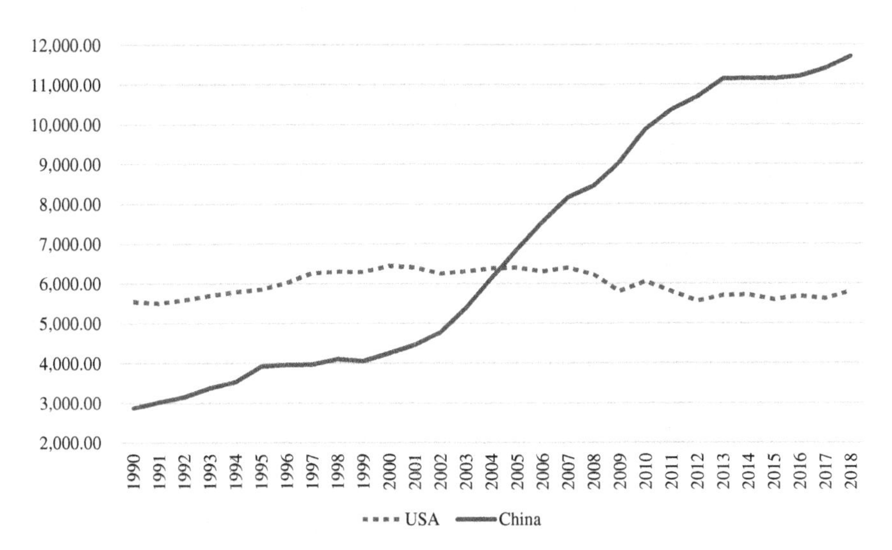

Figure 6.4. China and USA GHG Emissions Including LUCF (in $MtCO_2e$)
Source: By the authors based on CAIT Climate Data Explorer via Climate Watch (https://www.climatewatchdata.org/, consulted on April 21st, 2022).

Globally, 70% of greenhouse gas emissions are concentrated in 10 emitters (nine countries and the European Union). Only one Latin American country appears among the main emitters. As Figure 6.5 shows, in the period 1990–2018, Brazil ranked sixth in this group, contributing 4.3% of the total and accumulating during this period emission of 49,958 $MtCO_2e$. The third country of the American continent that appears on the list is Canada, in the 10th position, with GHG accumulated emissions of 23,778 $MtCO_2e$ (Figure 6.5).

In addition to identifying which countries contribute the most to global warming through GHG emissions, it is essential to know where these emissions come from, i.e., which sectors contribute the greatest proportion to total emissions. Undoubtedly, this information allows us to suggest mitigation strategies more effective and better targeted. The overall picture depicted in Figure 6.6 shows that 74.5% of emissions come from energy; almost one-fifth from agriculture and land-use change and forestry; and the remaining 8% from waste and industrial processes.

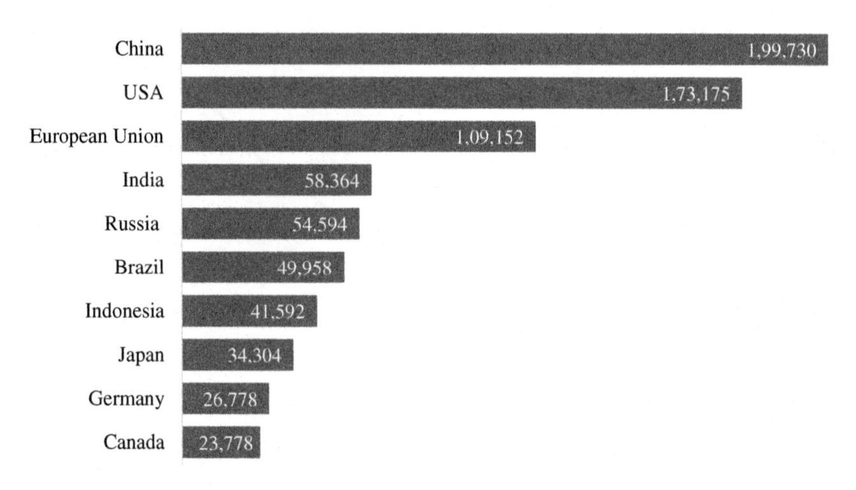

Figure 6.5. Top GHG Emitters since 1990 Including LUCF (in $MtCO_2e$)
Source: By the authors based on CAIT Climate Data Explorer via Climate Watch (https://www.climatewatchdata.org/, consulted on April 21st, 2022).

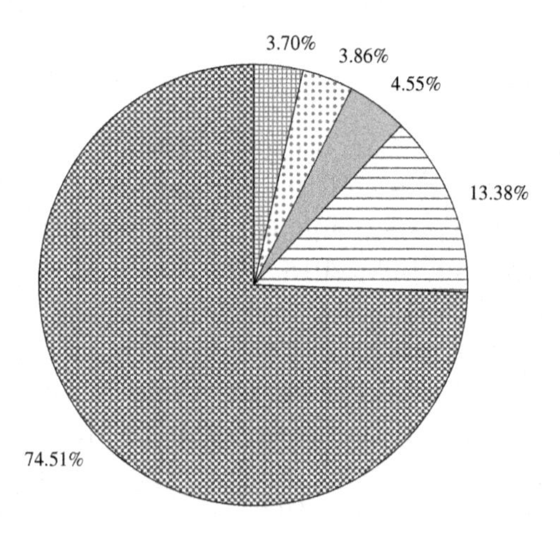

Figure 6.6. Total GHG Emissions by Sector Since 1990 (in $MtCO_2e$)
Source: By the authors based on CAIT Climate Data Explorer via Climate Watch (https://www.climatewatchdata.org/, consulted on April 21st, 2022).

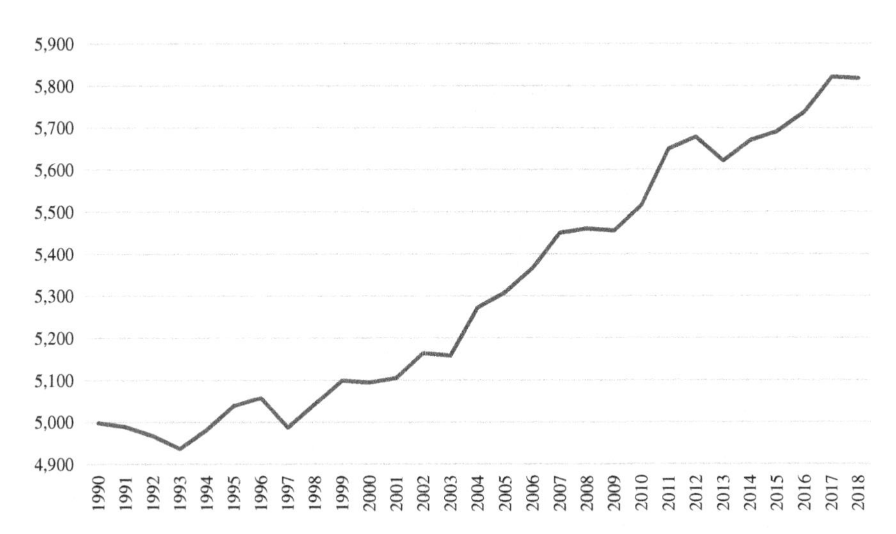

Figure 6.7. GHG Emissions Produced in Agriculture since 1990 (in $MtCO_2e$)
Source: By the authors based on CAIT Climate Data Explorer via Climate Watch (https://www.climatewatchdata.org/, consulted on April 21st, 2022).

With regard to the agriculture sector, data show that from 1990 to 2018 GHG emissions have increased by about 16%, with a growing trend practically since 1993 (Figure 6.7). In 2018, world total agriculture emissions reached 5.8 billion tons of carbon dioxide equivalent ($GtCO_2e$). Methane is the main gas emitted by this sector with around 60% of the total, the remaining 40% is related to nitrous oxide (N_2O) emissions. This relative contribution of each gas has not changed significantly during the past three decades (see Figure 6.8).

6.1.3 *The emissions gap: Signed agreements vs. real emissions*

The main purpose of major climate agreements has been focused on the reduction of GHG emissions. As mentioned earlier, the main goal of the Kyoto Protocol was to reduce GHG emissions by an average of 5% compared to 1990. However, real emissions figures are different for each country that signed the agreement. Table 6.1 shows what

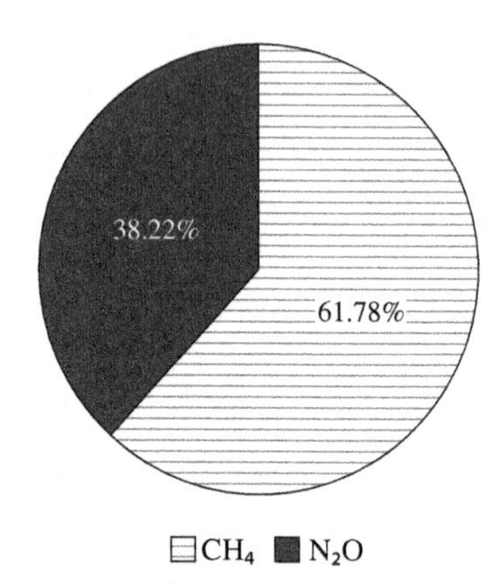

Figure 6.8. GHG Emissions Produced in Agriculture by Gas since 1990
Source: By the authors based on CAIT Climate Data Explorer via Climate Watch (https://www.climatewatchdata.org/, consulted on April 21st, 2022).

the target established in the Kyoto Protocol was and what actually happened in 2012. The last column shows the percentage change in emissions between 1990 and 2012.

As can be noted, some countries achieved their target while others did not. The countries and regions that achieved their goal (decreased their GHG emissions) are Australia, Belgium, Bulgaria, Croatia, Czech Republic, Denmark, Estonia, the European Union, Finland, France, Germany, Italy, Latvia, Hungary, Liechtenstein, Lithuania, Luxembourg, Monaco, the Netherlands, Norway, Poland, Romania, the Russian Federation, Slovakia, Slovenia, Sweden, Ukraine, and the United Kingdom. The countries that decreased their GHG emissions but did not achieve their goal are Iceland, Portugal, and Switzerland. Finally, the countries that did not achieve their goal since their GHG emissions increased are Austria, Canada, Greece, Ireland, Japan, Liechtenstein, New Zealand, Portugal, Spain, and the USA. Although Mexico is not part of this protocol, it also increased its GHG emissions by almost 50%.

What Table 6.1 shows is an example of the different levels of commitments and standard results delivered by the Parties of the CC international agreements. Despite the agreements reached in

Table 6.1. GHG Emissions Kyoto Protocol Target vs. GHG Emissions in 2012 Including LULUCF (in $ktCO_2e$)

Party	**1990**	**2012**	**Kyoto Protocol Target (%)**	**Change from 1990 to 2012 (%)**
Australia	615,477.99	560,441.05	+8	−8.94
Austria	66,224.24	73,981.01	−8	11.71
Belgium	142,316.73	119,324.44	−8	−16.16
Bulgaria	80,849.66	50,572.03	−8	−47.22
Canada	544,707.24	707,736.88	−6	29.93
Croatia	24,939.60	20,287.98	−5	−18.65
Czech Republic	190,111.06	125,261.06	−8	−34.11
Denmark	77,606.28	55,879.41	−8	−28.00
Estonia	38,085.75	16,060.78	−8	−57.83
European Union (Convention)	5,464,792.68	4,254,677.73	−8	−22.14
European Union (KP)	5,480,441.84	4,271,847.08	−8	−22.05
Finland	57,527.10	38,602.02	−8	−32.90
France	525,543.06	452,830.45	−8	−13.84
Germany	1,273,438.56	905,567.40	−8	−28.89
Greece	101,181.55	109,219.39	−8	7.94
Hungary	92,111.18	55,883.87	−8	−48.53
Iceland	12,875.10	13,919.84	+10	8.11
Ireland	59,531.40	63,238.00	−8	6.23
Italy	515,229.35	459,318.42	−8	−10.85
Japan	1,203,671.10	1,323,805.29	−6	9.98
Latvia	13,567.37	7,205.73	−8	−46.89
Liechtenstein	235.47	248.86	−8	5.69
Lithuania	42,341.62	11,241.49	−8	−73.45
Luxembourg	12,812.22	11,427.13	−8	−10.81
Monaco	102.74	87.50	−8	−14.83
Netherlands	225,676.39	198,036.27	−8	−12.25
New Zealand	41,114.77	55,250.05	0	34.38
Norway	39,507.38	32,103.82	+1	−18.74
Poland	445,550.64	364,950.51	−6	−34.84
Portugal	60,013.00	56,688.33	−8	−5.54
Romania	221,971.68	90,428.11	−8	−67.95
Russian Federation	3,086,562.30	1,417,395.23	0	−54.08
Slovakia	63,710.11	34,885.38	−8	−45.24

(*Continued*)

Table 6.1. (*Continued*)

Party	**1990**	**2012**	**Kyoto protocol target (%)**	**Change from 1990 to 2012 (%)**
Slovenia	14,168.27	11,846.45	−8	−24.12
Spain	254,004.57	314,877.20	−8	23.97
Sweden	34,712.52	18,034.73	−8	−48.05
Switzerland	51,615.52	49,555.31	−8	−3.99
Ukraine	884,223.01	397,366.28	0	−55.06
United Kingdom of Great Britain and Northern Ireland,	812,970.07	586,175.61	−8	−27.90
United States of America	5,541,854.70	5,778,924.68	−7	4.28
Mexico*	456,578.67	678,835.05	—	48.68

Note: Base year = 1990. *Mexico is not part of the Kyoto Protocol.
Source: By the author based on Kyoto Protocol Annex B and UNFCCC (2019). Greenhouse Gas Inventory Data — GHG Profiles — Annex 1. https://di.unfccc.int/time_series.

Kyoto and Doha and reaffirmed in Paris, the real actions to reverse global warming have so far been characterized by promises not yet fully materialized. The emissions gap is still far from what is required to reduce global warming (see Figure 6.9). If we consider the emissions goal set in Kyoto and compare it with the global 2012 emissions, we can identify that the gap between what was agreed upon and the actual figures is 46.5%. In other words, emissions grew by almost 50% beyond the goal set for 2012 in the Kyoto Protocol. Notwithstanding the concerns expressed by the Parties, this trend has continued in the last decade. If we look at the target set in Doha and the real emissions registered, the gap has not been reduced but rather the opposite, as emissions increased to almost 83% (Figure 6.9).

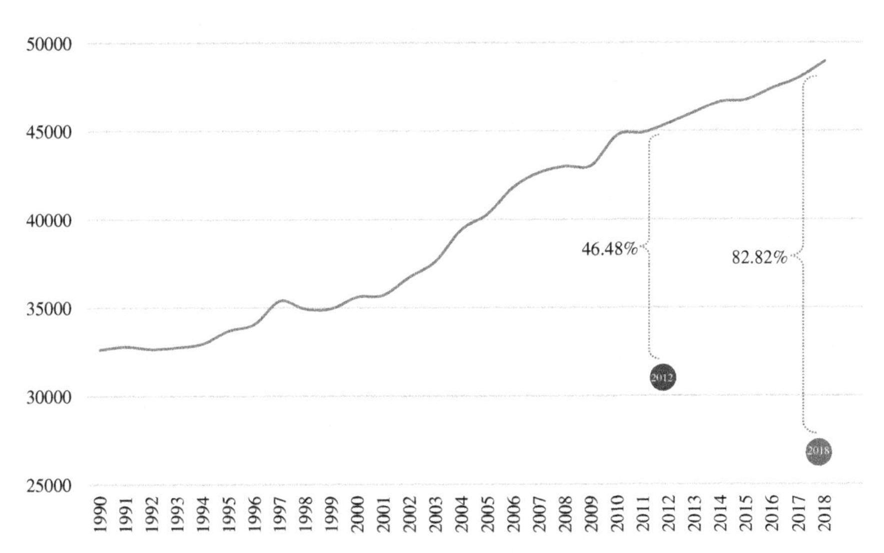

Figure 6.9. Total GHG Emissions Including LUCF and Kyoto Protocol Target Gap (in $MtCO_2e$)
Source: By the authors based on Kyoto Protocol Annex B and CAIT Climate Data Explorer via Climate Watch (https://www.climatewatchdata.org/, consulted on April 21st, 2022).

Without doubt, the time to take crucial actions and reduce global warming is running out. However, there is still hope as dozens of countries met again in Glasgow (COP26) at the end of 2021 to present more ambitious goals. Several announcements were made in this regard that led to the signing of agreements at COP26 (see Box 6.2 for some of the main agreements). The challenge is that nations must put in place policies and actions to meet their new commitments and implement them promptly. Human beings must wake up and act in the face of the imminent peril that we currently face from global warming. We must act quickly and firmly because the consequences of CC that we could face in the coming decades could be irreversible and put us at risk as a species.

Box 6.2. COP26's Main Agreements on Global Warming, Land, Agriculture, and Local Communities

Global Warming: Participants agreed to include reinforcing efforts to increase resilience to climate change, curb greenhouse gas emissions, and provide the necessary financing for both. Developed countries reaffirmed their commitment to provide 100 billion dollars a year to developing countries. In addition, they collectively agreed to work to reduce the gap between existing emission reduction plans and the actions required to reduce them so that the increase in global average temperature may be limited to 1.5°C. For the first time, countries are being asked to phase out coal power and inefficient fossil fuel subsidies. As part of those decisions, the countries also completed the Paris Agreement implementation rules regarding market mechanisms and non-market approaches, transparent reporting of climate actions, and support provided or received, including that for loss and damage.

Sustainable Land and Agriculture: Participants agreed that investment is necessary to make the agricultural system more efficient and resilient. While some participants emphasized the need for new financial resources, others suggested that existing financial capital could be unlocked by redirecting subsidies to more sustainable activities, e.g., in the form of transition funds for farmers. This may not be sufficient in all countries, so increasing available financial resources may still be required in countries with insufficient investment. In this regard, green financing products were mentioned as having great potential for driving the transition to climate-resilient and sustainable food production systems. Finally, 110 countries and hundreds of companies from around the world pledged to end deforestation by 2030 (Glasgow Declaration on Forests and Land Use).

Participants agreed to incentivize farmers to adopt best practices, but countries need financing to be able to provide incentives. A very important way of offering incentives and facilitating the

Box 6.2. (*Continued*)

adoption of best practices is to cover for the risks that farmers face when implementing proposed changes and new practices. Incentives are also needed that cover the short-term costs of practices that produce long-term benefits. Examples of successful incentive programs were shared, such as a public program that provides discounts on insurance premiums to farmers that use cover crops.

Participants agreed that scaling up implementation of best practices, innovations, and technologies that increase resilience and sustainable production in agricultural systems needs to be addressed by stakeholders in cooperation and partnership, with farmers at the core of considerations. A participatory approach is needed for the design of programs through implementation, monitoring and evaluation, and outreach. For example, research with land managers and following an iterative dialog help researchers and policymakers understand how farmers adopt and maintain certain practices. Working closely with farmers and empowering them to move towards more sustainable practices are key to success. Government accountability is also key to increasing confidence and motivating change. Some countries' formal mechanisms for sustaining multistakeholder participation, such as advisory committees and extended public consultation processes, were shared. Other countries have adapted participatory processes to suit the stakeholders.

Finally, the Koronivia Joint Work on Agriculture was launched at the COP23 and concluded at COP26. The original roadmap was set to discuss agriculture in the context of the UNFCCC and comprised six thematic workshops. At COP26, the Parties agreed to continue working together. Countries will discuss and propose a new roadmap at COP27, which will focus on new issues and means of implementation. The Koronivia decision addresses six interrelated issues on soils, nutrient use, water, livestock, methods

(*Continued*)

Box 6.2. (*Continued*)

to assess adaptation, and the socioeconomic and food security dimensions of climate change in the agricultural sectors.

Local Communities and Indigenous Peoples: The LCIP was established in 2015 and became operational in 2016. Its goal is to engage in dialog with and between local communities and indigenous peoples to exchange experiences and share best practices on mitigation and adaptation in a holistic and integrated manner. The decision seeks to take into account the interests and points of view of local communities and indigenous peoples, as well as the principles proposed by indigenous peoples' organizations: (a) full and effective participation of indigenous peoples; (b) equal status of indigenous peoples and Parties, including participation in leadership roles; (c) self-selection of representatives of indigenous peoples in accordance with their own procedures; and (d) adequate funding of the secretariat and voluntary contributions to enable the functions of the Platform. At COP26, participants agreed to (i) welcome the second 3-year work plan of the LCIPP for 2022–2024 and recognize that this work plan facilitates continued collaboration between Parties, Indigenous Peoples, and Local Communities (IPLCs) on climate change; (ii) continue the mandate of the FWG and recognize the full and effective participation of IPLCs in achieving the objective of the Paris Agreement; and (iii) continue to implement the activities of the second triennial work plan by facilitating the exchange of experiences between IPLCs and the Parties on approaches to ecosystem management.

Source: By the authors based on UNFCCC (2021b, 2021c), IFAD (2021), and ENB (2021).

6.2 Agriculture and Rural Policies

In this section, we extend the discussion of markets vs. state intervention presented in Chapter 3. This could help understand some of the reasons that may explain why commitments under the UNFCC have only partially been put into practice by signing countries with regard to agriculture.[3]

We present an overview of agricultural policies whose specific features result from agriculture's role in the attainment of sustainable food security and from the unique perspective of agricultural production. We include a discussion on the suitability of market-oriented agricultural policies designed to increase the productivity of subsistence rural households. As discussed in Chapter 3, special attention to rural households is required because of the prevalence of the billions of these types of actors in low- and medium-income countries facing market failures and high transaction costs, defined by their involvement in multiple activities and income sources that include forestry.[4]

6.2.1 *Markets vs. states*

The pro-market reforms followed by the government of Margaret Thatcher in Great Britain during the 1980s raised deep controversy between two views in the economic policy arena (Colclough and Manor, 1991). The disagreement can be synthesized by the following question: What policy is less harmful for growth and development: market failures or government failures? Thatcher's economic reform was based, among others, on deregulation and privatization of State entities and revealed that for her government, market failures were less pervasive. These political philosophical and economic policies

[3]The question of markets vs. states is related to the "neoliberal paradigm" linked to conventional economics and its policy recommendations based on market price signals. For some academic and professional circles of the Western Hemisphere, the increasing worldwide inequality and global warming require an analysis of the extreme economic liberalism. This is the case of the recent initiative called *Reimagining Capitalism* (https://omidyar.com/reimagining-capitalism-4/) and *Reimagining Capitalism: Major Philanthropies Launch Effort at Leading Academic Institutions* (hewlett.org).

[4]In Chapter 7, we adopt a general perspective to present hypotheses intended to explain why international commitments to reduce GHG emissions have only been partially followed in practice.

(frequently called neo-liberalism) were adopted by countries almost all over the world.

As to sustainable development policies, the question of markets vs. states can be incorporated in the positions held by economists and ecologists: In simple terms, their positions can be described as follows (details in Chapter 7, Section 7.1). Economists propose that to promote ecosystem conservation, governments require to impose restrictions, such as taxes, and then economic agents will follow market signals to maximize utility subject to these restrictions, whereas ecologists argue that the attainment of ecosystem preservation is only plausible by strong State regulations based on command-and-control measures.[5]

To reconcile these two philosophical and practical positions, only data availability and collection for serious diagnosis and policy designs and implementation are required. In addition, international negotiations to reduce global warming have not fully brought together economists and ecologists' positions, a situation that may be one of the reasons behind the poor progress in reducing global warming (see Chapter 7).

In regard to agricultural sustainability, it can be argued that the economists' markets-based approach has been recurrent. In its 2008 Report, the World Bank (WB) addresses the issue of the enormous heterogeneity of agricultural production systems among countries, regions, and rural household farmers. So, the WB proposes that these differences be considered in all efforts to enhance agriculture's role in development (Chapter 3). However, the WB agricultural reform proposals emphasize the role of markets and their access by small farmers: "The heterogeneity of smallholders, some market oriented and some subsistence oriented, calls for differentiated agricultural policies that do not favor one group over the other but that serve

[5]Command-and-control approach aimed at protecting the environment is a mandated level of performance enforced through a piece of legislation. Examples are the establishment of national parks to protect the ecosystem of a geographical area, the limits set on the volume of timber that can be harvested, and maximum levels legally allowed for pollution emissions.

the unique needs of all households *while speeding the passage from subsistence to market-oriented farming* ... Heterogeneity in the smallholder sector implies that a group of entrepreneurial smallholders is likely to respond when markets offer new opportunities. Improved access to assets, new technologies, and better incentives can enable more smallholders to become *market participants* in staples and high-value crops" (pp. 92–93; the italics are ours).

In the case of small farmers in Sub-Saharan Africa — formed by countries where most of the poor are in rural areas — the WB proposes that "In these regions, livelihoods depend on agricultural production, either as a source of income or for food-for-home consumption. The challenge is to improve the productivity of subsistence agriculture, diversify to new markets where possible, and open opportunities for nonfarm work and migration as pathways out of poverty" (p. 6).

With regard to agricultural sustainability, the WB places particular attention to the competition between agricultural expansion at the expense of forest land (Box 6.3) and proposes the following policy approach: "Getting the incentives right is the first step towards sustainability. Improving natural resource management in both intensive and extensive farming areas requires removing price and subsidy policies that send the wrong signals to farmers, strengthening property rights, providing long-term support to natural resource management, and developing instruments to help manage increased climate risks"... many opportunities exist to harness agriculture's potential as a provider of environmental services. The emergence of new markets and programs for payments for environmental services [i.e., carbon sequestration] is a promising approach that should be pursued by local and national governments as well as the international community. Agriculture's role is central to the mitigation of CC and the protection of biodiversity, and carbon financing may become an important source of funding for these global public goods. But in many cases, development of markets for environmental services at the local level, with close proximity between service providers and consumers of these services, may be

Box 6.3. Four Trajectories: Disappearing or Rebounding Forests, Misery or Growth

Expansion of the agricultural frontier into forested areas has been triggered by several factors, including population pressure, poverty, market conditions, road construction, and off-farm employment opportunities. Major new roads are another powerful driving force of deforestation. Intensifying agriculture can help reduce pressure on forest cover, but the outcome depends on how these factors play out. Sometimes, market opportunities make it profitable to continue expansion into forest areas despite intensification in existing fields. Four trajectories are possible.

Deforestation with intensification. Intensification can help slow deforestation if geography or tight labor markets prevent further expansion into forest areas. For example, intensification of rice farming in the valleys in the Philippines absorbed excess labor from hillside farms, allowing forests to recover. But deforestation can continue even with intensification. Forest areas dwindled in the Indian Terai where the green revolution increased the value of putting land into agriculture, until a 1980 ban on cutting forests for agriculture. The expansion of soybean cultivation in the Brazilian forest margins is another example of global economic forces at work.

Deforestation with impoverishment. When land use proves unsustainable — soil fertility declines and agricultural incomes collapse — natural regrowth of forests may not occur. Consequently, people leave the land, as with millions of hectares of *imperata* grasslands in Southeast Asia and large areas of apparently abandoned pastures near Belem, Brazil. If this type of unsustainable land use combines with high population pressure, the result is impoverishment and immiseration, as in Madagascar.

Reforestation with intensification. Reforestation is likely to accompany intensification when forest depletion leads to wood scarcity,

(*Continued*)

Box 6.3. (*Continued*)

raising the value of forests, and better tenure makes it possible for households and communities to manage forests. The result: a mosaic of croplands and managed forests, as in parts of Kenya, Tanzania, and the Sahel.

Reforestation with abandonment of rural areas. Forests are rebounding in some regions combined with out-migration (western Europe, Japan, North America, and more recently Eastern and Central Europe). Several developing countries appear to be making this transition from conversion to agriculture to forest regrowth, including parts of Asia (China, the Republic of Korea, peninsular Malaysia, and possibly parts of India and Vietnam), Central America (Costa Rica and the Dominican Republic), Cuba, and Morocco.

Source: World Bank (2008, p. 193).

more promising than putting into place national payment schemes when governance and fiscal capacities are weak" (*Ibid.*, p. 200).

Notwithstanding the WB's inclusion of the specific features of small farmers and of sustainability issues, its recommendations for policy reforms in agriculture are mainly defined by a market orientation. Among others, the WB suggests (1) decoupling supports to agricultural producers by eliminating supports directly linked to production prices, volumes, and area planted and by applying less distortive forms, such as income transfers to farmers, and (2) agricultural trade liberalization by reductions of agricultural goods import protection and the elimination of export taxes for these goods. According to the WB, the main role of the state in supporting the role of agriculture for development is to provide public goods, such as investments in transport and communications.

So, the WB's "Key elements of the future agenda [for agriculture for development] are to continue to get prices right through trade and domestic policy reform, to ensure complementary tax reforms to replace lost trade revenues for reinvestment in the sector, to ensure that the quality of public spending improves, to provide support to complementary programs to facilitate transitions, and to invest massively in core public goods for longer-term sustained growth. All of this requires a comprehensive approach beyond price and adjustment; governments must focus on improving market infrastructure, institutions, and support services" (World Bank, 2008, pp. 116–117).

A market mechanism included in the Kyoto Protocol is the carbon emissions market and the concept of carbon pricing (see Chapter 3, Box 2.3). This mechanism consists in setting a limit or cap on GHG emissions creating a type of value: the right to emit. With these market principles and rules, the countries or companies that reduce emissions below their cap have something to sell, an unused right to emit, measured in tons of CO_2 equivalent. Countries and companies that don't meet their target can buy these one-ton units to make up for the shortfall. This is called emissions trading, or cap and trade. The net effect on the atmosphere is the same, provided measurements are accurate — i.e., each unit represents a true one-ton reduction below the cap — and each unit is used only once. This market mechanism requires clear rules and transparency (https://unfccc.int/topics/what-are-market-and-non-market-mechanisms, consulted on December 12th, 2021).

According to the World Bank (2008), "The emerging market for trading carbon emissions offers new possibilities for agriculture to benefit from land uses that sequester carbon. The main obstacle to realizing broader benefits from the main mechanism for these payments — the Clean Development Mechanism (CDM) of the Kyoto Protocol — is its limited coverage of afforestation and reforestation... No incentives were included in the protocol for developing countries to preserve forests, despite the fact that deforestation contributes close to a fifth of global GHG emissions, largely through agricultural encroachment" (World Bank, 2008, p. 201).

There has been some progress since the Kyoto Protocol in the design, implementation, and evaluation of market and non-market approaches to contain global warming. Article 6 of the Paris Agreement includes non-market-based approaches to catalyze international cooperation that is not based on market mechanisms. As regards agriculture and forestry, non-market approaches may be convenient since their GHG emissions are frequently less concentrated, too small and their production outcomes too uncertain with respect to other sources such as stationary combustion of fossil fuels. So, non-market-based measures may be more appropriate, such as performance standards, regulations, taxes, and incentives.

It is now a widespread recognition that non-market-based mechanisms form an important component of the fight against human-induced CC, along with market-based mechanisms. However, these two policy instruments are complex, their implementation depends on specific conditions, and often one kind of instrument will, to a certain degree, also reflect elements of the other kind.

As shown in Box 6.4, the European Union's efforts to combine non-market and market instruments to reduce global warming reflect progress and challenges to put into practice these two approaches.

According to the Climate Markets & Investment Association, "The non-market-based approach needs guidance, tools, case studies, examples, etc. under the umbrella of the FVA (Framework of Various Approaches of the UNFCC) to ensure consistency and avoid perverse incentives. Parties need financial support from other related sources such as international development banks, donor agencies, and the Green Climate Fund where mechanisms such as payment by results (but not necessarily GHG results) may be used as a means of financing specific programs. Parties need institutional and capacity-building support to develop and implement the regulations and legislation required to put non-market mechanisms in place. The private sector needs IP protection, reductions in political risk, and removal of barriers to investment. It may help to develop a registry of non-market-based activities to help track actions, share experiences, and ensure comparability and transparency" (Climate Markets & Investment Association, 2013, p. 6, https://www.cmia.net/, consulted on January 20th, 2022: see Chapter 7 for a discussion of these and other requirements to reduce global warming).

Box 6.4. Climate Change Non-Market-Based and Market-Based Instruments in the European Union

The climate policy mix in the European Union (EU) contains instruments of two different types: non-market-based and market-based instruments. The purpose of this article is to introduce criteria to evaluate the various instruments and to discuss the pros and cons of both instrument types.

1. Differentiating non-market-based and market-based instruments

Non-market-based instruments work through the imposition of certain obligations or by installing non-monetary incentives to change behavior. Market-based instruments are indirect regulatory instruments, which influence actors' behavior by changing their economic incentive structure. Costs resulting from environmental pollution, such as GHG emissions, are added to the price of the original emitting process to signal and incentivize the polluter to reduce this impact. Nevertheless, this binary distinction by definition simplifies the complexity of policy instruments. Often one kind of instrument will, to a certain degree, also reflect elements of the other kind.

2. Simultaneous application of various policy instruments can have synergetic and opposing effects

There is no agreed set of criteria to evaluate climate policy instruments that are universally accepted. Often, policies are evaluated with a bias towards the concept of present cost minimization (static efficiency). However, it can be argued that a broader evaluation framework is necessary, including three main criteria, which influence practical feasibility; these criteria are environmental effectiveness, cost effectiveness, and additional impacts on society, i.e., income distribution or employment. All climate policy instruments differ in their score on these criteria and their introduction is highly embedded into societal processes. In addition, the simultaneous application of various instrument types can have synergetic but

Box 6.4. (*Continued*)

also contradictory effects, considering that the exploitation of the theoretical potential of policy instruments depends on the final details in policy design and its implementation.

3. Non-market-based instruments alone may fall short in cost effectiveness
The different types of climate policy instruments all entail advantages and disadvantages regarding environmental effectiveness, cost effectiveness, and additional impacts on society, i.e., income distribution or employment, which stem from their own characteristics. Command-and-control regulation (a non-market-based instrument) is a direct means of addressing GHG emissions and can therefore perform well in terms of environmental effectiveness. However, considering the varying costs of possible GHG abatement measures, a direct intervention might not result in the most cost-effective measures. Moreover, if applied alone, a purely regulatory approach might have to become increasingly intrusive to address possibly occurring rebound effects.

Nevertheless, command-and-control measures can play an important role in innovation and technology development. By supporting and developing currently not profitable technologies, the range of available abatement options can be increased by bringing these technologies to market maturity. Together with price mechanisms, command-and-control can create a market for new technologies.

4. Market-based instruments alone may face problems of acceptance and environmental effectiveness
Pricing instruments ideally perform well in terms of (static) cost effectiveness. Their revenue (where such is generated) can also help fund other policy programs. However, applied alone, they would likely require very high price levels to trigger desired changes, which could have a negative effect on low-income households and vulnerable industry sectors. Market-based instruments have

(*Continued*)

Box 6.4. (*Continued*)

a high distributional impact. Furthermore, humans do not always respond to price signals in the desired way; reaction can also lag behind for a certain time span. Given incumbent interests and technology lock-in effects, market-based instruments alone are likely to not provide sufficient incentives for innovation and innovation diffusion. A combination of command-and-control tools and dedicated technology support might therefore be necessary.

5. Hybrid instruments can reduce shortcomings of both instrument types

Due to their complementary characteristics, diversity within the policy instruments can effectively combine environmental and economic motivations. Smart policy design should take the respective characteristics of the different policy types into account and choose the most suitable policy based on the function it is meant to fulfill — in the respective context. A hybrid-policy approach can thereby reduce the shortcomings of each single instrument and lead to an improved outcome in comparison to the introduction of a single policy type.

Source: https://climatepolicyinfohub.eu/node/103/pdf#:~:text=Non%2Dmarket%20based%20instruments%20work,their%20economic%20incentive%20structure1, downloaded March 23rd, 2022.

Based on national food security concerns, non-market government interventions have been a generalized fact all over the world.[6] This practice goes against the precepts of conventional trade theory. In simple terms, according to the static version of this theory, trade liberalization would maximize consumers' welfare in countries

[6]State intervention is enlarged when national governments pursue "food sovereignty" by prioritizing production for local and national markets over international trade. It may also prioritize family farming and peasants' access to land over agribusiness and restricts the introduction of technologies such as genetically modified organisms (FAO, 2008).

involved in this process. Trade liberalization leads countries to specialize in the production of goods and tradable services according to comparative advantages determined by relative factor endowments between trading countries through price signals established by free trade (see Chapter 13 in Taylor and Lybbert, 2015).

Negotiating trade liberalization between member countries is one of the major objectives of the World Trade Organization (WTO). With regard to agriculture, following trade theory principles, the WTO position is that trade restrictions and State domestic intervention in the sector reduce global food security. In 1995, an agreement on agriculture was reached, aimed at establishing a fair and market-oriented agricultural trading system under the multilateral trade rules and disciplines. To promote the use by farmers of prices settled internationally, WTO partners agreed to reduce trade-distorting subsidies. However, a market-oriented agricultural trade has not been fully put into practice yet, partly because of WTO countries' concerns about national food security. The situation is revealed by the failure of WTO member countries to agree to take necessary actions towards a free agricultural trade since 2001, when the Doha Round was held.[7,8]

[7]The Doha Round is the latest round of trade negotiations among the WTO membership. Its aim is to achieve major reform of the international trading system through the introduction of lower trade barriers and revised trade rules. The Round is also known as the Doha Development Agenda that has a fundamental objective to improve the trading prospects of developing countries. See https://www.wto.org/english/tratop_e/dda_e/dda_e.htm#:~:text=The%20Doha%20Round%20is%20the,about%2020%20areas%20of%20trade; https://www.theigc.org/blog/food-security-international-trade/, both sites consulted on March 13, 2022.

[8]Global food security is not only negatively affected by inappropriate government interventions since food insecurity is also driven by market swings, trade wars, political unrest, or a global pandemic, such as COVID-19. To these drivers current war in Ukraine has been recently added since it is disrupting world grain and fertilizers supplies. Government intervention in agriculture is in place even in the United States of America (USA), one of the most market-oriented economies (for national security concerns related to USA agriculture see https://www.farmprogress.com/government/agriculture-crucial-security-risk-variety-threats consulted on March 13, 2022).

According to the United Nations Conference on Trade and Development (UNCTAD), while the 1995 agreement under the WTO was a major multilateral achievement, its incomplete implementation and the lack of use of provisions for special and differential treatment have limited the ability of some developing countries to deal with food security concerns. Pending requirements to promote agricultural trade and development are as follows: banning export restrictions on essential foodstuffs for food deficit countries; enhancing the support to resource-poor agricultural producers and facilitating support to vulnerable producers, including women; finding a permanent solution to public stockholding for food security purposes; and increasing financial and technical support to foster agricultural productivity in developing countries. So, for UNCTAD to enhance food security in low-income countries entails cooperation and a firm commitment from WTO members to finally remove the limitations and asymmetries of the agreement on agriculture (Bicchetti *et al.*, 2021).

The problems of implementing the UNFCC commitments by its members resemble the failure of the WTO to reach agreements to liberalize the agricultural sector. However, the reasons for these two unsuccessful efforts are different, among others, because agreements to contain global warming are not subject to legal enforcement, whereas trade liberalization agreements under the WTO are.

6.2.2 *Subsistence rural households and sustainable development policies*

Based on their empirical analysis of the impact of climate variability and extremes on agriculture and food security, Holleman *et al.* (2020) conclude that their findings are compelling and bring urgency to the fact that climate variability and extremes are proliferating and intensifying all over the world, and contributing to a rise in global hunger. The world's 2.5 billion small-scale farmers, herders, fishers, and forest-dependent people, who derive their food and income from renewable natural resources, are the most at risk and affected. They conclude that actions to strengthen the resilience of livelihoods and food systems to climate variability and extremes urgently need to be scaled up and accelerated.

As well as documenting the level of vulnerability billions of rural households have, Holleman and associates' findings reflect failures to accomplish United Nations Sustainable Development Goals (SDGs) in face of the myriad of challenges to design and implement measures that reduce rural households' vulnerability and food security in a sustainable way.

As we have discussed, one approach is to reduce transaction costs in rural goods and services markets through investments in infrastructure in order to create incentives for rural economic agents to follow price signals. In addition, and as the WB proposes, "Smallholders can act collectively to overcome high transaction costs by forming producer organizations .... Cooperation between larger commercial farmers and smallholders is another possibility. Smallholders sometimes can also benefit from economies of scale in input or output markets by renting out their land and working on the larger farms. Increasing the bargaining power of smallholders in this type of arrangement can help guarantee that benefits are shared by smallholders and the larger farms" (World Bank, 2008, p. 92).

Farmers' cooperatives have a long history all over the world. A recent approach, called in some countries Productive Territories (PT), has been implemented in several Latin American rural areas. Basically, it consists of promoting and/or creating rural households' productive organizations aimed at facilitating their access to markets through the design of collective projects. These projects will be presented to the government and, if approved, the organizations will receive state support to implement them. So, the PT strategy is a combination of market orientation and government intervention (Berdegué *et al.*, 2015).

The experience of PT shows that there are challenges for its implementation. An example is provided by the experience of a pilot exercise applied in rural Mexico, financed by FAO's International Fund for Agricultural Development (IFAD) and Mexico's central government. Notwithstanding that in several rural communities, the design of reasonable productive projects was reached under the guidance of trained independent supervisors, the corresponding government ministry did not evaluate and support the projects.

In some measures, the failure was due to problems of governance and lack of political will (i.e., local states' authorities' priorities of rural supports were not those related to households' PT projects) (see Chapter 7).

Neither the WB nor the PT approach considers in depth the issue of sustainability of collective rural projects. In addition, these strategies are centered on those rural households with "productive potential." This means that billions of subsistence households are left out. An option for this population may be to migrate to the cities. The problem is that these migrants carry poverty conditions with them and also millions of them remain in rural areas using natural resources to support their livelihoods.

In face of these phenomena and the loss of ecosystems, the question that requires answers is as follows: How to accomplish the SDGs and the commitments to reduce global warming under the UNFCCC agreements in rural areas? This leads to another question: Do rural households in medium- and low-income countries have or may have a role in preserving natural resources, and if so, how to promote this function while maintaining their livelihoods?

The easy answer to these questions is that market orientation together with non-market interventions are required to promote the accomplishment of the UN conventions' commitments regarding rural areas. The challenge is to specify the characteristics of this combined approach in light of a wide number of phenomena and situations such as the following: (1) Many rural households have common access to scarce natural resources (i.e., private property rights are absent), which leads to the controversy of what is called "the tragedy of the commons."[9] (2) There are rural households that preserve natural resources and there are others that do not because they have no subsistence options (the former includes the cultivation of biodiverse native crops by small subsistence farmers such as corn and other crops in Mexico and potatoes in Peru). (3) The access

[9]See Chapter 7 and Ostrom (2010). The issue of common-pool natural resources also applies to commercial farmers' access to groundwater for irrigation (see, e.g., Madani and Dinar, 2012).

and control of natural resources by indigenous populations and their communities.

Notwithstanding those deep analyses of these and other complexities and their implications as regards sustainable development are pending, UNFCCC Parties of COP26 have taken steps to consider the role of indigenous people and communities in the preservation of nature (see Box 6.5).

The declarations presented in Box 6.5 are framed under the Glasgow COP26 Declaration on Forests and Land use that stresses the need for transformative steps to move the world onto a sustainable and resilient land-use path (Box 6.6).

It is worth noting that in the official decisions that emerged from COP26-Glasgow, protection of forests was clearly acknowledged by the Parties, who did not only rely on conservation. This change indicates the recognition on the part of the signing Parties that state interventions in rural areas are necessary to combat global warming. However, policy actions that countries can take towards a sustainable land use — and for forest and agriculture land use in particular — have not been published as of the end of March 2022 (in the UNFCCC website we did not find literature on these actions, e.g., https://unfccc.int/news/nations-and-businesses-commit-to-create-sustainable-agriculture-and-land-use).

In its considerations of rural households, the UN work on CC and its recommendations single out indigenous populations from the rest of the rural households. The question is how convenient it is to separate this population from the remaining rural households in low- and medium-income countries. This is so because, notwithstanding that indigenous peoples' livelihood conditions are generally less favorable, they share similar problems with other rural (subsistence) households, i.e., extreme poverty conditions, discrimination, no access to assets and markets, production of biodiverse crops, and/or dependency on natural resources for their livelihoods (this is the case of *mestizo* population in many Latin American countries). So, it may just be that an adequate approach would be to include all subsistence rural households in a diagnostic of their unique situation and in the design of sustainable policies and then account for the specificities of

Box 6.5. COP26 on Indigenous Populations and Communities

With reference to the Glasgow Leaders' Declaration on Forests and Land Use of November 2nd 2021 and its commitment to working collectively to halt and reverse forest loss and land degradation by 2030 while delivering sustainable development and promoting an inclusive rural transformation.

We, the Ministers and representatives of the countries and organizations, listed the following:

Recognize the critical guardianship provided by Indigenous Peoples and local communities in protecting tropical forests and preserving vital ecosystem services, and the global contribution they make to climate change mitigation, biodiversity preservation, and inclusive and sustainable development.

Acknowledge the land and resource rights of Indigenous Peoples and local communities, in accordance with relevant national legislation, the UN Declaration on the Rights of Indigenous Peoples, and other international instruments, as applicable, and that, despite the important role they play in protecting forests and nature, only a small fraction of these communities enjoy secure rights to own, manage, and control land and resources and have access to the support and services required to protect forests and nature and pursue sustainable livelihoods.

Note with concern the rising cases of threats, harassment, and violence against Indigenous Peoples and local communities.

Welcome the political leadership and steps taken by many countries to recognize and protect Indigenous Peoples' and local communities' land and resource rights, in accordance with relevant national legislation and international instruments, as applicable.

Welcome the initiatives and efforts of Indigenous Peoples and local communities in securing the legal recognition of land and resource

Box 6.5. (*Continued*)

rights and in strengthening their institutions, organizations, and networks to support concerted action to protect their land, forests, and resources.

Commit to renewed collective and individual efforts to further recognize and advance the role of Indigenous Peoples and local communities as guardians of forests and nature, in partnership with governments and other stakeholders, with a particular focus on strengthening land tenure systems, protecting the land and resource rights of Indigenous Peoples and local communities, and protecting indigenous and community defenders of forests and nature.

Commit to promote the effective participation and inclusion of Indigenous Peoples and local communities in decision-making and to include, consult, and partner with them in the design and implementation of relevant programs and financial instruments, recognizing the specific interests of women and girls, youth, persons with disabilities, and others often marginalized from decision-making.

We are demonstrating our commitment today by announcing an initial, collective pledge of $1.7 billion of financing, from 2021 to 2025, to support the advancement of Indigenous Peoples' and local communities' forest tenure rights and greater recognition and rewards for their role as guardians of forests and nature. We call on other donors to significantly increase their support to this important agenda.

This financing will be directed at

- channeling support to Indigenous Peoples and local communities, including through capacity building and financial support for group activities, collective governance structures and management systems, and sustainable livelihoods;

(*Continued*)

Box 6.5. (*Continued*)

- activities to secure, strengthen, and protect Indigenous Peoples' and local communities' land and resource rights, including, but not limited to, support to community-level tenure rights mapping and registration work, support to national land and forest tenure reform processes and their implementation, and support to conflict resolution mechanisms.

Endorsed by the Federal Republic of Germany, Kingdom of Norway, Kingdom of the Netherlands, United Kingdom of Great Britain and Northern Ireland, United States of America, Ford Foundation, Good Energies Foundation, Oak Foundation, Sobrato Philanthropies, The David and Lucile Packard Foundation, The William and Flora Hewlett Foundation, The Christensen Fund, Children's Investment Fund Foundation, The Protecting Our Planet Challenge: Arcadia, Bezos Earth Fund, Bloomberg Philanthropies, and Gordon and Betty Moore Foundation.

Source: https://ukcop26.org/cop26-iplc-forest-tenure-joint-donor-statement/, consulted on March 27th 2022.

indigenous people. This approach could help evaluate if non-market-oriented policies can also apply to "non-indigenous" subsistence rural households.

The resemblance between global commitments vs. facts to reduce global warming under the COPs and the failure of the WTO in reaching a global agreement to reduce agricultural protection show that world leaders are yet not prepared to commit their countries to take necessary actions to halt CO_2 emissions and liberalize agricultural trade. To us, there is a major difference between these two forums though: up to now, the commitments under the UNFCCC do not have an enforcement mechanism (i.e., a legally binding one in terms of what countries need to do), whereas when agreed among WTO member countries, trade liberalization measures are compulsory. This may be one reason why contemporary agreements have been reached under the UNFCCC and not under the WTO.

Box 6.6. COP26: Forests and Land Use

The Glasgow COP26 Declaration on Forests and Land use endorsed by 141 countries stresses the need for transformative steps to move the world onto a sustainable and resilient land-use path — inextricably tying forests and the fight against climate change.

In international arenas, strong and clear language on policy is key. As such, COP26 is notable in the crafting of language giving specific importance to "ecosystem integrity" in fighting climate change, and on indigenous and community rights. In official decisions that emerged from Glasgow, Parties' "protection" was expressly acknowledged for forests rather than just relying on the term "conservation" that includes sustainable use as is usually the case in UN discussions, in the context of the role of forests in limiting global temperature increase to 1.5°C. The Policy Action Agenda for Transition to Sustainable Food and Agriculture sets out pathways and actions that countries can take to repurpose public policies and support to food and agriculture — to deliver these outcomes and enable a just, rural transition. It also sets out actions and opportunities for other stakeholders (international organizations, food producers, financial entities, researchers, civil society, and others) to channel their expertise, knowledge, and resources in support of this agenda.

From the Glasgow COP26 Declaration on Forest and Land Use, leaders from 141 countries committed to halt and reverse forest loss and land degradation by 2030 by strengthening their efforts to conserve and restore forests and other terrestrial ecosystems and accelerate their restoration. The Declaration identifies specific actions in terms of policies that promote sustainable production and consumption on the one hand while ensuring the resilience of communities by supporting their livelihoods and respecting their fundamental rights as a priority. Importantly, the Declaration on Forest and Land Use [did not find it on COP26 website] reaffirmed

(*Continued*)

Box 6.6. (*Continued*)

an accelerated and increased financial commitment for forests which was seen in the several financial announcements made during COP26 that amount to $19 billion in public and private funds, such as in the Congo Basin, with indigenous people and local communities, in the forest, agriculture, and commodity trade areas, focused on regenerative food systems, and through a just rural transition, among many others. In addition, the United States of America launched the Forest Investor Club and Forest Finance Risk Consortium (FFRC) which includes a network of leading public and private financial institutions and other investors and aims to unlock and scale up investments that support sustainable, climate-aligned outcomes in the land sector.

Nature-based Solutions resonated more than ever in Glasgow, for both mitigation and adaptation efforts. NbS [an integrated global platform for everyone involved in the design, supply, and construction of the built environment] for mitigation implemented in forests include protection, restoration, and management of working lands — among these, there are several types of solutions to be implemented that lock carbon in high-carbon stock ecosystems (protection of natural ecosystems), generate emission removals (reforestation and restoration) and reduce emissions in productive land uses (improved practices). A recent joint UNEP-IUCN report raises the importance of implementing NbS holistically where reducing emissions from the land sector should be maximized while investments are directed to permanent carbon removals.

The roles of the world's forests are vital in the fight against climate change, and the Parties at COP26 are not only acknowledging this complex reality but also taking strong steps towards a more inclusive approach to combatting climate change (Friday, December 17, 2021).

Source: https://www.iucn.org/news/forests/202112/what-cop26-does-forests-and-what-look-2022, consulted on March 27, 2022.

The discussion presented in this chapter is associated with questions related to the valuation of non-priced ecosystem services and to institutions, whose consideration is the purpose of the next chapter.

References

Bicchetti, D., Razo, C., and Shirotori, M. (2021). *Trade and food security: When an Agreement Delayed Becomes a Human Right Denied.* United Nations Conference on Trade and Development. https://t.ly/0-rZ.

Climate Focus. (2015). *Forests and Land Use in the Paris Agreement.* Climate Focus Client Brief on the Paris Agreement I. https://climatefocus.com/wp-content/uploads/2022/06/20151223-Land-Use-and-the-Paris-Agreement-FIN.pdf.

Climate Markets & Investment Association. (2013). *Submission to Subsidiary Body for Scientific and Technical Advice. On the Role and Technical Design of the Non-market-based Mechanism.* https://unfccc.int/files/cooperation_support/market_and_non-market_mechanisms/application/pdf/nmm_projectdeveloperforum_06092013.pdf.

Colclough, C. and Manor, J. (1991). *States or Markets? Neo-liberalism and the Development Policy Debate.* Clarendon Press, Oxford, UK.

Consultative Group for International Agricultural Research (CGIAR). (2015). *Paris Climate Agreement Unlocks Opportunities for Food and Farming.* Climate Change, Agriculture and Food Security. https://www.cgiar.org/research/program-platform/climate-change-agriculture-and-food-security/.

Crippa, M., Guizzardi, D., Muntean, M., Schaaf, E., Solazzo, E., Monforti-Ferrario, F., Olivier, J., and Vignati, E. (2020). *Fossil CO2 Emissions of All World Countries — 2020 Report.* Publications Office of the European Union. https://publications.jrc.ec.europa.eu/repository/handle/JRC121460.

Dupraz-Dobiaz, P. (2021). *At COP26, Indigenous Leaders Welcome Funding but Demand More of a Say. Those Who Pollute the Most and Cut the Most Trees are the Ones Who Make the Most Money.* The New Humanitarian. https://www.thenewhumanitarian.org/news/2021/11/10/COP26-Indigenous-leaders-welcome-funding-but-demand-more.

Earth Negotations Bulletin (ENB). (2021). *Glasgow Climate Change Conference,* 31 October–13 November 2021. A Reporting Service for Environment and Development Negotiations, *12*(793). https://enb.iisd.org/sites/default/files/2021-11/enb12793e_1.pdf.

Food and Agriculture Organization of the United Nations (FAO). (2008). *The Right to Food and Access to Natural Resources. Using Human Rights Arguments and Mechanisms to Improve Resource Access for the Rural Poor* [L. Cotula, M. Djiré, and R. W. Tenga (eds.)]. https://www.iied.org/sites/default/files/pdfs/migrate/G03065.pdf.

Holleman, C., Rembold, F., Crespo, O., and Conti, V. (2020). *The Impact of Climate Variability and Extremes on Agriculture and Food Security — An Analysis of the Evidence and Case Studies.* Background paper for The State of Food Security and Nutrition in the World 2018. FAO Agricultural Development Economics Technical Study No. 4. https://doi.org/10.4060/cb2415en.

International Fund for Agricultural Development (IFAD). (2021). *IFAD and COP26: What Next?* Executive Board — 134th Session, Rome, 13–16 December 2021. https://webapps.ifad.org/members/eb/134/docs/EB-2021-134-R-2.pdf.

Intergovernmental Panel on Climate Change (IPCC). (1990). *Climate Change: The IPCC Scientific Assessment.* Report prepared for IPCC [J. T. Houghton, G. J. Jenkins, and J. J. Ephraums (eds.)]. Cambridge University Press, Cambridge, UK. https://www.ipcc.ch/site/assets/uploads/2018/03/ipcc_far_wg_I_full_report.pdf.

IPCC. (1995). *IPCC Second Assessment Climate Change 1995.* A report of the Intergovernmental Panel on Climate Change. https://www.ipcc.ch/site/assets/uploads/2018/05/2nd-assessment-en-1.pdf.

IPCC. (2001). *Climate Change 2001: Synthesis Report.* A contribution of Working Groups I, II, and III to the Third Assessment Report of the Intergovernmental Panel on Climate Change [R. T. Watson and the Core Writing Team (eds.)]. Cambridge University Press. https://www.ipcc.ch/site/assets/uploads/2018/05/SYR_TAR_full_report.pdf.

IPCC. (2018). Summary for Policymakers. In: Global Warming of 1.5°C. An IPCC Special Report on the impacts of global warming of 1.5°C above pre-industrial levels and related global greenhouse gas emission pathways, in the context of strengthening the global response to the threat of climate change, sustainable development, and efforts to eradicate poverty [Masson-Delmotte, V., P. Zhai, H.-O. Pörtner, D. Roberts, J. Skea, P. R. Shukla, A. Pirani, W. Moufouma-Okia, C. Péan, R. Pidcock, S. Connors, J. B. R. Matthews, Y. Chen, X. Zhou, M. I. Gomis, E. Lonnoy, T. Maycock, M. Tignor, and T. Waterfield (eds.)]. Cambridge University Press, Cambridge, UK and New York, NY, USA, pp. 3–24. https://doi.org/10.1017/9781009157940.001.

IPCC. (2019). Summary for Policymakers. In: Climate Change and Land: an IPCC special report on climate change, desertification, land degradation, sustainable land management, food security, and greenhouse gas fluxes in terrestrial ecosystems [P. R. Shukla, J. Skea, E. Calvo Buendia, V. Masson-Delmotte, H.-O. Pörtner, D. C. Roberts, P. Zhai, R. Slade, S. Connors, R. van Diemen, M. Ferrat, E. Haughey, S. Luz, S. Neogi, M. Pathak, J. Petzold, J. Portugal Pereira, P. Vyas, E. Huntley, K. Kissick, M. Belkacemi, J. Malley, (eds.)]. In press. https://www.ipcc.ch/site/assets/uploads/sites/4/2020/02/SPM_Updated-Jan20.pdf.

IPCC. (2021). Summary for policymakers. In V. Masson-Delmotte, P. Zhai, A. Pirani, S. L. Connors, C. Péan, S. Berger, N. Caud, Y. Chen,

L. Goldfarb, M. I. Gomis, M. Huang, K. Leitzell, E. Lonnoy, J. B. R. Matthews, T. K. Maycock, T. Waterfield, O. Yelekçi, R. Yu, and B. Zhou (eds.), *Climate Change 2021: The Physical Science Basis.* Working Group I Contribution to the Sixth Assessment Report of the Intergovernmental Panel on Climate Change. https://www.ipcc.ch/report/ar6/wg1/downloads/report/IPCC_AR6_WGI_SPM_final.pdf.

Madani K. and Dinar, A. (2012). Non-cooperative institutions for sustainable common pool resource management: Application to groundwater. *Ecological Economics, 74*, 34–45. https://doi.org/10.1016/j.ecolecon.2011.12.006.

Ostrom, E. (2010). Beyond markets and states: Polycentric governance of complex economic systems. *American Economic Review, 100*(3), 641–672. doi:10.1257/aer.100.3.641.

Taylor, J. E. and Lybbert, T. J. (2015). *Essentials of Development Economics.* University of California Press, California, USA.

United Nations Framework Convention on Climate Change (UNFCCC). (1992). *United Nations Framework Convention on Climate Change.* https://unfccc.int/resource/docs/convkp/conveng.pdf.

UNFCCC. (1998). *Kyoto Protocol to the United Nations Framework Convention on Climate Change.* https://unfccc.int/resource/docs/convkp/kpeng.pdf.

UNFCCC. (2011). *Fact Sheet: The Kyoto Protocol.* https://unfccc.int/files/press/backgrounders/application/pdf/fact_sheet_the_kyoto_protocol.pdf.

UNFCCC. (2015). *Paris Agreement.* https://unfccc.int/files/essential_background/convention/application/pdf/english_paris_agreement.pdf.

UNFCCC. (2018). *Issues Related to Agriculture.* https://unfccc.int/topics/land-use/workstreams/agriculture.

UNFCCC. (2021a). *COP26 Strengthens Role of Indigenous Experts and Stewardship of Nature.* https://unfccc.int/news/cop26-strengthens-role-of-indigenous-experts-and-stewardship-of-nature.

UNFCCC. (2021b). *Sustainable Land and Water Management, Including Integrated Watershed Management Strategies, to Ensure Food Security.* Workshop report by the secretariat. https://unfccc.int/sites/default/files/resource/sb2021_03a01_E.pdf.

UNFCCC. (2021c). *Local Communities and Indigenous Peoples Platform.* Advance unedited version. Decision-/CP.26. https://unfccc.int/sites/default/files/resource/cop26_auv_2f_cover_decision.pdf.

World Bank. (2008). *World Development Report.* Quebecor World, Washington, D.C., USA.

Chapter 7

Challenges to Reduce Global Warming

There is no doubt that in market-oriented economies of all countries the attainment of sustainable development requires State and/or government intervention. What is under debate is how deep and extended this involvement must be to achieve sustainability. The discussion has to include the proposals of economists and ecologists on how to valuate natural resources.[1] In addition, the debate involves issues related to institutions and political economy (in other words, to government policies with an economic impact), as well as issues in the realm of democracy.

In this chapter, we document these aspects. Based on the fact that many natural resources and their services lack market prices, Section 7.1 examines the answers provided in the literature to valuate biodiversity and ecosystem services. In Section 7.2, we discuss the role of institutions to address the problem of global warming as regards democracy, corruption and states, markets and rural areas. In the last instance, the valuation of natural capital and understanding how institutions function and evolve can help understand why national and international commitments to halt global warming have only been partially fulfilled.

[1]The SAMSs and socioeconomic models presented in Chapter 5 either ignore that some natural resources are not valued by markets or assign a value to them using different monetary measurement strategies (see for example, Yúnez-Naude and Aguilar-Mendez, 2018; López-López and Yúnez-Naude, 2019).

7.1 Valuation of Natural Resources

An important part of nature and its services are public and hence, do not have a market value (such as clean air and fresh water). This characteristic is related to externalities and requires the valuation of nature to promote sustainable development; it also calls for answers related to property rights and access to natural resources or natural capital and a serious discussion about the appropriate scope of state intervention in market-oriented economies (Section 3.3, Chapter 3).

The non-existence of relevant markets for services provided by nature implies that these do not have a price, a situation that does not mean that nature and nature's services have value (see Box 7.1 and "value pluralism" below). Hence, policies designed to promote sustainability must, somehow, valuate nature and its services. The answer to this requirement is complex and not straightforward and depends on the approach to be followed that diverges between economists and ecologists.

Box 7.1. The Diversity of "Values"

The word "value" has interrelated but distinct dimensions and is understood and analyzed differently in the biophysical sciences, social sciences, economics, and from indigenous and local knowledge perspectives. Moreover, the word "value" has different meanings.

Values as principles, preferences, and subjective importance are assigned to things on the basis of people's experiences, beliefs, and understandings. People attribute values to nature, nature's contributions to people and constituents of a good quality of life and we assign measures to quantify them.

- Values associated to nature and its contributions to people can be non-anthropocentric such as intrinsic values, which are independent of any human experience and evaluation. They refer to the inherent value of nature and its components which is not ascribed or generated by external agents (such as human beings).

Box 7.1. (*Continued*)

- There can also be anthropocentric such as instrumental values, which often relate to nature's contributions to people and refer to the value attributed to something as a means to achieve a particular end.
- They can also be relational values, which reflect symbolic relationships with natural entities to the extent that such relationships are embedded in people's identity and every day they reveal elements of cultural identity, social cohesion, social responsibility, and moral responsibility toward nature. This type of relationship with nature is also part of the set of nature's contributions to people that impinge on people's good quality of life, such as those associated with learning and artistic inspiration, symbolic meanings, and cultural identity connections.

Source: Intergovernmental Science-Policy Platform on Biodiversity and Ecosystem Services (IPBES). https://ipbes.net/diverse-values-valuation, consulted on February 9, 2022.

Economists and ecologists' position in regard to the attainment of sustainable development is divergent since they follow a different school of knowledge. Economists point of departure is relative scarcity and follow Newtonian physics to build well-established instrumental models, leading to optimal solutions and equilibrium, whereas ecologists' point of departure is absolute scarcity, follow a Darwinian vision adopting the notions of unstable and non-predictable systems whose evolution is irreversible. Ecologists add that ecosystems and societies dynamics are inherently linked.

Many economists that include the environment in their analyses adopt an anthropogenic stance to promote ecosystems conservation, proposing government intervention to impose restrictions, and then economic agents follow market signals to maximize utility subject to these restrictions (i.e., a tax on the use of fossil fuels). By contrast, ecologists adopt an eco-centered position, arguing that nature must be respected and not exploited. Ecologists claim that the environmental management proposed by economists may cause an ecological collapse.

Economists' proposed mechanisms to promote sustainability can be summarized as consisting of two stages: (1) The establishment of some contractual arrangement, incorporating ecological principles, and environmental ethics to establish the rules applicable to the development policy (e.g., motor cars emission control). (2) Within those rules, the utilitarian stance of economic maximization following market signals can be adopted. The outcome of this process is that society obtains as much economic development as possible after the attainment of a certain degree of environmental quality has been assured (the aggregated economy variable that will be maximized can be output growth, per capita income, etc.).

This means that for economists, the attainment of sustainability does not require an administered economy. State intervention has to focus on providing the appropriate incentives to private agents within the context of market economy. Among others, these incentives go from taxing GHG emissions to promoting the development and application of green and efficient technologies (see Section 3.3, in Chapter 3).

On their part and among others, ecologists are risk averse and propose the use of small-scale productive technologies. In a nutshell, ecologists' objective is to change how the world functions toward what is desirable for the preservation of nature and humanity. Sustainable development is viewed by them as eco-protection based on minimizing the use of the natural environment even at the expense of economic growth. According to ecologists, achieving this goal requires State regulation based on command-and-control institutions.

7.1.1 *Economic value*

In the literature, economists' approach to assign values to natural resources is referred to as instrumental-anthropocentric, whereas ecologists are considered non-anthropocentric since they argue that nature has an intrinsic value (Box 7.1).

Economists conducting research on sustainable development propose that measures designed to protect the environment must consider human well-being, but only after considering that natural capital is unique, cannot be substituted and its loss is irreversible.

Economic value is a measure that the utility society gets from the consumption of goods and services. As regards the assessment of the environment it is necessary to know the value of all goods and services exchanged and not the marginal value of a specific good and/or service as conventional microeconomic theory states. Total value of a good-service is the sum of individual values. These values are subjective and not all measurable in monetary terms. Total economic value is expressed indirectly, not by the expenditure of individuals on consumer goods and services, but rather by what they are willing to spend to acquire these goods and services (an example is in Box 7.2).[2]

Box 7.2. Willingness to Pay to Preserve Galapagos

An example of willingness to pay for services of natural resources comes from a study on eco-tourism in the Galapagos Islands. A survey was conducted among international tourists at the Galapagos airport when leaving the Islands. The survey focused on the tourists' willingness to pay to preserve the Galapagos ecosystem. The purpose of the survey was to obtain information as to the appropriate fees the Ecuadorian government should charge to international tourists visiting the Islands to finance public expenditure on protection while maintaining international visitors. The results showed that international tourists were willing to pay a fee significantly higher than the fee they had paid as long as the Galapagos ecosystem remained safe.

The survey was conducted by Micki Stewart, a University of California-Davis Ph.D. student. Unfortunately, the results of the

(*Continued*)

[2]An alternative for value assessment is to inquire about what individuals are willing to receive for disposing of goods and/or services they own.

Box 7.2. (*Continued*)

survey were not published. Notwithstanding the foregoing, the data provided by this and other surveys applied to businesses and households in Galapagos were the basis to evaluate the multisectoral impacts of eco-tourism on the Islands' fragile ecosystem.

Source: Taylor *et al.* (2009).

The willingness-to-pay approach has limitations, out of which, the differences of individuals' income and/or financial capacity as well as different preferences stand out. (i.e., persons with similar preferences may differ as regards their willingness to pay for conserving the environment).[3]

An issue relevant to the concern about agricultural sustainability is related to the existence of billions of small farmers in low and medium-income countries surrounded by market failures including high transaction costs and the valuation of the crops they produce and consume (see Chapter 3). Many of these farmers are part of subsistence rural households producing staples for family consumption whose economic decisions are based on their own valuation of these goods and not on market prices, that is to say, on what economists call "shadow prices." When market failures in rural economies are explicitly considered, there is recent empirical evidence that subsistence rural households' own valuation of their staple production is considerably higher than the regional and/or national market price (see Box 7.3). As discussed below, the IPBES suggests that this type of valuation must be included in the designing of sustainable policies.[4]

[3]The challenge posed by the absence of markets for environmental services is exemplified by the limitations of Cost-benefit Analysis to evaluate the economic and environmental impacts of a development project (see Taylor and Filipski, 2014, pp. 55–58).

[4]In addition to what we write in footnote 6, Chapter 3, subsistence rural farming households in Mexico producing corn cultivate this grain in a system called *milpa*, characterized by the cultivation in the same plot biodiverse corn together with

Box 7.3. Estimating Shadow Prices in Economies with Multiple Market Failures

The complex behavior of households in rural developing areas is due only in part to the increasing diversification of their income sources ... It is also owed much to the fact that their activities depend on productive factors and inputs that they own, rent or sometimes borrow ... It is difficult even to estimate the net income of households that consume (either entirely or partially) the final goods that they produce ... In principle, under properly functioning markets, how much to produce or consume is a function of market prices. Yet when failures occur, these decisions depend on endogenous, non-observable shadow values that may differ widely from market prices ...

Shadow and market prices can differ under various types of markets failures, including transaction costs, often linked to poor transportation. Such costs make buying and selling goods difficult. As they rise, self-sufficiency ultimately becomes the best option, allowing gaps between shadow and market prices ... A gap in the price of output is to be expected also when markets do not recognize certain qualities that subsistence households' value ... For instance, corn farmers in Oaxaca, Mexico, reportedly prefer their own grain to that sold in the market when preparing special meals or herbal medicines, yet they also grow the crop to preserve their culture and traditions ... Another seemingly common market failure is the imperfect substitution of family and hired labor that encourages household members to employ themselves at home rather than in the market ... Both circumstances tend to create a gap between market and shadow wages ...
In this article we propose a theoretical model of household behavior in a mixed, subsistence/commercial economy with two market

(*Continued*)

biodiverse beans and pumpkins, allowing the growth of several eatable weeds. This biodiverse practice conducted by indigenous and mestizo households is relevant in the discussion of sustainable development policies.

Box 7.3. (*Continued*)

failures ...: in subsistence goods and ... labor. Based on the theoretical solution to this problem we propose a protocol to estimate shadow wages using nationally representative data of Mexican rural households, and in turn, use these results to estimate the shadow price of corn grown in monoculture by this population. This restriction enables us to control the value of other crops often grown in polyculture in Mexico in our corn production estimates ...

Unemployment and the highly heterogeneous nature of subsistence goods are arguably common occurrences in developing rural areas around the world, reflecting the simultaneous presence of multiple, interacting market failures. Such circumstances are bound to help explain the complex and sometimes puzzling behavior of rural households, influenced by shadow prices. Since shadow and market prices can differ under various types of markets failures, accurate estimates of shadow prices can have important policy implications ...

In the case of rural Mexico, we find that the shadow wage of family labor was significantly lower in 2007 than the market wage, i.e., MX$ 93.2/day in average versus MX$132.3. This fact has enabled us to derive unbiased estimates of the shadow price of corn at the time, which was MX$32.37/kg — that is, nearly an order of magnitude greater than its market counterpart, MX$3.19/kg. Such estimates have enabled us, in turn, to correct errors in the measurement of rural poverty, particularly food poverty ...

Our estimates have additional applications not developed further here. For instance, in Mexico, accurate estimates of the shadow price of corn could be used to explain households' lack of participation in programs meant to bolster their income, such as the current guaranteed-prices scheme for corn and other staples,

Box 7.3. (*Continued*)

the major agricultural program since 2019. More specifically, estimates could be used to assess the rate of exclusion of subsistence farmers both in and above poverty — that is, the percentage of those not supported by the program since their shadow value for corn exceeds guaranteed prices.

Since shadow households' incomes are an important determinant of their labor decisions, more precise estimates should also help yield better estimates of the supply of family labor than are now available. Estimates could yet prove indispensable inputs to realistic general equilibrium modeling of developing rural economies. More generally, our methods allow for the estimation of shadow prices of both products with missing markets and products derived entirely from household labor. These imply common activities across developing rural areas, such as fetching water for domestic use, wildlife hunting or fuelwood collection.

Source: Hernández-Solano *et al.* (2020).

7.1.2 *Value pluralism*

The IPBES (https://www.ipbes.net/) discusses the contrasting approaches between economists and ecologists to assess biodiversity and ecosystem services, and proposes an integrated approach called "value-pluralism."[5]

IPBES proposes that in the discussion of sustainable development policies, there are two contrasting approaches to values and valuation: instrumental-anthropocentric value vs. intrinsic, non-anthropocentric, value of nature. Dominant approaches tend to emphasize the dichotomy; instead, IPBES argues that there is a relational value perspective that emphasizes the value of the

[5]The following summary comes from IPBES contributions in https://ipbes.net/contrasting-approaches-values-valuation, consulted on February 9, 2022.

interactions between people and nature and those among individuals in society; i.e., IPBES proposes a value pluralism approach (Box 7.1).

IPBES adds that much of policy discourse on the need for valuation of nature's contributions to people relies on either a one-dimensional value lens (value-monism) that derives from a utilitarian economic perspective or on an environmental ethics stance of nature–human relationships, furthering the instrumental vs. intrinsic dichotomy. Instead, a plural value lens can encompass a wide variety of dimensions that assess the interdependence between nature and societies, including biophysical, health, sociocultural, or holistic approaches.

IPBES also proposes that acknowledging and fostering the use of diverse conceptualizations of multiple values of nature and its contributions to people is required for adequately addressing the challenge of achieving global sustainability. Other challenge to valuate nature is that people hold often different views of nature. In addition, the lack of recognition or exclusion of some of these views cause an uneven participation or cost bearing among those holding different perspectives, triggering conflicts.

Alternative worldviews, foci of value, policy objectives, valuation approaches, value indicators, as well as policy support tools and instruments can be incorporated in very different ways. For the IPBES a value pluralism acknowledges the role of institutions (formal and informal), the existence of a diversity of values and valuation approaches. In addition, value pluralism would allow for developing the conditions for the design of more comprehensive and deliberative policy support tools and policy instruments to enhance nature, nature's contributions to people, and good quality of life. This alternative approach highlights that valuation process needs to account for multiple worldviews in a more integrated and iterative way, both within and among the different valuation steps. All this is based on the premise that human (social and economic) activities ultimately depend on ecosystems and that there are strong feedback mechanisms linking nature, nature's contributions to people, and a good quality of life. Hence, value pluralism sees that nature and its contributions to people for a good quality of life are interdependent.

As the IPBES argues, the pluralism approach would require applying deliberative measures toward potential conflict resolution over values. This is associated with the need to leverage power relations through participatory negotiations among stakeholders holding incommensurable values over human–nature relations (see Section 7.2). This integrative approach opens the opportunity to bridge biophysical, sociocultural, economic, health, or holistic perspectives on valuation.

So, the IPBES pluralistic valuation approach recognizes intrinsic, instrumental, and relational values of nature. These multiple values may be formed and elicited within different cultural, social, and institutional frameworks. Values are assigned to things in alignment with people's experiences, beliefs, and understandings, which are in turn influenced by their sociocultural context. These values shared by people in groups or that inform shared identity of a particular group, cannot be elicited by valuation tools that focus on values only as a measure. Underlying worldviews determine which types of value and valuation approaches and methods may be perceived as appropriate in any given context.

In summary, the IPBES approach to valuate biodiversity and ecosystems for decision-making proposes that different types of values need to be accounted for and promoted. While for this, intrinsic values of nature are important, decision-making relies to a greater extent on instrumental values of nature's contribution to people. However, these contributions can embody symbolic relationships with nature to the extent that these relationships are inextricably linked to people's sense of identity and spirituality and to a meaningful life. In this sense, nature's contributions are associated with relational values, i.e., with values that do not directly emanate from nature but are derivative of people's relationships with nature and our responsibilities toward it.

The IPBES concludes that acknowledging, assessing, and explicitly including the diversity of values while identifying their specific uptake into policy design is challenging, as it requires an equally integrative vision and "toolbox."[6] Decision-making processes would benefit from pluralistic ways of valuation, and this means finding and supporting means to include values held by the full range of stakeholders with different worldviews of nature, nature's contributions to people, and a good quality of life, at different spatial and temporal scales.

7.2 Institutions and Sustainable Development

As noted in the previous section, using the pluralistic approach to valuate biodiversity and ecosystem services requires considering institutions, among others. Knowledge of the various types of contemporary institutions and their role in economic development is also needed to discuss policies designed to promote sustainable development. This also applies to democracy, a political institution.

There is a myriad of institutions — including bad ones, such as that of institutional corruption — that encompass a wide variety of human rules and behaviors that have been studied by social scientists since Adam Smith's proposal of the role of markets as the "invisible hand" for economic agents' decision-making process, and also by Karl Marx argument that claims that markets hide the exploitation of workers under capitalist systems.[7]

In the beginning of the 1970s the study of institutions and their role in economic development boomed with the contributions of prominent Nobel Prize economists like Ronald Coase, Douglass North, Elinor Ostrom, and Oliver Williamson. This area of knowledge is called New Institutional Economics and it covers fundamental

[6]In an assessment report the IPBES presents scenarios and models based on best-practice "toolkit" for their use in decision-making on biodiversity, human–nature relationships, and the quality of life. The aim of the report is to help governments, private sector, and civil society to anticipate change — such as the loss of habitats, invasive alien species, and climate shifts — to reduce the negative impacts on people and to make use of important opportunities (IPBES, 2016).

[7]For a discussion of the origins of institutions see Taylor and Lybbert (2015, pp. 190–193, 203–206).

issues for the study of development, including democracy, governance (transparency, corruption, enforcement of contracts, etc.) as well as formal and informal social norms (some basic definitions are in Box 7.4).

Box 7.4. Governance, Institutions, and Democracy

Governance can be defined as a complex process whereby some sectors of a society wield power, and design and put into practice public policies that directly affect human, human–nature, and institutional interactions, and, in the last instance socioeconomic and sustainable development, by using resources in a proper, efficient, and effective manner. In principle, three groups of actors interact in the course of governance: the public sector, the private sector, and civil society (https://www.insightsonindia.com/governance/governance-an-introduction/). In other words, governance is the system by which entities are directed and controlled. It is composed of structures and processes for decision making, accountability, control, and rules at the top of an entity.

Institutions: In general, an institution is composed of formal and informal rules that structure and limit the behavior of members of society along with enforcement mechanisms.
Characteristics and role of institutions:

- Institutions do not determine what is to be done, but rather, how it should be done.
- Institutions affect the behavior of individuals, economic agents, and groups whose decisions enable the creation of markets and affect society as a whole.
- Institutions may be susceptible to "path dependency": an institution that was created under certain historical circumstances may persist after these initial conditions disappear (see below, Acemoglu and Robinson (2008) on the persistence of power, elites, and institutions).

(*Continued*)

Box 7.4. (*Continued*)

Examples of institutions:

- The market
- Public entities such as public schools and universities and the British National Health services
- Private established organizations or corporations such as banks
- Informal institutions may emerge when well-developed markets are missing; i.e., shared cropping in the agricultural production in low-income countries.

Democracy:
A system of government by the whole population or all the eligible members of a state, typically through elected representatives. A government in which the supreme power is vested in the people and exercised by them directly or indirectly through a system of representation usually involving periodically held free elections. https://www.merriam-webster.com/dictionary/democracy.

To consider the contributions of new institutional economics is necessary in any reflection about the challenges the United Nations face to fully put into practice the agreements reached under the Conferences of the Parties on Climate Change, and also to inquire on why national and international commitments to reduce global warming have not been realized.

In Chapter 8, Taylor and Lybbert (2015) state institutions act as operating systems of computers for economies and societies. Institutions provide rules, conventions, norms, and processes that enable people to know the outcomes they can expect arising from their decisions and interactions with others. Institutions often function in the background of human lives and are often only fully acknowledged when they crash (an example is the take-off of the United States of America (USA) Congress by the moods questioning Biden's triumph in the presidential election).

It is difficult to determine empirically the role institutions play in economic performance as it is difficult to know the cause and effect. For example, institutions determine how development takes place, but at the same time, development enables countries to invest in the creation of better institutions. Other example can be presented as a question: Since corruption and crime are interrelated with poverty, do corruption and crime cause poverty, or *vice versa*?

Notwithstanding the problems to empirically assess the role of institutions in development, Acemoglu and Robinson (2012) provide evidence as to why nations have failed to develop. The authors adopt an institutional approach using data on world patterns of economic development and conclude that differences in economic and political institutions among countries are the main reasons some nations have failed to develop.

Acemoglu and Robinson support this conclusion with three arguments.[8]

(1) There are two types of institutions: extractive and inclusive, and the countries that failed to develop are characterized by the former. Extractive institutions have a concentrated political power and economic institutions that reinforce and often enrich the powerful few (i.e., gold and/or oil extraction without processing these resources). The governing elite of extractive institutions extracts value from the resources it controls (land, minerals, monopoly rights, public coffers, people, foreign aid, etc.), with little regard for making investments that create value and improve welfare for the society at large. By contrast, inclusive institutions encompass political systems that are pluralistic, protect individual rights, and create the conditions that reward innovation and entrepreneurship, including securing private property and competitive markets.[9]

[8]The following summary is taken from Taylor and Lybbert (2015, pp. 200–202).
[9]As we will discuss in Section 7.2.1, Acemoglu and Robinson add that societies with inclusive institutions also have governing elites who try to cash in their power and influence for personal profit. In the last Section 7.2.3 of this chapter we discuss the issue of private property rights as regards natural resources.

(2) Institutions can be an influential economic force because of the positive or negative dynamics they trigger (i.e., inclusive institutions foster and encourage innovation). As with any dynamic process, small institutional differences today often become big differences tomorrow.
(3) Some policies are known to be "bad" in the sense that they inhibit the economy and cause people to stay poor (i.e., corruption). Elites may not want to combat these institutions since their dissolution may deteriorate the power of the elites. Through this approach, the ruling elite often pretends to want change and promotes the change publicly while privately ensuring that little actually gets done (see Sections 7.2.1 and 7.2.2).

One important implication of Acemoglu and Robinson study is that institutions are all that mater in explaining underdevelopment. So, if extractive institutions prevail in low-income countries, the international aid to support their development will not achieve the goal.

In his review of Acemoglu and Robinson's book, Sachs (2012) disagrees with their arguments. Sachs's position can be summarized as follows. (1) It is incorrect to assume that authoritarian elites are necessarily against economic progress. There is evidence of authoritarian regimes that introduced economic and political reforms, which led to more inclusive institutions through domestic and/or international pressures. (2) Notwithstanding those inclusive institutions promote innovation, the dissemination of technologies from other countries with authoritarian institutions also matter. (3) In addition to corrupt agents not wanting institutional change, there are other constraints for development such as adverse geography; insufficient food availability; limited access to suitable technologies; lack of appropriate essential public services such as health, education, clean water, and infrastructure (Taylor and Lybbert, 2015).

The discussion between Sachs and Acemoglu and Robinson shows how complicated it is to find out what the main drivers of development are, a challenging question if one includes sustainability as a major component of development.

7.2.1 *Democracy*

The paper of Acemoglu and Robinson (2008) on persistence of power from elites in democratic regimes provides insight into the potential limits of democracy as a requirement to attain sustainable development as proposed in the literature.

Acemoglu and Robinson's main purpose is to explain why changes in political institutions (i.e., from an authoritarian regime to democracy) do not necessarily lead to expected economic outcomes. For example, why changes in political institutions such as the independence of Latin America from Spain and/or Portugal in the early 19th century and the abolition of slavery in southern USA did not lead to substantial economic outcomes, whereas the democratization of Great Britain during the 19th century did. The answers to these differences are mixed in the empirical literature. Studies based on regressions and/or comparisons between democratic and authoritarian regimes either find significant effects of political institutions on economic outcomes, or no differences at all.

According to Acemoglu and Robinson, these mixed results can be explained when we distinguish *de jure* from *de facto* political power by constructing a model with this distinction to study the likely implications that changes in political institutions have on economic institutions. Among others, Acemoglu and Robinson's model results indicate that a change in political institutions alters the distribution of *de jure* political power, but creates incentives for elites to invest in *de facto* political power to partially or even fully offset change in *de jure* power. "The model can imply a pattern of captured democracy, whereby a democratic regime may survive but choose economic institutions favoring an elite. The model provides conditions under which economic or policy outcomes will be invariant to changes in political institutions, and economic institutions themselves will persist over time" (p. 267).

In Acemoglu and Robinson's model equilibrium institutions and the distribution of resources are the outcome of the interplay between *de jure* political power allocated by political institutions and investments in *de facto* political power to influence the course of politics through other means such as lobbying, bribery, and use of extralegal force. For our purpose, we select the following findings of the authors.

- By virtue of their smaller numbers and greater expected gains, the elite is more likely to invest in their *de facto* political power than the more numerous citizens. This asymmetry has important implications for the structure of political equilibria: the persistence of institutions and the relationship between changes in political institutions and economic performance.
- Changes in *de jure* power driven by reforms and political institutions can be partially or entirely offset by changes in *de facto* political power.
    - An extreme form of offset, even though political institutions change along the equilibrium path of the model, the stochastic distribution of economic outcomes remains invariant (this type of persistence in economic institutions and outcomes is broadly consistent with a number of historical examples).
- The model also shows the conditions under which changes in political institutions translate into corresponding changes in economic outcomes.
    - An effective democratic reform that creates a sufficiently level political playing field so that it becomes no longer profitable for the elite to invest heavily in their *de facto* political power. Such democratization will lead to significant changes in economic outcomes.
    - In contrast, more moderate steps toward democracy may lead to little or no change in economic outcomes.
- In addition, when political and economic reforms take place simultaneously, their effect on the structure of equilibrium could be much larger.
- The interplay between *de facto* and *de jure* political power leads to a number of new comparative static results. For example, the analysis shows that elites that have fewer members, that can

benefit more from controlling economic institutions and that are more forward looking are more likely to dominate politics.

- Somewhat paradoxically, over a certain range, a greater democratic advantage for the citizens leads to greater elite domination of politics. The reason for this result is that when there is a greater democratic advantage for the citizens, elites intensify their investments in *de facto* political power in order to avoid democratic institutions, which are more costly for them after the change (*Ibid.* pp. 268–270).

Notwithstanding that, as Sachs argues, a focus on institutions is not sufficient in explaining economic development, the work of Acemoglu and Robinson provides clues as to why commitments to reduce global warming have only been partially fulfilled by many high, medium, and low-income countries with democratic regimes. For high-income countries an example is the long-term investment of Exxon-Mobil oriented to prevent the USA Congress from approving measures (i.e., tax bills) whose purpose was to reduce oil consumption.[10] In regard to low and medium-income countries an example are the frequent bribes to officials from the wood and agricultural sectors to obstruct government actions intended to stop deforestation.

Acemoglu and Robinson's results and evidence of the exercise of political *de facto* power to offset reforms show the importance of considering scientifically based research and policy design and the potential limits of democracy as well as the role of (bad and good) institutions in the study about the types of institutions required to promote sustainable development. This type of inquiries should be

[10]The documentary "The Power of the Big Oil" published by FRONTLINE, part of USA Public Broadcasting Service or PBS, presents journalistic evidence that this is the case of the recent public recognition of Exon-Mobil of the anthropogenic basis of global warming, while privately doing "business as usual." https://www.pbs.org/wgbh/frontline/film/the-power-of-big-oil/, consulted on May 4, 2022. Another case of the influential and powerful economic elites is the empirical study of lobbying related to power and water distribution in Spanish irrigated agriculture (Esteban *et al.*, 2019).

independent of political and economic powerful groups; in particular, from those interested in short-run outcomes for their own benefit. Since the international UN efforts to reduce global warming are based on partner governments agreements, the challenge for independent scientists is to incorporate their results on the role of institutions in CC international negotiations.

7.2.2 *Corruption*

Corruption can be singled out as one of the most pervasive institutions for development since it hinders "good governance" by deviating domestic and international financial resources allocated for sustainable development policies.[11]

Corruption is a complex pervasive institution and hard to define in simple terms. This is due to the fact that corruption adopts many forms and can involve politicians, government officials, members of the army, public servants, business, and/or members of the civil society. In addition, corruption is a two-party activity: the one party who takes the bribe and the one who offers it. Corruption takes place anywhere: in the government, businesses, in the courts and legal system and in the media, and also across all sectors, from health and education to infrastructure projects and sports.

Corruption influences behaviors and promote public servants asking for and receiving money in exchange for services, politicians misusing public budget funds, and/or receiving bribes from the private sector to be award public bids such as infrastructure building or projects that deplete natural resources (i.e., construction of touristic resorts) and officials granting public jobs or contracts to their sponsors, friends, and families.

In general terms, International Transparency (IT) defines corruption as the abuse of entrusted power for private gain (https://www.transparency.org/en/what-is-corruption, consulted on April 21, 2022),

[11]In many low and medium-income countries powerful organized crime has become increasingly involved in economic and political decision-making, through corruption and violence.

a definition that falls short in considering the practices of organized crime, among others.

To the problems of empirically evaluating the effects of corruption on sustainable development arising from the ample coverage of corrupted activities and agents, data restrictions are added since corruption is an illegal activity. As IT states: "Corruption happens in the shadows, often with the help of professional enablers such as bankers, lawyers, accountants and real estate agents, opaque financial systems and anonymous shell companies that allow corruption schemes to flourish and the corrupt to launder and hide their illicit wealth" (https://www.transparency.org/en/what-is-corruption, consulted on April 21, 2022).

What is generally accepted is that corruption deteriorates democracy, corrodes certainty and, in the last instance hinders sustainable development. As Fisman and Miguel (2008) report, the concurrence of corruption, violence, and the persistence of poverty is so pervasive that it is hard to dissociate the study of poverty from that of corruption and violence.

Notwithstanding that the difficulties to study empirically the hypothesis that corruption causes economic underdevelopment, what is easily calculated is the relationship between corruption and income levels using country data provided by IT and the World Bank development indicators; i.e., the corruption perception index (CPI) and per capita income, respectively.[12] We worked on this exercise using data for 170 countries — the ones included by both international institutions — and for 2020, and estimated the correlation coefficient between CPI and per capita income measured in PPP. We obtained a correlation coefficient of 0.78, which is very high. This result indicates that as income rises corruption falls (Figure 7.1 shows this result).

[12] In order to compare countries using per capita income levels the World Bank measures this income in terms of purchasing power parity or PPP that measures the cost of life in each country. The PPP is necessary because the purchasing power of say \$10 in country X in general differs from the purchasing power of this amount in country Y; i.e., a consumer in a low-income country can get more of a good than a consumer in a high-income country.

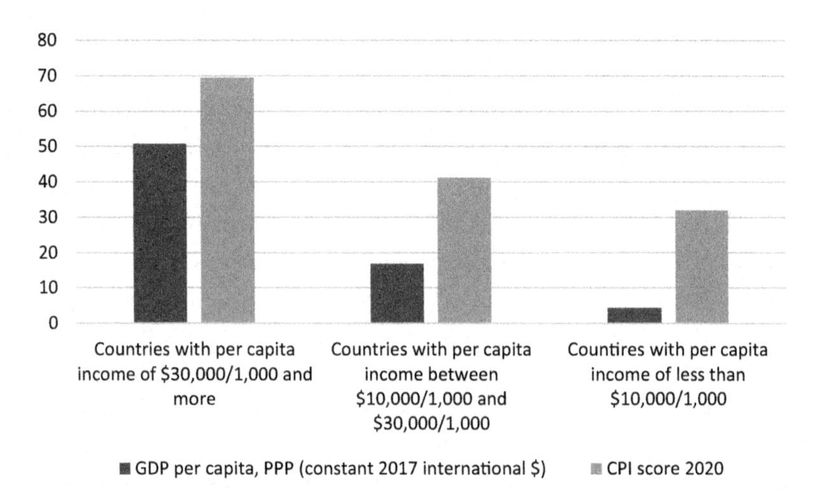

Figure 7.1. Per capita Income and Corruption Index in 2020 by Groups of Countries.*

Note: * Per capita income in thousand international dollars based on Purchasing Power Parity (PPP).

Sources: Income data from the World Development Indicators, updated on November 15, 2021 (https://data.worldbank.org/indicator/NY.GDP.MKTP.PP.KD). CPI data from Transparency International (https://images.transparencycdn.org/images/CPI2020_Report_EN_0802-WEB-1_2021-02-08-103053.pdf, consulted on November 24, 2021).

Our correlation coefficient estimation is in line with the findings of Fisman and Miguel (2007) in their study on corruption. The authors took data available from the New York City (NYC) police and combined this information with TI's CPI. Until 2002 diplomats working in the UN building in Manhattan were granted immunity from parking citations issued by NYC police. Fisman and Miguel found that diplomats from highly corrupt countries were much more likely to accumulate more parking citations than those from less corrupt countries.

7.2.3 *States, markets, and rural areas*

Questions related to the billions of small farmers and rural households prevailing in low and medium-income countries as well as their use of natural resources need special consideration. Notwithstanding these facts, the context in which they take economic decisions is, at best, not fully incorporated in sustainable development policy design by either international institutions or governments. Other questions that require special attention are related to gender and common pool natural resources.

It can be argued that one basic and general reason behind those who overlook specific rural households' economic functioning and the communities where they are located lies in the conventional proposition that low and middle-income countries should follow the path followed by high-income countries and adopt these countries institutions such as market and democracy. This proposition is characterized by the view that all fits in the experience of a stylized high-income country experience that can be described as a "top-down" view of institutions. However, there is also a distinct approach: a "bottom-up" view of institutions that allows for the possibility that societies develop with institutions different to those of the high-income world.

The discussion between a top-down vs. bottom-up approach is shown in the controversy between Jeffrey Sachs (from UN) and William Easterly (ex-World Bank researcher) about the convenience of international aid for development. Easterly argued that international aid promoted by the UN and the WB does not consider local conditions of low-income countries — such as corruption — whose presence may even revert the expected outcomes, such as poverty reduction (details in Chapter 8 of Taylor and Lybbert, 2015).

Top-down vs. bottom-up policy design also applies to actions oriented to rural development. As we discussed in Section 6.2 of Chapter 8, the promotion of market access of small farmers is a major argument of those adopting the first view, whereas proposals of rural farmers and rural households' participation in the design of government supports for them are a basic component of the second view.

We suggest the bottom-up approach should be considered in rural sustainable development research and policies. Several reasons support this suggestion. An important one being rural households' diversification of their economic activities and/or income sources in divergent contexts in which they take decisions (i.e., access to natural resources and public services).

To start the reflection on rural households' inclusion in rural sustainable development policy design we propose a conceptual distinction between them: households located in towns or villages with relative but limited access to markets, and households relatively isolated from the first. Although this differentiation does not capture the diversity and complexity of the contexts where rural households take their decisions, it helps frame our reflection on appropriate development policies.[13]

Many rural households and communities engaged in productive activities and having access to goods and services provided by urban centers experience limitations to sell their production mainly due to the small scope of their activities. The promotion or creation of democratic economic cooperatives of men and women of these households can be a way to enhance their participation in regional markets. This bottom-up strategy is in line with the top-down markets perspective. The difference is that as well as including women, the former is based on the planning of productive and marketing projects by rural households' organizations on the basis of their specific living economic conditions and what they need in order to sell their production and services under better conditions. These projects are submitted to the corresponding government agency for its evaluation and approval to later provide them to the cooperative public support. Cooperative projects shall include components designed to purchasing the required productive inputs under better conditions (see reference to "Productive Territories" in Section 6.1, Chapter 6). Lastly, the cooperative projects must be economically and ecologically sustainable and their governmental assessment is to take this into consideration.

As for the second conceptual category of relative isolated rural households and communities in low and medium-income countries, many of them have informal institutions based on culture and

[13]Our reflection does not rule out rural migration. However, considering the fact that migration to the urban sector has not significantly reduced poverty incidence in urban areas of many low and medium-income countries, there can be better alternatives for a portion of the households to remain in rural areas.

tradition, some are positive for development and others are negative. An example of the former is the conservation of native biodiverse crops such as corn in Mexico and potatoes in the Andes, and discrimination against women in the case of the latter. Communities where these households are located are generally found in remote areas, and a large number of them are inside or near rich natural resources areas.[14] Many, but not all of them, are formed by indigenous populations.

It can be argued that the combined market oriented top-down and bottom-up approaches can be also applied to isolated-second-type households and communities. However, the strategy needs to consider the differences between this group and the first one. Two considerations stand out: First, to properly connect remote and disperse communities to the regional economy (i.e., to well-connected villages or urban centers), a major governmental investment in communications and infrastructure works is required. Second, new infrastructure can affect ecosystems and livelihoods of rural population.[15] Hence, an option could be public investment in small-nature friendly infrastructure together with measures to promote the production of these relatively isolated households of biodiverse crops, agroforestry and other goods such as art-crafts for special small markets (i.e., farmers' markets and markets for tourists). As regards natural resources such as forests, this strategy can be coupled with the scheme of payments for environmental services (see Chapter 6, Section 6.2). Again, and due to the divergent situations in the rural world, these strategies must be based on a bottom-up perspective.

---

[14] People in several regions in low and medium-income countries are mestizo who retain some of the indigenous population informal institutions (examples are rural regions in Mexico, Central America and the Andes). The category "indigenous population" referred to in COP agreements may exclude mestizo rural population. The issue requires clarification in the design of development policies as they can exclude mestizo rural populations.

[15] An emblematic contemporary case is the construction of a railroad in south-east Mexico, called *Tren Maya*. Ecologists from all over the world claim that the project will affect the underground fresh water ecosystem of the Yucatan Peninsula (see, for example, https://www.expoknews.com/impactos-ambientales-del-tren-maya/, consulted on May 6, 2022).

A challenge in sustainable rural policy design for both relatively connected and relatively isolated communities is to contribute to the eradication of discrimination against women. To achieve this, bottom-up strategies must include women's empowerment; i.e., women must take part in the design and implementation of community projects. Furthermore, women participation will enhance sustainable development by incorporating their longer view perspectives such as their major concerns with regard their daughters and sons' future in these projects.[16]

An alternative for rural sustainability policy could be to extend and/or create protected natural areas, also called natural parks. The problem this option poses is that in many cases its implementation would require the displacement of rural populations living in these areas, a process that ultimately may have to be forced by the state. In addition, not all rural populations live in rich ecosystems and so, the question as to their inclusion in the sustainable development paths remains.

A relevant development issue for rural areas in low and medium-income countries is the existence of common access to natural resources. The question has been a matter of discussion in the economic development literature. As Elinor Ostrom writes: "Garrett Hardin's portrayal of the users of a common-pool resource — a pasture open to all — being trapped in an inexorable tragedy of overuse and destruction has been widely accepted since it was consistent with the prediction of no cooperation in a prisoner's dilemma or other social dilemma games. It captured the attention of scholars and policymakers across the world. Many presumed that all common-pool resources were owned by no one. Thus, it was thought that government officials had to impose new external variables (i.e., new policies) to prevent destruction by users who could

[16]The conditional income transfers to female household heads in poverty applied all over the low and medium-income countries is a way to empower women. This is a lesson that should be included in all bottom-up development actions. Women's participation in productive projects was the starting point of Productive Territories in Mexico (see Berdegue *et al.*, 2015).

not do anything other than destroy the resources on which their own future (as well as the rest of our futures) depended" (Ostrom, 2010, p. 649).[17]

Ostrom and colleagues propose the Institutional Analysis and Development (IAD) framework, and with it, criticize the foundations of the problem, called "the tragedy of the commons". The formulation of this dilemma was done in the mid-20th century, when social scientists fit the world into simple models and used to criticize institutional arrangements that did not fit as arrangements to use common natural resources.

In laboratory studies based on experiments of different situations, Ostrom and her team found that isolated, anonymous individuals overharvested from common-pool resources, and that simply allowing communication enables participants to reduce overharvesting and increase joint payoffs contrary to game theoretical predictions. In addition, studies of irrigation systems and forests challenge the presumption that governments always do a better job than users in organizing and protecting important resources.

Ostrom proposes a more general theory of individual choice that recognizes the central role of trust in coping with social dilemmas. However, due to the complexity of broader field settings, it is necessary to develop more configural and situational approaches to the study of factors that enhance or detract from the emergence and robustness of self-organized efforts within multilevel, polycentric systems. As regards policies, Ostrom argues that the application of empirical studies to the policy world leads to stressing the importance of fitting institutional rules to a specific social-ecological setting (*Ibid.*)

The contents of this chapter show that "one size fits all" policies are not effective and so, bottom-up approaches are necessary in the

[17]The prisoner's dilemma is a problem considered by game theory to answer the question of why two people might not cooperate even if cooperation is in their best interest. The formalization of this game is based on prison sentence payoffs (Wikipedia provides a good account of the prisoner's dilemma, https://en.wikipedia.org/wiki/Prisoner's_dilemma).

design and implementation of rural sustainable development policies. A similar conclusion also applies to the argument that low and medium-income countries actions for development shall follow the experience of high-income countries described by their proponents in a very stylized-general manner. Furthermore, in view of the inability of high-income countries to substantially contribute to halt global warming, the later proposition should be subject to serious discussion.

We can conclude that humanity faces major challenges to formulate and implement effective sustainable development policies. Since solutions to these challenges are pending, they are part of the explanation as to why global warming caused by humans remains.

References

Acemoglu, D. and Robinson, J. A. (2008). Persistence of power, elites and institutions. *American Economic Review, 98*(1), 267–293. https://doi.org/10.1257/aer.98.1.267.

Acemoglu, D. and Robinson, J. A. (2012). *Why Nations Fail: The Origins of Power, Prosperity, and Poverty.* Random House Digital, Inc. New York City, USA.

Berdegue, J. A., Franco, G., Gordillo, G., Robles, H., Scott, J., Soloaga, I., Toledo, C., and Yúnez-Naude, A. (2015). *Territorios productivos: Un Programa articulador para reducir la pobreza rural a través del incremento de la productividad, la producción y los ingresos.* RIMISP/Centro Latinoamericano para el Desarrollo Rural. https://rimisp.org/wp-content/files_mf/1427203794DocdertabajoPTPfinalmarzo2015.pdf.

Esteban, E., Dinar, A., and Albiac J. (2019). Determinants of water lobbying: Irrigators' behavior in a water-stressed basin. *Water Policy, 21*, 1107–1122. https://doi.org/10.2166/wp.2019.148.

Fisman, R. and Miguel, E. (2007). Corruption, norms, and legal enforcement: Evidence from diplomatic parking tickets. *Journal of Political Economy, 115*(6), 1020–1048. https://doi.org/10.1086/527495.

Fisman R. and Miguel. E. (2008), *Economic Gangsters: Corruption, Violence, and the Poverty of Nations.* Princeton University Press, Princeton, New Jersey, USA.

Hernández-Solano, A., Ávila Foucat, S., and Dyer, G. A. (2020). *Estimating Shadow Prices in Economies with Multiple Market Failures.* Working Paper.

Intergovernmental Science-Policy Platform on Biodiversity and Ecosystem Services (IPBES). (2016). *The Methodological Assessment Report on Scenarios and Models of Biodiversity and Ecosystem Services.* In S. Ferrier, K. N. Ninan, P. Leadley, R. Alkemade, L. A. Acosta, H. R. Akçakaya,

L. Brotons, W. W. L. Cheung, V. Christensen, K. A. Harhash, J. Kabubo-Mariara, C. Lundquist, M. Obersteiner, H. M. Pereira, G. Peterson, R. Pichs-Madruga, N. Ravindranath, C. Rondinini and B. A. Wintle (eds.). IPBES. https://doi.org/10.5281/zenodo.3235428.

López-López, J. and Yúnez-Naude, A. (2019). *Hacia la incorporación de los recursos naturales de México en estudios multisectoriales.* El Colegio de México, Centro de Estudios Económicos. https://cee.colmex.mx/documentos-de-trabajo/2019.

Ostrom, E. (2010). Beyond markets and states: Polycentric governance of complex economic systems. *American Economic Review, 100*(3), 641–672. http://www.aeaweb.org/articles.php?doi=10.1257/aer.100.3.641.

Sachs, J. D. (2012). Review essay: Government, geography and growth: The true drivers of economic development. *Foreign Affairs, 91*(5), 142–150. http://www.jstor.org/stable/41720868.

Taylor, J. E. and Filipski, M. (2014). *Beyond Experiments in Development Economics: Local Economy-Wide Impact Evaluation.* Oxford University Press. https://doi.org/10.1093/acprof:oso/9780198707875.001.0001.

Taylor, J. E., Hardner, J., and Stewart, M. (2009). Ecotourism and economic growth in the Galapagos: An island economy-wide analysis. *Environment and Development Economics, 14*(2), 139–162. doi:10.1017/S1355770X08004646.

Taylor, J. E. and Lybbert, T. J. (2015). *Essentials of Development Economics.* University of California Press, California, USA.

Yúnez-Naude, A. and Aguilar-Mendez, P. (2018). Effects of water availability and policy changes for irrigated agriculture. In H. Guerrero (ed.), *Water Policy in Mexico.* (pp. 55–74). Springer. https://link.springer.com/chapter/10.1007%2F978-3-319-76115-2_3.

Chapter 8

Summary, Policy Implications, Conclusion, and Final Questions

Humans and Nature are witnessing increasing global warming. A process that, if not stopped, will be catastrophic for life on earth. Current scientific research findings show that there is no doubt that human activities are the primary drivers of climate change (CC) tendencies since industrial times. In recent decades, human-induced global warming has increased at a rate of 0.2°C per decade. However, detractors of this evidence remain as well short sighted powerful economic and political interests even in prominent democratic countries. Notwithstanding the fact that relevant actors are increasingly recognizing the anthropogenic roots of CC, their actions to reduce greenhouse gas (GHG) emissions do not reflect their concern.

To this day, the economic consequences of the COVID-19 pandemic and the war in Ukraine have led to a bleaker panorama. The urgency of countries all over the world to recover economic growth before Russia's invasion to Ukraine shows that growth based on fossil fuels is the priority of vested interests with respect to efforts to reduce global warming. Now, the Ukraine war has been added in limiting the accomplishment of the United Nations Sustainable Development Goals (SDGs). We are witnessing the huge rise of oil and gas prices triggered by the limitations of the European Union to buy these fossil fuels from Russia, as well as global price increases and supply reduction of fertilizers, grains, and oilseeds to the world from Ukraine and Russia, who are the major worldwide suppliers of these agrochemical and food crops. The former tendency has increased revenues from the non-Russian oil and gas companies promoting their production of fossil fuels. And the latter is very likely to reduce food security in food-staple dependent countries, especially in the Middle East and African countries that import these commodities from Ukraine. It is necessary to add that the way countries are dealing with these two crises is centered on self-interests, a situation contrary to what is required to attain global sustainable development.

8.1 Summary

To learn about economic development, agriculture, and CC one must first set up the framework and define related basic notions such as Biodiversity, Natural Capital, Sustainable Development, and Valuation of non-priced natural resources. The first two chapters of this book addressed all of these.

With regard to the framework, in Chapter 2 we offered scientific evidence showing that global warming has increased since the Industrial Revolution and that the major drivers of this shift are related to human activities and population growth. Based on this evidence the United Nations (UN) has organized several conferences aimed at discussing this trend and reached agreements between its member states to reduce GHG emissions. In these efforts the Kyoto Protocol (1992), the Paris Agreement (2015), and the Glasgow Conference or COP26 (2021) stand out.

In addition, the UN member states adopted the 2030 Agenda for Sustainable Development based on 17 SDGs. These goals range from the reduction of worldwide poverty, hunger, and overall gender inequality to the protection and restoration of natural resources. However, UN member states' commitments to attain SDGs and to reduce GHG emissions have so far been at most just partially fulfilled.

In Chapter 3, we revised the literature on the role of agriculture in economic development, from the classical and neoclassical dual growth models to the studies that consider agriculture sustainable development. In this chapter, we concluded that studies on agriculture and development must consider rural areas and the prevalence of billions of rural households in the world, especially so in low and medium-income countries. We also presented an initial approach to agricultural and rural development policies, with special attention on the different views about markets vs. State intervention for development.

We pointed out that dual models are too aggregated since they describe a less developed country as being formed by just two sectors: a traditional/agricultural and a modern/industrial sector. Another limitation of these models is the role they assign to agriculture: either as the provider of surplus labor (Lewis's classical model) or as cheap labor and food supplier (neoclassical models). In contrast, contemporary studies consider that agricultural production is heterogeneous and that this sector is different from that of industry in ways that go well beyond the dichotomy proposed by dual models; that is to say, farming is disperse, conducted in extensive territories by billions of agents using as inputs considerable amounts of natural resources such as land and water.

In more recent research, agriculture is included as a part of rural areas, a perspective that allows, among others, the study of the competition of natural resources used by other human activities. As regards the latter, access to fresh water and forest land is worth mentioning.

In regard to rural households, we proposed that their inclusion in the study and policy design for development must consider the particular decision-making process followed by these agents and the context of market failures under which decisions are taken.

Our proposals are similar to those listed in the Intergovernmental Panel on CC (IPCC) approach and other research instance methods based on the notion of Agriculture, Forestry and Other Land Uses (AFOLU). This approach is critical in assessing the role of agriculture and rural areas for sustainable development, and it is necessary as it includes the function that AFOLU as a sink of GHG emissions did not consider in the standard literature on agriculture discussed in Chapter 4.

We finished Chapter 3 with a brief account of agricultural development policies proposed in the seminal work of the World Bank *Agriculture for Development* and by the UN Food and Agricultural Organization (FAO) contributions. We also introduced the question of markets vs. State interventions.

Chapter 4 focused on issues related to sustainable development in agriculture and rural areas based on the IPCC concept of AFOLU. We presented first mitigation and adaptation strategies aimed at, respectively, reducing global warming and taking actions to deal with CC in the AFOLU sector. In our discussion, we included fresh water, another component of natural capital which, just like land, is a major input in agricultural production. We considered then the vulnerability of CC in rural areas, with special focus on rural households. Chapter 4 was concluded by discussing sustainable development policies in regard to the AFOLU sector.

Among others, in Section 4.1 we considered the fact that land is both a source and a sink of GHG emissions. In rural areas agriculture is the major polluter, whereas forests are one of the most important natural resource sinks of GHG emissions. Since agriculture competes with forests for land use, this implies there is a trade-off between increasing food production and preserving forests that must be considered in policy design for development.

Section 4.2 focused on discussing how to deal with CC through mitigation measures and adaptation processes in AFOLU. Mitigation through human intervention aims to reduce the sources or enhance the sinks of GHG emissions by reducing both loss of natural habitat and deforestation. These actions can result in significant biodiversity, soil and water conservation. As for agriculture, appropriate technology development can increase the sector's productivity and along with it, per capita food availability and a reduction in per capita agricultural land area. Other mitigation actions are related to improved crop land management based on agronomy such as tillage/residue management, more efficient irrigation and drainage systems, and agroforestry.

Section 4.2 addresses the existing challenges to put into practice for mitigation measures in agriculture. Among others is the fact that the effectiveness of these practices depends on climate, soil type, and farming systems around regions of the world and that most of the "green" technology is not designed for, or accessible to small farmers.

Evidence proves that forests are fundamental for achieving low-cost global mitigation that will give rise to synergies with adaptation and sustainable development. Forest mitigation includes reducing emissions from deforestation and forest degradation thus enhancing the sequestration rate in existing and new forests.

An aspect discussed in Section 4.2 is the fact that CC makes people and economic agents more vulnerable, and therefore, adaptation to this phenomenon is crucial. The factors leading to vulnerability are complex and context-specific. After discussing the different notions of vulnerability adopted in the literature, we focused on approaches that define vulnerability to CC as an external stressor and on studies aimed at answering questions as to who is more vulnerable to this climate phenomenon among rural households, and why. The answers to these questions provide a starting point for the design and implementation of actions than can promote and facilitate adaptation.

Following the IPCC definition of adaptation — the process of adjustment to actual or expected climate and its effects — we presented the different types of adaptation to CC (e.g., *ex-ante* and *ex-post*). For agriculture, there is a considerable number of adaptation measures such as modifying planting and harvest times and applying new production practices. Unfortunately, literature with detailed research on adaptation options, strategies, and experiences for agriculture is scarce.

In Section 4.3, we focused on rural households' adaptation to CC, as these agents' characteristics, contextual settings, and their use and dependency on natural resources for their livelihoods make rural households extremely vulnerable to CC. In addition, rural households' behavior and context are frequently overlooked in the literature on sustainable development. In other words, these studies do not take into account that a considerable proportion of these households in low and medium-income countries produce for family subsistence in small land plots, among others.

Based on our review of studies on rural households' vulnerability and adaptation options we concluded that it is evident that vulnerability — hence, adaptation options and strategies — differs across regions as well as across rural households. Much research is still needed to explore the determinants of rural households' vulnerability and to better understand the link between their adaptation capacity and vulnerability. Chapter 4 ends with a discussion on adaptation and mitigation policies in agriculture and rural areas (see Section 8.2).

We dedicated Chapter 5 to introduce the main features of the major applied modeling approaches for the study of socioeconomic phenomena and development. These modeling efforts are part of the contributions of economists who study sustainable development and the effects of CC and policy options regarding the economy and society.

In Section 5.1, we analyzed migration models critical to explain why people migrate from rural to urban areas and international destinations. There is no single migration model that can broadly explain the economic, social, and environmental factors leading to rural outmigration. Instead, there is a range of theories, frequently segmented by disciplinary areas, which lead to a better understanding of how migration processes influence agriculture and economic development within the context of CC.

Since the main drivers behind migration decision-making are multiple given that migration is a multicausal process, we listed the main characteristics of migration models, ranging from neoclassical models through worldwide systems and cumulative causation theories up to the New Economics of Labor Migration (NELM). The main proposition of the NELM approach is that decisions involving migration are not made in isolation by individual actors, but by groups of related people (typically families or households) who act collectively not only to maximize the expected income but also to minimize risks and reduce the market restrictions these agents face. Additionally, in this section we also reviewed some of the key arguments related to climate conditions as drivers of migration.

Considerable efforts to study the effects of CC on agriculture have been made with partial equilibrium models inspired on Ricardian economics. This approach automatically captures farmers' adaptive responses, assuming that the cross-sectional samples incorporate partial equilibrium decisions with respect to their production choices. We summarized the main characteristics of the Ricardian models in Section 5.2.

A more comprehensive modeling approach to study empirically the effects of exogenous shocks such as those coming from CC is based on multisectoral models, also called economy-wide models, since they represent the functioning of a whole economic system and the linkages between its components. We included a summary of these models in Section 5.3.

There is a wide range of economy-wide models that can be separated in two general categories: multiplier models and general equilibrium models. The first type is inspired on Keynesian economics and the second type is based on neoclassical economics. Both approaches often use Social Accounting Matrixes (SAMs) as their data base.

A SAM is a representation of a specific full economy and society for a period (generally a year). A SAM captures the relationships or linkages between the components of a particular socioeconomic system. Among others, these components are: the inputs for a particular productive activity resulting from another activity; value added on factors of production (labor, capital, land, water, etc.); and its transfer to the owners of these factors (workers, capitalists, landowners, etc.); and the expenditures these latter agents do to obtain goods and services produced domestically or abroad.

There are also micro multisectoral models that incorporate rural households' economic behavior when high transaction costs and/or market failures prevail. Section 5.3 stresses the fact that the application of these disaggregated rural economywide models (DREM) is convenient when rural households make their economic decisions in situations of market failures and/or high transaction costs. This is the case of vast rural regions in low and medium-income countries. A DREM captures situations where the effect of an exogenous shock on rural households facing high transaction costs will differ with respect to economic agents that produce for the markets (examples of applied DREMs are provided in this section and in Box 2.2 of Chapter 2).

In Section 5.4, we summarized features of some eco-physical models. The main purpose of these models is to analyze the natural processes that shape cultural systems. These models are based on the notion that the relationships between ecological and social systems represent links with cultural meanings and material relationships within eco-physical systems. The purpose of some studies using this framework is to analyze sustainable development and are aimed at finding a balance in the space and time of the ecological, social, and cultural functions that seek to provide goods and services in the decades to come.

So, Chapter 5 examines the progress in modeling economic agents' behavior to measure the likely socioeconomic impacts of global warming and state policies. We also included some features of the eco-physical models. Notwithstanding the progress in the construction of applied models, much research is still needed to fully measure the complexities of CC drivers and impacts, as well as the potential effects of alternative policies to reduce global warming. Data gathering is also required to feed applied economic and physical models (e.g., to incorporate natural resources in SAMs).

The purpose of Chapter 6 was to discuss in greater detail the topics included in Chapter 2 related to trends and perspectives of global warming with special focus on land, rural areas, and agriculture. We also discussed agricultural and rural policies.

Section 6.1 focused on reviewing the drivers and trends of global GHG emissions and compared the latter with countries' commitments to reduce global warming under the United Nations Framework Convention on Climate Change (UNFCC). We reflect on the reasons that may explain why these commitments have at most only partially been fulfilled.

We presented the history and some details of the main international agreements signed by UN Partners to reduce global warming. Our review included summaries of the scientific basis leading to these agreements as provided by the IPCC. Likewise, we included our estimations of global trends in GHG emissions during the last three decades and set them against the commitments agreed to by UN Parties.

Among others, our findings indicate that, if we consider the emissions goal set in Kyoto and compare it with global 2012 GHG emissions, we can argue that the gap between what was agreed and the actual figures is as high as 46.5%. In other words, emissions grew by almost 50% beyond the goal set for 2012 in the Kyoto Protocol. Notwithstanding the concerns expressed by the Parties, this trend has continued in the last decade. However, some countries did accomplish the Kyoto emission goals reductions, among which Australia and several European countries stand out.

In Section 6.2, we extended the discussion presented in Chapter 3 about the role of markets and/or states in promoting sustainable agricultural and rural development. The purpose of this was to understand some of the reasons that can explain why actions to reduce GHG emissions under the UNFCC have mostly failed. To answer this question, we presented an overview of agricultural policies and the role of this sector in the attainment of food security. We also discussed market-oriented agricultural policies designed to increase productivity of subsistence rural households.

Based on the review of the policy proposals by international institutions such as the World Bank (WB) and the UN to enhance worldwide agricultural sustainable production and food security, we concluded that it is now widely acknowledged that non-market-based mechanisms form an important component of the fight against human-induced CC, along with market-based mechanisms. However, both, the WB and the UN privilege the latter approach. In particular, the WB proposes the reduction of transaction costs in rural areas as a way to promote access to markets by small farmers. This strategy is based on State investments in public goods and services (e.g., in roads). The WB adds that small farmers' cooperatives are a way for these agents' market access in better trade conditions.

Going back to the combination of market and non-market-oriented approaches, in Section 6.2 we point out that the challenge is to specify the characteristics of this combined strategy in light of a wide number of phenomena and situations found in rural areas of low and medium-income countries.

Finally, we considered the inclusion of indigenous populations in COP26 and suggested that indigenous people be included as part of rural households in the diagnosis and design of actions to enhance sustainable development, as both these populations live under similar social and economic circumstances such as poverty, subsistence production, and access and dependency on the use of natural resources. Furthermore, in rural areas of many low and middle-income countries rural households are mestizos and many of them share the values of indigenous populations. However, it is a must that the special characteristics of isolated indigenous populations be considered in rural sustainable development policies.

Chapter 7 is both informative and thoughtful, aimed at discussing challenges faced by humanity to reduce global warming. Our reflection arises from the need to assess natural resources and from the way institutions function. Hopefully, the contents of this chapter will contribute to the understanding of why anthropogenic global warming continues. We determined that part of this problem is related to the different views between ecologists and economists and their dissimilar proposals to attain global sustainable development. We framed these disagreements in the discussion of markets vs. State intervention. As in previous chapters we place special attention to agriculture and rural areas.

In Section 7.1, we presented the first challenge explained by the different approaches of economists and ecologists to valuate natural resources and their services with no market prices, that is to say, those resulting from their characteristics as public goods causing externalities. We presented the appealing proposal of the Intergovernmental Science-Policy Platform on Biodiversity and Ecosystem Services, called value pluralism, that integrates economists and ecologists approaches to valuate biodiversity and ecosystem services.

Policy design value pluralisms acknowledges, assesses, and explicitly includes the diversity of values. To follow this approach is challenging, since pluralistic ways of valuation require to include values held by the full range of stakeholders with different worldviews of nature and its contributions to people at different spatial and temporal scales.

In Section 7.2, we discussed the role of institutions in the pursuit of sustainable development and reduction of global warming. As in the debate between economists and ecologists with regard to the valuation of natural resources, there are discrepancies about the roles of institutions. In part this is because it is hard to distinguish cause from effect in empirical studies, i.e., when good institutions as democracy promote development or *vice versa*. However, and notwithstanding the foregoing, institutional economists provide evidence in this regard.

Based on historical data on developed and underdeveloped countries and using the notions of inclusive-democratic and extractive-authoritarian institutions, Acemoglu and Robinson conclude that extractive-authoritarian institutions are fundamental to explain why countries fail to develop, and *vice versa*. Sachs criticized this conclusion arguing that institutions are not all that matter since, among others, there is evidence of authoritarian regimes that introduced economic and political reforms that led to more inclusive institutions through domestic and/or international pressures, leading to economic development. The role of institutions and other phenomena in development is an open question that has to be addressed in the study of sustainable development as well as the reason why some countries have failed to accomplish UN sustainable development goals.

In Section 7.2, we analyzed the notion that points out that democracy is an institution that favors development. However, based on Acemoglu and Robinson contributions, it can be argued that changes in political institutions (i.e., from an authoritarian regime to democracy) do not necessarily lead to economic development. According to these authors this can be explained when we distinguish *de jure* from *de facto* political power. Among others, Acemoglu and Robinson's analysis indicate that a change in political institutions alters the distribution of *de jure* political power, but creates incentives for elites to invest in *de facto* political power to partially or even fully offset change in *de jure* power. In Section 7.2, we proposed that the work of Acemoglu and Robinson provides clues as to why commitments to reduce global warming have only been partially fulfilled by many high, medium, and low-income countries with democratic regimes.

In Section 7.2, we also discussed the issue of corruption and development. It is generally accepted that this bad institution is pervasive for development and we added that corruption limits the application of international commitments to reduce global warming. We performed an empirical exercise to relate corruption indexes and per capita income for 170 countries and found a very high correlation coefficient (0.78), indicating that as per capita income rises, corruption falls. Again, this may be one of the reasons why low and medium-income countries are in general the ones that have failed the most in reducing its GHG emissions.

In Section 7.2, we also addressed issues related to states, markets, and rural areas. We included this reflection because of the prevalence of billions of small farmers and rural households in low and medium-income countries as well as their use and dependence on natural resources for their livelihoods. And also, because the context in which these agents make economic decisions is, at best, not fully incorporated in sustainable development policy design by either international institutions or governments. In addition, we discussed issues related to gender and the use of common-pool natural resources. We ascertained that these phenomena have to be seriously considered in policy design and implementation.

We also discussed the fact that in many low and medium-income countries common access to natural resources is frequent. For some economists and policymakers, the users of a common-pool resource such as forests are trapped in a tragedy of overuse and destruction of nature. Nobel Prize in Economics, Elinor Ostrom and colleagues criticize the foundations of the problem, called "the tragedy of the commons," arguing, among others, that the formulation of this problem adopts the view that "one size fits all." Ostrom goes on to propose a theory of individual choice that recognizes the central role of trust in coping with social dilemmas such as common-pool natural resources.

We concluded in Chapter 7 that the attainment of sustainable development and its requirement, that is, to contain global warming, is a challenge that humans must urgently address. We have to seriously try to reconcile the visions from economists and ecologists and incorporate rural agents in the analysis of their role in the protection of nature.

8.2 Policy Implications

Preconditions to put effective policies for rural sustainable development and to reduce GHG emissions into practice in these areas, as well as to promote the role of land as sinks for these gases are many-fold. Some of the critical ones can be grouped as the following questions. (1) In what context and/or situation market signals are appropriate to encourage agents to reduce their activities on GHG emissions and when is State intervention required? (2) When necessary, what is the appropriate mix of market and State interventions? (3) When are command and control measures needed to enhance land to function as sinks of GHG emissions through land quality improvement and forests conservation, reforestation, etc.? (4) In democratic regimes, how can the differences between *de jure* and *de facto* political power be reduced in order to put sound policies aimed at promoting sustainable agriculture and rural development into practice? (5) What is the required mix of top-down and bottom-up policies for rural sustainable development and how to include indigenous population and women empowerment in this approach? (6) How to eradicate corruption practices, including the misuse of international aid and investments for sustainable development? and (7) What are the conditions required to promote data gathering and analyses for diagnosis, policy implementation, monitoring, and evaluation of impacts of sustainable development policies?

All these questions are bluntly formulated and so, they exclude the fact that some countries and/or regions within them have successfully addressed challenges to reduce GHG emissions. These experiences can be considered as lessons of policy options to reduce global warming that range from the promotion of research of green technologies and their dissemination and application by farmers, to policies aimed at preserving crop biodiversity and forests by rural households, women, and indigenous populations.

The design of these policies must consider the conditions and contexts where farmers make their decisions such as their plot size, market, and natural resources access and agroecological production conditions.

An area of opportunity for a sustainable agricultural sector is the dissemination and adoption of green technologies mainly developed in high-income countries by scientific institutions and commercial medium and big-sized farmers. In the case of adaptation to CC, we are referring, for example, to the use of improved seed varieties resistant to global warming effects such as droughts, among others. With regard to mitigation, technologies to produce low carbon fertilizers are currently in the experimental phase as well as the development of perennial cereals such as wheat to replace annual crops as a way to enhance soils sequestration of GHG emissions. Other technologies to reduce water requirements in crop production, including urban farming, are available.

The increasing demand of animal proteins by consumer preferences changes and income and/or population growth is a major problem to attain sustainable global food security goals. One solution is the production of high protein vegetables such as peas; another is the processing of proteins from insects (the British Broadcasting Corporation or BBC has produced a documentary serial of these new green technologies for food production: https://www.bbc.com/future/bespoke/follow-the-food/).

The above technologies can be adopted by commercial farmers in any income-type countries. However, research involved is mainly financed by private corporations that own the property rights for their use. Promoting and accelerating the dissemination and adoption of these technologies by other farmers requires arrangements that call for governments' involvement. In the case of low-income countries, the commitments of high-income countries under the Paris Agreement and COP26 to finance mitigation strategies can include the adoption of these green technologies by commercial farmers.

An option for sustainable use of land that can be adopted by farmers of all sizes, including rural households engaged in agricultural production, is agroforestry, either by planting crops or cattle rising. An example of this strategy is the current Mexican government program designed for rural households called "cropping for the future" based on subsidized plantation of trees in crop fields (this program is currently extended to the three northern countries of Central America). Other policy options are related to forest conservation, reforestation, and to the reduction of forest degradation and fires. These aims have been already agreed by many COP26 partners (details in Chapter 6, Section 6.2). In addition, farmers that enhance GHG sequestration in their cropping and forests lands are eligible to receive payments for environmental services as long as markets for these services are promoted by the private and public sectors.

In regard to small farmers an appropriate analytical and policy-design approach is to consider that in low and many medium-income countries agricultural production is mainly carried out by rural households that are also engaged in other activities and income sources; for example: forestry and the receipt of remittances of family members working in cities and/or abroad. It is also convenient to make a distinction between commercial and subsistence rural households.

In general, market-oriented policies can be applied to small commercial farmers, whereas additional and/or other supports may be adequate for subsistence households. In both cases government interventions must have a sustainable orientation. For example, subsidies to rural households to preserve the biodiversity of local seeds they use to produce foods and the promotion of local-regional markets.

Due to their small size, the expansion and/or creation of small farmers and rural households' economic cooperatives is essential, as well as a combination of bottom-up and top-down processes in policy design; i.e., the design of productive and/or conservation projects by these agents under cooperation schemes and the evaluation of these projects by governments, according to their policies for sustainable rural development.

Finally, in order to be coherent, and hence effective and efficient to enhance sustainability, government interventions require coordination among its agencies and at all levels; e.g., between Department or Ministry for the Environment and the Department for Agriculture at the national, state, and municipal levels.

8.3 Conclusions

How the world economy will come out from the pandemic health crisis, the consequences of the Ukraine war, and both of their impacts on CC are open questions. What is clear to us is that several complex challenges remain as regards the attainment of global sustainable development and the reduction of global warming. As we document in this book, some of the most important challenges are related to extending scientific research, data collection and availability, coherent and complete valuation of natural resources, and adequate policy design and implementation in agriculture and in rural areas. We need to take actions now; it is time to reduce myopic economic interests of powerful groups and intensify real diplomacy in concrete actions and no more broken promises.

CC has been the result of several connected phenomena as history, geography, ecosystems degradation, bad institutions, short-sighted decisions, and lack of appropriate technology. These facts call for open-minded multidisciplinary and interdisciplinary approaches in scientific research based on dialogue and understanding between ecologists and economists with different approaches, and between disciplines. To ensure the success of this type of efforts, research has to be independent of vested interests.

The IPCC has been a major contributor in scientific knowledge. However, its results are subject to the approval of governments whose interests widely vary. This situation also limits the effective inclusion of civil society proposals in the Conferences of the Parties' (COPs) negotiations on measures to reduce CC. In light of the governments-based policy design, the challenge to attain global sustainable development is the incorporation of all relevant scientific research and the involvement of civil society in the preparation of its national position in the negotiations to define actions toward a more sustainable world.

As regards agriculture, CC, and sustainable development, there are several lessons that derive from our presentation and discussion in this book. We highlight some of them as follows:

- In research and policy design it is not appropriate to separate agriculture from rural areas and from other sectors of the economy. Among others, the former because agriculture is one of a myriad of activities and the source of income of billions of rural households in low and medium-income countries. And the latter because agriculture competes with industry and services for natural resources, where scarce fresh water stand out. These types of connections are captured by multisectoral models that can be improved by further steps to disaggregate the social components of the economy; by linking national-regional models with worldwide models as well as by incorporating the use of natural resources and physical models.
- If non-market alternatives to preserve natural resources in high-income countries are required, this approach is even more necessary for agriculture and rural areas in low and medium-income countries.
- In research and in policy designs, rather than separating indigenous people from the rest of the world's population, it is better to consider this population as part of rural households and local communities, and then, consider the specificities of this vulnerable group when designing and implementing climate actions.
- To lay down and facilitate actions to empower women is also a must; among others, because women usually have the longer view required to transit to sustainability.

Notwithstanding that scientific evidence shows that CC and global warming are facts triggered by human activities since the Industrial Revolution, extreme views prevail on how to contain these phenomena. The answer to this question requires efforts to reduce divergent philosophical, ideological, and/or political positions. So, we invite both, students and readers to reflect on these issues, bearing in mind the urgency we humans have to take effective actions to preserve our planet.

Finally, it is essential to note that the topics addressed in this book are a small piece of the puzzle of the economic and social impacts and challenges caused by global warming. Much research and reflections remain to be done on global response to the threat that CC poses. Political will is required to put into practice these actions that are critical to achieving the United Nations SDGs and solving some of the major challenges faced by humanity.

8.4 Final Questions

In addition to the questions raised at the beginning of Section 8.2, the following is a sort of homework assignments intended to enhance reflections by students and overall readers of the topics addressed in this text book.

8.4.1 *General questions*

- What are the scientific bases to conclude that global warming is, since the Industrial Revolution, mainly caused by anthropogenic phenomenon?
- In face of the prevailing global inequality, how reasonable is it to argue that global population growth in general is another fundamental phenomenon that has caused global warming?
- What are the most influential international agreements on Climate Change?
- Are the commitments made under the Paris Agreement and the COP26 adequate to reduce GHG emissions, and why?
- Why have international commitments to reduce global warming failed?
- According to the literature, what are the main roles and contributions of agriculture for development and for sustainable development?
- Why it is necessary to provide context to agriculture as part of human activities in rural areas?

8.4.2 *Economic models*

- What are the main contributions of socioeconomic modeling to explain global warming and the effects of CC?
- Is it time to mainstream the environment as a driver into the migration decision-making models?
- What are the steps and data required to incorporate natural capital in social accounting matrixes?
- What are the differences between partial and general equilibrium economic models?
- What are the differences between macro and micro multisectoral models?
- If household and general equilibrium micro economic models assume that rural households are rational economic agents, why do they react to price changes in an unexpected way?
- Household and general equilibrium micro economic models take the household as the decision-making unit. Is this assumption a limitation to consider discrepancies between family members? (e.g., between male and female household heads).
- What are the major pending research issues in economists' contributions to the knowledge of CC and how can this problem be addressed?
- How can we link socioeconomic models with eco-physical models or *vice versa*?

8.4.3 *Policies*

- Is it feasible to reconcile ecologists and economists' proposals for sustainable development, and why?
- What are the pros and cons of market-oriented policies and of command-and-control measures for sustainable development of agriculture and rural areas?
- How convenient is the goal to include all rural households in market-oriented policies?
- What are the limitations of the idea to promote the adoption of green technologies developed in high-income countries?

- Is it necessary to single out the situation and functioning of rural households' decision-making in the diagnosis and actions designed to reduce global warming, and why?
- How convenient, efficient, and effective is to consider rural indigenous population as part of rural households?
- Under what approaches rural women empowerment can be enhanced?
- How the concerns of the civil society in regards the future of humanity can influence effective State actions to reduce global warming and how can professionals and students of social sciences contribute to this objective?

Index

H

I

U

V

W

Y

Printed in the United States
by Baker & Taylor Publisher Services